Socially Responsible Investing

Making a Difference and Making Money

Amy Domini

DEARBORN™
TRADE

A **Kaplan Professional** Company

This publication is designed to provide accurate and authoritative information in regard to the subject matter covered. It is sold with the understanding that the publisher is not engaged in rendering legal, accounting, or other professional service. If legal advice or other expert assistance is required, the services of a competent professional person should be sought.

Vice President and Publisher: Cynthia A. Zigmund
Senior Managing Editor: Jack Kiburz
Interior Design: Lucy Jenkins
Cover Design: DePinto Studios
Typesetting: Eliot House Productions

© 2001 by Amy Domini

Published by Dearborn Trade, a Kaplan Professional Company

Printed in the United States of America

01 02 03 10 9 8 7 6 5 4 3 2 1

Library of Congress Cataloging-in-Publication Data
Domini, Amy L.
    Socially responsible investing: make money while you make a
    difference/Amy Domini.
        p. cm.
    Includes index.
    ISBN 0-7931-4173-7 (alk. paper)
    1. Investments—Moral and ethical aspects—United States. 2. Stocks—
United States. 3. Social responsibility of business—United States. I. Title.
    HG4910 .D655 2001
    332.63'2—dc21
                                                    00-011148

Dearborn Trade books are available at special quantity discounts to use as premiums and sales promotions, or for use in corporate training programs. For more information, please call the Special Sales Manager at 800-621-9621, ext. 4514, or write to Dearborn Financial Publishing, Inc., 155 N. Wacker Drive, Chicago, IL 60606-1719.

30% Post-consumer
100% Recycled

Dedication

My sons, Jotham and John Kinder, never signed on to give their mother up to another book but took it in stride nonetheless. Whenever I feel that the efforts are too little, too late, the image of their faces refocuses my energy and commitment.

Thousands of starfish washed ashore.

A little girl began throwing them in the water so they wouldn't die.

"Don't bother, dear," her mother said, "it won't make a difference."

The girl stopped for a moment and looked at the starfish in her hand.

"It will make a difference to this one."

Contents

List of Sidebars

Chapter 4. Direct Dialogue: Speaking Up as an Investor to Make a Difference   83

Chapter 5. Community Economic Development: Investing to Make a Difference Locally   107

Chapter 8. The Power of SRI: Better Investing Will Result in a Better Tomorrow   178

Acknowledgments

Lindsey Parsons continuously demands better of me. Whenever I feel discouraged about the future, I remember that it is populated with leaders of her caliber and feel secure.

Two giants of socially responsible investing shaped my thinking 20 years ago. Tim Smith and Chuck Matthei, each in different ways, have changed the lives of hundreds of thousands for the better. Tim, the charismatic father of shareholder activism, convinced me that responsible investors did not stop with screening portfolios. Chuck, the Johnny Appleseed of community lending, forever humbled me with his selfless dedication to serving the poor, the voiceless, and the most desperate.

So many of my thoughts have been shaped by peers who have taken the time to retreat with me, to help me to articulate the concepts, philosophical underpinnings, and goals of socially responsible investing. Principal among these is Francis Coleman, a rigorously dedicated man who has earned my gratitude, my respect, and my admiration. Without much formal structure, we call ourselves the Morelos Forum. Thank you: Jack Allard, Ricardo Banyon, Michelle Chan-Fischel, Ann Crompton, Marc deSousa-Shields, Tonya deSousa-Shields, Deb Elliott,

Patricia Farrar, Anita Green, Emilio Heradia, Victor Heradia, Trish Hylton, Michael Jantzi, Tim Johnson, Michael Lent, David Levi, Adine Meese, Sigward Moser, Lindsey Parsons, Ann Partlow, Sheridan Pauker, Kevin Ranney, Greg Ratliff, Blaise Salmon, Judy Samuelson, Eric Steedman, Coro Strandberg, Robert Walker, and Heather White.

Over the past few years, I have been given a special introduction to social investing in the rest of the world. Thank you to Joshua Mailman for creating the infrastructure of connectedness to this network. Also thank you to Jan Van Oosterwijk, Joyce Meuzelaar, Amanda Haworth-Wiklund, Carlos and Heidi Boudin, Prada Tiasuwan, Maria Alexandra Eisenmann, Mark Lee, Dan Gertsacov, and most especially to the effervescent Robert Rubenstein.

Many contributors to my thoughts and efforts on this book helped so much in making it come together: David Borenstein, Stephen Davis, Ralph DeGennaro, Adam deSola Pool, Roberto Eisenmann, Carsten Henningston, Paolo Ivo, Bobby Julian, Steven Lydenberg, Grant McCracken, Patrick McVeigh, Thomas Thijssens, Mizue Tsukushi, and Axel Wilhelm.

Cynthia Zigmund, who heard me speak and urged me to write, has been a dedicated and insightful editor. Her clarity and patience have been extraordinary; her understanding of the importance of the message gave me energy when I flagged. Jane Heeckt conducted research and reviewed the manuscript. Monisha Saldanha and Margaret Domini also reviewed the manuscript and gave me valuable feedback. Monisha especially kept me focused on international contributions to the field.

Others stand out as giants in the field of social change through investments. Thanks to Robert Reich, Joan Bavaria, Robert Zevin, Joan Schapiro, and Peter Kinder, all of whom shaped both the field and my thoughts.

Preface

As a financial advisor I work and live in two different worlds. The world I live in is populated with caring people who strive continuously to make the lives of their children, their communities, and often the world at large a little bit more livable. The world I work in is populated with people who ceaselessly work to achieve superior investment results for their clients. These two worlds are occupied by the same people. When at home, they care, and when at work, they care. But what they care about in each locale is at conflict with what they care about at the other. As a result, they work long days to achieve a goal that jeopardizes all that they hold dear when at home.

Financial advisors should know better; we feel the relentless pressure from our clients and understand the rules; our job is to maximize financial rewards for our clients so that they can enjoy the fruits of life. But the result is that we maximize financial results by allowing companies to do whatever it takes. A corporate management team might understandably argue that it is their duty to buy the science needed to sell a product of questionable benefit, buy the public opinion needed to get the useful legislation that allows them to avoid taxes, and buy the workforce that can produce it most cheaply even if they work in chains. Company managements take no personal responsibility for the outcome, hiding in the presumption that they are playing by the rules and they didn't make the rules. If people cared, they'd make different rules. Are we actually enabling our clients to enjoy the fruits of life? No, we are fattening their wallets; but we are not giving them what we claim. Financial well-being ought not to come at the expense of health, personal safety, or the capacity to take enjoyment from simple everyday pleasures.

I believe that by integrating deeply held personal or ethical concerns into the investment decision-making process, investors can bring about a world that values and supports human dignity and environmental sustainability. Through socially responsible investing, the investor reengineers the equation of success. We want to make money because we want a better life, more security, a legacy for our children or our planet, or even simply because we like to feel that we played and won. But socially responsible investors ask that first we do no harm. The world is shrinking, time to fix the environment is running out, too many lives are still subjected to realities that a civilized people would never allow, and somehow money lies at the root of these facts. These are things we know. Social investors seek to address them.

The Context

In *Socially Responsible Investing* I introduce the underlying philosophy of a socially responsible approach to investing. The financial services industry is fast becoming a form of global "government," and the well-being of the whole person is not a mandate that finance feels. The result is a ticking time bomb as our environment is assaulted, and human dignity becomes a forgotten concept. Lenders put whole nations into bankruptcy to repay a loan they never should have made; investors demanding cheaper raw materials stand by as peasants are seized and chained to work the pipeline. These actions are immoral. Yet they happen every day on my behalf. An amoral financial services industry sees maximizing shareholder return as such a noble endeavor that it must take not just precedence, but an exclusive position of power.

The history and the development of social investing owe much to the lessons learned in the debate over the appropriate role for U.S. companies doing business in South Africa. That debate landed in fertile soil in part due to the tumultuous period of the 1960s and 1970s and in part due to a history of individuals and groups that sought to align their investments with their convictions. The strategy and mechanics of social investing evolved out of faith-based standards for investments, moved through the early environmental movement, the influence of the war in Vietnam, the civil rights struggle in the United States, and came of age during the synthesis of international efforts geared toward alleviating suffering in South Africa.

The Methods

Three tools help social investors make money while making a difference. I begin by carefully selecting stocks on the basis of social and ethical considerations. I filter potential investments through a sieve, and purchase only those that are not in the most egregious industries and, moreover, are better-than-average corporate citizens. Screening is a means of both intentionally investing in ways that are more consistent with your values and building an ongoing structure for corporate accountability oversight.

My second tool is engagement in active dialogue with companies' management teams. Through responsible voting of shareholder resolutions, through filing resolutions on issues of concern to us all, and through less forceful means, I work with other socially responsible investors and with management at companies to seek solutions to emerging problems like sweatshops and a repressive régime in Burma. Direct communication with companies' management teams helps both sides to find reasonable first steps for addressing issues ranging from appropriate environmental practices to enhanced diversity efforts and for alleviating the human suffering caused by world debt.

My third tool is using community lending to work outside the dominant paradigm. To bring about a world of justice and environmental sustainability, I argue that we must support small community development financial institutions. In our inner cities, on Native American reservations, and in emerging economies, whole populations are at risk of losing generations before stabilizing to the point of being able to create healthy communities. Extraordinary institutions that combine lending with lessons on finance and personal skill building do what they can to assist these populations, but they need funds. Assisting them can be as easy as being deliberate about where you do your banking.

The Impact

The world has become too small to think in terms of national boundaries either when buying products or when buying stocks. Our demand for products is the cause of gross injustice abroad. Our ownership of stocks of foreign companies has already led companies to make decisions contrary to the way that business has been conducted for generations and is harmful to native populations. On the other hand, the close-knit nature of our one world could be a tremendous asset in the struggle to build a world within which human dignity and environmentally sound practices can flourish. Certainly the investment challenges of a global economy are myriad.

Can you make money as a socially responsible investor? Yes, clearly it is possible to make money. The track record speaks for itself and there are real reasons that it should be so. Social investment mutual funds have had above-industry-average returns, as has the benchmark for the industry, the Domini 400 Social Index. I build the case that this investment record may well be the result of the social-screening process, which I believe helps reveal both the quality of management and the corporate culture at work.

Can you influence outcomes by the way you invest? Socially responsible investing has contributed to alleviation of suffering, to building a cleaner world, and to constructing a framework within which companies can be brought into the problem-solving side of emerging issues facing society. Most powerfully of all, a new owner of the corporations of the world is gaining a voice, an owner that believes that there is a difference between making money and stealing money from our children, our neighbors, our natural environment. As this new owner grows in number and in power, responsible and sustainable business practices will result.

Money Makes the World Go Round

The goal of management is to make money for the investor. Yet most investors operate on the concept that money is value neutral and that investing is an act without real-world consequences. This is not the case. There is a world of commerce, within which goods and services are distributed, and there is a world of finance, within which money flows. Finance both fuels commerce and is fueled by it. But the partnership is unequal. Investors from the world of finance own our corporations. One partner, the partner whose only purpose is to fatten the wallet, owns the other.

NIMBY—not in my backyard—is a label for a community's outrage in response to plans to build a federal penitentiary, a landfill, or a superhighway in the vicinity. No one wants a problem in his backyard, even for services never thought of as a problem before. But the world is very small today. Within six hours I can travel from my home in Cambridge to the rain forest in Panama and visit with indigenous people whose language is undocumented. Or I can be in the desperately poor squalor of Port au Prince, Haiti, where illiteracy is 80 percent and standards of living have been dropping for 25 years. My backyard is this fragile planet.

The Way We Invest Matters

Defining the Goals of
Socially Responsible Investing

I can't think of anything more important to teach young people today than this: that ordinary people working together can change history. They can look for a new Martin Luther King or Rosa Parks or Malcolm X to tell them how to make a difference—but they can also look in the mirror.

—ROSA PARKS

Times are good. Employment is full; the economy is humming. In the United States, people that never before had a chance at getting jobs are being hired and trained by employers desperate for a workforce. Around the world people have access to global markets and global communications systems. A steady rise in stock prices has raised the wealth levels of millions, giving them discretionary spending dollars and some comfort that they will be able to retire in dignity. Nonetheless, our pristine wilderness is disappearing; our natural heritage of species is being decimated. Our rich cultural and ethnic diversity is all but gone, and vast ghettoes scar every metropolis. Millions live in slavery, or prisons, or as captives in their own homes. Children of eight are forced into the advance guard of armies. Others are sold into bonded apprenticeship or prostitution. Each day, hundreds of thousands of people die of malnutrition, cholera, and a dozen other poverty-created causes.

Slavery Is Not a Thing of the Past

Article 4 of the 1948 Universal Declaration of Human Rights guarantees that "no one shall be held in slavery or servitude, slavery and the slave trade shall be prohibited in all their forms." Yet slavery still occurs. Contemporary slaves still work in the fields, and provide manual labor for many industries in both rural and urban settings. Attempts to eradicate contemporary forms of slavery have been much less successful than the past century's campaigns against the traditional slave trade. Today's slaves include forced labor in Burma, child carpet weavers in Pakistan, bonded charcoal burners in Brazil, and bonded brick kiln workers in India.

Source: "Contemporary Forms of Slavery Requiring Action by Governments: Examples of a Large-Scale and Persisting Problem in the 1990s," prepared in June 1995 by Anti-Slavery International for the United Nations Working Group on Contemporary Forms of Slavery and <www.antislavery.org>.

How can these two worlds coexist? Perhaps the questions are, How long can we allow these two worlds to coexist and what is the natural outcome of the world we are building? Is it one in which a few coddled and blinded individuals live lives of peaceful luxury, cleanliness, and grace, while earnestly doing their best to assist those unfortunate billions whose lives are ones of relentless suffering? It would seem we are already living this life.

A change is needed. We no longer can accept the adages that "the business of business is business" and that "the rising tide will lift all ships." It hasn't, it won't, and it cannot without a rewriting of the definition of success. Business is run on a set of rules that solely values making money for the few owners. These rules have made business the most powerful social change force on the planet. Our large companies have revenues that far exceed the incomes of most emerging nations, or even whole continents. Nothing can stand in their way as they strive to achieve their primary mandate: making money for shareholders.

The symbolism of architecture reveals a startling trend. From ancient times through the Renaissance, almost all of the largest structures on the landscape were built in tribute to deities. The soaring cathedrals of Europe and the Wats of Southeast Asia taught people that a universal goodness and purpose exist and must be honored. Next came the age of government. Through much of the past 300 years the largest buildings were the houses of Parliament or great palaces. These tell us that civil society's social structure is of primary importance and must be honored. While somewhat narrower than universal goodness, they still indicate that the good of the majority is paramount.

During the past century until quite recently, the largest buildings present in our cities became company headquarters. Whether you drive into Cincinnati or Milan, you see a skyline dominated by huge monuments to the company that chose this place to settle in. The Chrysler and Pan Am Buildings of New York became landmarks to guide tourists to Grand Central Station. These tributes to the great engines of commerce, to the power of commerce to provide people with food, clothing, shelter, and desired goods and services, replaced those of civil society.

But now even this is shifting. Today the Pan Am Building has a new name and a new owner; it is now the Met Life Building. Today our largest monuments belong to the financial services industries, and we acknowledge and honor the power of money movers. No universal goodness, no respect for social fabric nor even a tower of admiration for commerce is symbolically raised above our city roofs. Today money movers have replaced God, government, and commerce.[1]

The investments we make today shape the world we will live in tomorrow. If our investments are made in a vacuum, without consideration for the social or environmental impact they may have, the result will be a continual slide toward rewarding that which is profitable at the cost of that which is life enhancing. Today two worlds exist side by side and already most of us with money cannot see the other world. As the symbols displayed in our cities show, we see only the power and the glory of money.

The fundamental belief that socially responsible investors share is this: that the way we invest matters. Our reasoning is simple: there is a basic conflict between making the highest possible profit for the few that have investments and building the most livable world for the many that inhabit it. It is cheaper to use slave labor than to pay living wages; it is cheaper to pollute than to clean; it is cheaper to tar over a parking lot than to build one around planted trees and benches. If civilized people continue to define monetary rewards to investors as the reason that corporations exist, the future we hope for cannot be realized.

After 10,000 years of advancing civilization, now is the time for humankind to realize its potential for peace, loveliness, human dignity, and shared values. We have the capacity; we probably have the will. What we have lacked is a commitment to integrate the goal of creating a livable world into the day-to-day management of our most powerful institutions: business and finance.

Today a growing number of individuals and institutions recognize the basic truth that the way we invest matters. Because of this, the field of socially responsible investing (SRI) has experienced explosive growth over the past few years. A recent Gallup poll found that one out of every eight households has some form of socially responsible investments.[2] According to the Social Investment Forum's biannual survey, assets managed with social criteria, or with active shareholder dialogue, or in community development initiatives have almost doubled every two years since 1996 and now stand at $2 trillion in the United States alone.[3] Two of the three largest money managers in America, TIAA/CREF (the teachers' retirement system) and Vanguard Group, launched mutual funds for the socially responsible investor in the first half of 2000 alone. Socially responsible investing has come of age.

Growth of the SRI Market

- Thirty-five percent of companies in the United States of America with defined contribution plans offer SRI options to employees. This list includes two of the largest: Ford Motor Co. (F) and General Motors (GM).
- 401(k) plan administrators are offering SRI options as well. For instance, one large administrator, Fidelity Investments, offers 9 SRI funds out of 97 non-Fidelity funds their 401(k) plan administration services offer.
- Significant funds are also now invested in SRI funds through variable annuity products. These include TIAA/CREF Social Choice Account ($4.1 billion) and Lincoln National Social Awareness Fund ($1.8 billion).

Sources: "What's New in Social Investment" (April 2000). Prepared for the members and affiliates of the U.K. Social Investment Forum and Social Investment Forum. The Social Investment Forum Web site is located at <www.socialinvest.org>.

Corporate social responsibility was not discussed in annual reports 15 years ago, but it is now routinely discussed both there and on the Web sites of our largest companies, where we read about a commitment to communities, diversity, and the environment. Consulting firms have sprung up to advise on building a reputation as a responsible corporation. Ethics chairs and curricula are appearing at the nation's business schools; University of Alabama's Durr-Fillauer Chair of Business Ethics and Harvard's John Shad Chair of Business Ethics are but two.

The effect of this interest is nonetheless quite limited. Companies do not own themselves but are owned by their shareholders, and so long as these shareholders put profit maximization ahead of all other considerations, so will corporations. If we desire a future in which human dignity, environmental sustainability, and basic freedoms can exist, then we must take responsibility for our world today in more positive ways. We have the building blocks: capitalism, finance, and world trade. We must face the fact that corporations have an impact on many constituencies. By tracking that impact over time, by continually reminding both investors and corporations about the effect of actions they take, and by seeking alternative models for economic development, socially responsible investors are emerging as a powerful voice that will positively impact the future of our planet.

In Switzerland: Investing for Sustainable Development

As of year-end 1999, Ethos Foundation administered approximately 460 billion euros in global equities and bonds on behalf of 74 pension funds from all over Switzerland. Director Dr. Dominique Biedermann describes his organization: "The Ethos Foundation was created by pension funds for pension funds. The aim was to forge an instrument of asset management enabling them to analyze companies according to the criteria of sustainable development, in an approach based on classical financial criteria and on a set of environmental and social criteria. A further aim was to exercise shareholders' voting rights in a responsible fashion." The investment strategy includes a mixture of avoidance, positive selection, and engagement.

Source: "What's New in Social Investment" (April 2000). Prepared for the members and affiliates of the U.K. Social Investment Forum.

The Dominance of Global Capitalism

There are alternatives to corporations as we know them in Europe, Japan, and the United States. Cuernavaca, Mexico, enjoys a large, vibrant central marketplace in which thousands of vendors hawk their wares. They show up at the same place every day, and are self-organized into blocks that sell children's clothing, blocks that sell electrical parts, blocks that sell flowers, and so forth. There are no shareholders; no central purchasing office negotiates prices; no marketing department designs advertisements; no corner office distributes bonuses at the holiday season. Yet an extremely effective exchange of products takes place. Not only do consumers find the goods they desire, but also hundreds of individuals are able to earn a livelihood and support their families.

In the United States, we have huge flea markets, temporary fair sites where dozens of entrepreneurs converge for a few days to sell crafts, secondhand furniture, and other goods. These entrepreneurs act as a cooperative, frequently through an umbrella trade organization. Again, there are no shareholders, purchasing offices, marketing departments, or corner offices. In many ways, these flea markets are a holdover of the ancient fairs from which contemporary retail businesses emerged.

Only during the past 300 years or so have people had ready access to desired goods outside of central city marketplaces. In medieval times, a village might hold one or two fairs a year, giving its inhabitants a chance to purchase frying pans, needles, axes, or whatever goods they chose. Gradually, people's tastes changed. Fashion became almost as important as function.[4] We began to expect to be able to purchase goods whenever we desired them, and stores emerged as an answer. As commerce became more routine and as shops became established, so, too, did the means of financing this engine. Individual speculators would buy shares in (parts of) a shipping venture or in a textile manufacturing plant. Laws were developed to protect these investors from being held accountable for actions that they did not themselves undertake. Means of collecting debts or of seizing property when debts were not paid were codified.

In the meanwhile, the great powers of Europe had sailing ships and gunpowder, allowing them to travel to the far corners of the earth and take over the management of whole countries as "protected colonies" from which natural resources and certain goods could be gathered. To accomplish what government could not or would not undertake, corporations were chartered. The British East India Co. was one such chartered company. The return to shareholders was achieved by killing thousands of

Indians and so outraged British statesman and philosopher Edmund Burke that he declared:

> Every rupee of profit made by an Englishman is lost forever to India. With us are no retributory superstitions, by which a foundation of charity compensates, through ages, to the poor, for the rapine and injustice of a day. With us no pride erects stately monuments which repair the mischiefs which pride had produced, and which adorn a country out of its own spoils. England has erected no churches, no hospitals, no palaces, no schools; England has built no bridges, made no high roads, cut no navigations, dug out no reservoirs. Every other conqueror of every other description has left some monument, either of state or beneficence, behind him. Were we to be driven out of India this day, nothing would remain, to tell that it had been possessed, during the inglorious period of our dominion, by anything better than the ourang-ourang or the tiger.[5]

Eventually, Parliament did revoke the company's charter and placed management under direct control of the Crown in an acknowledgment that unwritten rules of decency should come before the company's mandate to maximize profit for shareholders.

Stocks and bonds are the two primary forms of investments that result from the development of commerce. Their roots are simple. Occasionally, for instance, a shopkeeper would need funds. Perhaps it was to build up an inventory of supplies or to build a new outlet. But if the shopkeeper did not have enough saved to meet the need, the need could be met in one of two ways. The shopkeeper could borrow money or could sell a piece of the business. Either transaction involved an individual who was an outsider to the business making cash available in exchange for potential financial gain. In the case of a loan, the moneylender was said to be buying a bond. In the case of purchasing a piece of the business, the investor was said to be buying a share of the company.

What Is a Stock and Why Do People Buy Stocks?

Stock is ownership. The owner of the stock is the owner of a piece of the business. And just as the owner of a small corner ice-cream shop must pay off interest due on loans before taking any profits, so also do the stockholders' rights to profits take a back seat to bank loans or loans from other sources. Why then would someone own a stock and not a bond? Because as an owner of a piece of a business, the stockholder has the chance to see his or her ownership value grow as the business grows. The real reason to own stocks is because you think you are going to be able to sell your investment at a profit that is greater than the profit you might make by purchasing and selling another potential investment such as a piece of real estate. But remember that many things influence stock prices. You can be right about everything at the company, but if a corner of the world goes to war or a plague breaks out or any one of a number of external events occurs, your stock may still fall in value.

Stocks and bonds are the basic instruments of the financial services industry. They are inventions of the needs of business and were constructed to grease the wheels of commerce. This fundamental fact has been forgotten as finance has grown in strength and now even dictates the way in which business is conducted. But society both needs and desires food, clothing, shelter, health care, and other goods and services. Financial systems were invented to assist commerce, which in turn gives society ready access to these things; finance is meant to be a means to an end.

Imagine two worlds: The first is the enormous world of commerce within which goods and services are created and delivered. Factories, shipping services, communications, and a host of other familiar entities inhabit this world. The second world is one of finance. Here currency is exchanged for debt, for owner-ship, and, increasingly, simply for a bet on rising or falling for-tunes of a nation. Trillions of dollars move each and every day, much of it to support the world of commerce. But there is a junc-ture where these two worlds touch and that juncture is the investor, the source of the fuel to both world engines.

What Is a Bond and Why Do People Buy Bonds?

A bond is a loan. If you buy a U.S. Treasury bond, you're making a loan to the U.S. government. If you purchase a municipal bond, you're making a loan to a city or state. When you buy a corporate bond, you are making a loan to that corporation. Each bond has a stated rate of interest and a date of repayment. If you need to sell the bond before the date of repayment (called the maturity), you have to negotiate a sale price based mostly on how interest rates have changed since the time your loan was created. Because they are paid off in a relatively short period (compared to ownership of a stock which is never paid off—you have to sell) and because they have clearly stated interest payment schedules, bonds are not nearly so volatile as stocks. A high-quality bond is therefore frequently thought of as a safe harbor. It is a good place to keep the portion of your investments that you want to have readily available when a large expense is coming up in the next five years or so. It is also good to own bonds if you want something safer than stocks in your "rainy day fund."

Increasingly, that investor becomes involved in finance through the ownership of mutual funds. Although the mutual fund industry is about 70 years old, it has grown to prominence only over the past quarter century. It began with the U.S. Employee Retirement Income Security Act of 1975. Employed individuals were given tax incentives to save for their own retirement through the creation of an individual retirement account (IRA). Suddenly, virtually every working American had an incentive to save for retirement.

What Is the Difference between Income, Yield, and Return?

Income, yield, and return are perhaps the three most misunderstood words that investors use.

Simply stated, investment income is the money you get paid from the dividends (which are a piece of the profits) that a company elects to distribute to its shareholders and from the interest payments received from bonds and money market investments. Although you pay tax on capital gains, capital appreciation is not considered income.

Yield is found by dividing the number of dollars in anticipated income by the total value of the portfolio. Today, it is quite common to see stock portfolios that yield less than 2 percent because most companies pay very small dividends, but the investor should not be tricked into believing that that is all he or she will get out of such a portfolio.

Return—or, more correctly, total return—combines both the capital appreciation (the increase in market value) the portfolio has enjoyed and the income from dividends and interest payments and divides that combined figure by the starting value of the portfolio at a certain moment in history. The formula is a bit more complicated, but that's the basic idea. A mutual fund that had a total return of 20 percent in 1999 would have received some of that return in the form of dividends and some of that return in the form of capital appreciation (whether or not its stocks were actually sold, their appreciation would be counted in the calculation). This total return is more commonly called performance.

In the 1980s, a second but equally dynamic source of new mutual fund investors appeared. Until that time American corporations generally guaranteed retirement benefits to their workforce, just as they still do in many nations. But the U.S. economy was going through a wrenching transformation, downsizing workforces and driving for greater efficiency. Corporation after corporation abandoned the defined benefit pension plan and replaced it with a defined contribution pension plan, generally a 401(k).

Defined contribution pension plans are in several ways quite similar to IRA plans. They largely transfer asset management decisions to the employee and can "follow" the employee from employer to employer. Their tax treatment is favorable. Further, if he or she so chooses, an individual can determine what the account is worth every day. With so many benefits, and with the dismantling of other social safety nets, employees are greatly encouraged to set aside as much as possible into a retirement plan. Fueled by growth from this sort of demand, mutual funds became an almost universally understood investment vehicle in the United States. Virtually every working American understands something about the vocabulary of investing, and what was once the exclusive jargon of Wall Street has gone mainstream.

Now, the history of the past 20 years in the American financial services industry is being repeated in other developed nations. Europe's history of offering its population a social safety net, which included a guaranteed pension, is crumbling, and Europeans are investing in mutual funds as they learn how best to save for their own retirement. In Europe, Japan, and Australia, old-fashioned norms, such as relying on your local bank for advice, are giving way to magazines, newsletters, and Web sites that serve the new individual investor, just as in the United States. In emerging economies, there have been essentially two classes of people: those with money and those without. Those with money are financially sophisticated investors and are comfortable with investment decision making. If these nations begin to experience a gradual rise in the per capita income of their populations and a strong middle class, more of their citizens will become investors. All these trends will fuel the growth of the mutual fund industry.

There is much that is positive about this. Mutual funds are essentially empowering and allow small investors access to highly qualified portfolio management at an extremely reasonable cost. They make it possible for just about anybody to benefit from the growth of corporations and therefore from the growth of the global economy. Mutual funds make a good deal of sense for most of us. However, they have grown in size to a point that has ramifications for the sovereignty of the rest of the world. Financial services companies now build the tallest skyscrapers in our cities. To understand social investing globally, you must recognize the power that the financial services industry holds.

What Motivates the Socially Responsible Investor?

The investor stands at the juncture between the engine of the world's economy and the fuel, money. This is the reason that the way we invest today will shape the world we live in tomorrow. Investments are both the link and the engine upon which both commerce and finance rely. By not accepting responsibility for this, investors have built the world we inhabit today, the shrinking world with so little time remaining. There are two basic reasons for integrating social or ethical criteria into the investment decision-making process: the desire to align investments with values and the desire to play a role in creating positive social change. Consistency is almost always the motivation that causes investors to start down the path of becoming socially responsible in their investments.

The decision to invest in a socially responsible way allows us to define the role of the corporation in society by evaluating the corporate impact of various stakeholders. We can identify and clarify emerging issues both through shareholder activism and through creating bellwether indicators in the screening process that will track these new areas. We work to build healthy communities through designating portions of our portfolios to community development financial institutions. If you are, for instance, a high school teacher, then it might well strike you as inconsistent to invest in alcohol manufacturers that seem to advertise to youth. If your personal philanthropy primarily goes to environmental causes, then it is only being consistent to invest in a way that supports your philanthropic giving. Investing is a purchasing decision. Caring about it is like caring about what you eat or how you choose to lead your life.

Socially Responsible Investor. . . Why Do We Do What We Do?

In the words of Boston orator and abolitionist Wendell Phillips, "The price of liberty is eternal vigilance." As nation after nation is liberated from famine and poverty by the capitalist system and its inherent financial instruments, society must be constantly vigilant in assuring that corporations, including those in the financial services industry, continue to provide civic society with desired goods and services, and that they strive to reduce the harm their practices might create.

My own first step toward becoming a responsible investor was in 1978. I was a stockbroker at the time and had come of age during the Vietnam War. The fact that I had "sold out" and "become a cog in the military-industrial machinery" bothered me less and less as the money got better and better, but was always there somewhere in the back of my mind. Meanwhile, I built up relationships with people with whom I did business and tried to give them recommendations of good stocks to buy.

One day the research department at the firm I worked for sent out a recommendation for a company that they thought had good prospects for winning a major military contract. On the basis of this expectation, most of my fellow brokers were calling their best customers and recommending a purchase of the stock. I felt sick. How far had I fallen that I might consider calling people I was fond of and urging that they make an investment in a killing machine?

Taxpayers for Common Sense

Ralph DeGennaro is cofounder and president of Taxpayers for Common Sense. What really make Ralph and his colleagues mad are wasteful government spending and subsidies, including corporate welfare. He pledges that TCS will continue to save taxpayers an average of more than $1 billion a year. Here are some of Ralph's current initiatives against corporate welfare.

Boeing (BA) has a $1.6 billion, three-year contract to oversee development of a National Missile Defense system, which it shares with **TRW (TRW), Raytheon (RTN), and Lockheed Martin (LTM)**. These companies favor rushing to deploy a missile defense system, even though it has not passed required tests, will destabilize the nuclear balance, and costs too much.

Weyerhaeuser (WY), Louisiana-Pacific (LPX), and Boise Cascade (BCC) have each received tens of millions of dollars of government subsidies to cut down taxpayer-owned trees in the national forests. Especially in the Pacific Northwest and Alaska, these companies have benefited from free trees, taxpayer-financed timber roads, and deceptive accounting by the forest service.

Source: You can reach Ralph at ralph@taxpayer.net or visit his Web site <www.taxpayer.net>.

It was a moment of realization for me, and since that day, I have come to recognize that most social investors have experienced a similar moment. There is value to being more consistent with yourself and with your value system. You don't need perfect consistency; every step in that direction feels better than no step in that direction.

Institutions also frequently invest in a way that is consistent with their mission. Health care organizations choose not to invest in tobacco companies. Organizations working for the protection of women and children often decide not to invest in alcohol and gambling companies, acknowledging the high cost families pay when these are abused. Church investors consider their tenets of faith when making investment decisions. Personal or institutional consistency is the first goal investors have when they decide to integrate social criteria into the way they manage their money.

Consistency is joined by a second goal: being part of a dynamic force for the process that creates positive social change. Like me, most social investors find the field out of a desire to bring their investments more closely in line with their values, and, like me, most stay because of a belief that the way that we invest can actually make both money and a difference in the world.

Global Facts

- The richest 1 percent of people in the world owns as much as the bottom 57 percent.
- Someone with an income equal to $25,000 is richer than 98 percent of the world population.
- The poorest tenth of Americans have average incomes higher than two-thirds of the world.
- The ratio between the average income of the world's top 5 percent and the world's bottom 5 percent increased from 78 to 1 in 1988 to 114 to 1 in 1993.

Source: "Global Facts," *Left Business Observer 93*, 10 February 2000, 5.

This second motivation, of being a change agent, is the reason the field has grown so quickly. Most people care and want to do what they can. Most of us are grateful for a chance to have so much impact for so little effort. We can invest and achieve results as good as those achieved by ordinary investors, yet we can be a part of something greater than we could give ourselves. We can be a part of shaping a world of justice and of environmental sustainability and one in which simple pleasures can be enjoyed by all.

When a large percentage of the owners of the world's business enterprises believe that profit must not come at the loss of human or environmental justice, then companies will respond. They will serve as effective means of delivering desired goods and services to the population in a manner that does not harm their owners, who are—after all—living beings. If the owners of the economic engine of the world recognize that money doesn't help if you can't breathe, then they will create rules that allow for both breathable air and financial return. Socially responsible investors recognize that at a certain level the owners of the economic engine dictate the management of that engine. The socially managed portfolio is a part of something larger than itself; it is a part of a global reformation of the way business is done. Why use investment portfolios to build a better world? Because, as bank robber Willie Sutton said, "That's where the money is."

Steve's Stakeholder Story Stocks: Corporations and Civic Values Community—Health and Lifestyles

Steven D. Lydenberg, research director at Kinder, Lydenberg, Domini & Co., Inc. (KLD), believes companies have the potential to greatly benefit society but that a corporation devoted solely to maximizing profit at the expense of other stakeholders can leave civil society poorer. To help highlight the kinds of broad-based returns companies can provide, KLD has inaugurated its Civic Values 500 project, which identifies companies, especially smaller, less well-known firms, that exemplify particular values based on civic respect and responsibility. Throughout this book, I'll include several baskets of stocks, chosen by Steve to reflect different values. These six corporations work to improve health and lifestyles:

- **American Water Works (AWK)** is a water utility company devoted to maintaining safe water supplies for local communities. Water is increasingly recognized as a dwindling resource.
- **Aphton Corp. (APHT)** is a pharmaceutical company working with the World Health Organization on the development of contraceptives for population control in developing nations.
- **Biomet Inc. (BMET)** is a producer of orthopedic products for surgical and nonsurgical use. These improve the quality of life of patients.
- **Gardenburger, Inc. (GBUR)** a food products company, produces innovative, meatless alternative food products designed to be consumed as main courses. The production of non-animal-based food products has a substantially less negative effect on the environment than the production of meat products.
- **Triangle Pharmaceuticals (VIRS)** develops drugs for AIDS, HIV, hepatitis, and other serious viral diseases. The treatment of these diseases is important for improving the quality of life and preventing the future spread of these infectious diseases. For example, individuals lacking HIV treatment face a dramatically increased likelihood of contracting AIDS, which threatens to become a worldwide epidemic.
- **Whole Foods Markets, Inc. (WFMI)**, is a food retailer promoting organically produced food products. By acting as a conduit between organic farmers and customers, the company helps create an economy that can support healthier food production.

Source: You can reach Steve at stevel@kld.com or visit his Web site <www.kld.com>.

The Three Basic Approaches Used by Socially Responsible Investors

Three basic aspects to socially responsible investing are screening portfolios, direct dialogue with corporations, and investments in community development financial institutions. Social investors try to use all three. While each has a different purpose and impact, each of the three serves to strengthen the impact of the other two.

The social screening process, which will be discussed in more detail in Chapter 3, allows investors to stay in companies with more positive profiles. It is constructed to avoid particularly harmful products or services and to evaluate the more positive initiatives the company has undertaken. You can do this in a portfolio of stocks you manage or by buying shares in a mutual fund that has been designed to meet the needs of the socially responsible investor. And while some funds do focus exclusively on a particular issue (such as animal rights or the environment), the vast majority of SRI mutual funds considers a company's overall impact. As one early client said to me when I asked what her concerns were, "Don't ask me to decide what matters more—women's rights, the environment, or South Africa. They all matter." It appears that most investors agree with her. The niche funds have not raised the assets that the broad-based ones have.

One way that the integration of social criteria in investments makes a difference results from the fact that portfolio screening cannot take place without good research. The demand for corporate social research by social investors has created a large amount of information about the ways in which companies affect our lives. Never before has society tracked data on the way business copes with diversity, environmental impact, community support, or a host of other issues. We do today, thanks to social investing. This information in and of itself is an instrument for positive change, as I demonstrate in later chapters.

Filtering or screening investments for consistency with personal values seems daunting. But finding ways to be consistent with financial goals while investing in more responsible companies is possible. Most can't claim to invest in perfectly responsible companies, for such a claim would be difficult to defend or even to define. However, mutual funds and professional investors in the field can state that we try to meet the needs of the socially responsible investor. To do this, we look at a company's overall impact on employees, customers, communities in which it operates, suppliers, shareholders, and the natural environment. This is called stakeholder analysis.

A responsible investor wants an evaluation of the company and wants to take a step toward consistency with his or her own values. This mandates a degree of flexibility because concepts of what is responsible shift. Years ago, when I started out researching companies, the word *sweatshop* referred to nonunion steel mills in the Ohio River Valley. But today I must find a way to evaluate a tiny tin-roofed factory in central Vietnam. Fortunately, social investing is adaptable and able to respond to emerging issues.

The filters are both negative and positive screens. The original approach was negative to avoid investing in something inconsistent with a set of values. This grew out of the fact that religiously motivated social investors sought to avoid profiting from industries viewed as detrimental to human society. But anyone can understand that alcohol, tobacco, and gambling are addictive and have done the most to tear the fabric of families. So even without a religious underpinning, an investor might feel that these industries are inconsistent investments for one who wants to build a better world.

Negative screens allow investors to avoid harmful industries, but they do not enable accentuating companies or industries that are attempting to improve their impact in terms of people and the planet. Socially responsible investors have thus stressed the positive, better described as qualitative, screens. These permit investment in companies with a better record than their peers have and industries that have demonstrated a commitment to achieving exemplary corporate citizenship. Qualitative screens both reward companies that have cleaned up their act and encourage other companies to follow suit.

This is accomplished by looking at the ways a company treats shareholders, customers, employees, communities, suppliers, and the natural environment. The research relies on carefully selected data points. Ideally, this information will be available without a company's help, can be counted (therefore is not subject to writing style), and is indicative of significance beyond itself (it is unlikely you have a high percentage of physically disabled executives unless you have a workplace that was particularly friendly for them).

Qualitative screening has created ongoing, systemwide collection and evaluation of corporate accountability data. This is a tremendous contribution to society. Until the modern era of socially responsible investing, no one was watching corporate social impact on Wall Street or anywhere else. Only the existence of social investors has created a structure for the review of the corporation in society.

Activist Success Story: Starbucks Bows to Consumer Pressure

On April 10, 2000, **Starbucks (SBUX)** announced that it had signed a contract to sell Fair Trade certified coffee in its 2,000 plus cafés, making the company the largest purchaser of Fair Trade coffee in the United States. The announcement came with only three days remaining before nationwide protests were scheduled to begin, demanding the giant retailer offer its customers the choice to buy coffee grown by small farming cooperatives, rather than through the cartels that control most coffee production. According to Deborah James, director of the Fair Trade Program at Global Exchange, the result is that "thousands of farming families in poor countries will see their incomes triple." Starbucks's decision clearly demonstrates the power citizens have to hold corporations accountable for their actions and reflects a growth in demand for products made under nonexploitative conditions.

Source: "Coffee Comes on Strong as Consumers Demand Fair Trade," *Connections Networking for Responsible Business and Investing* 30 (Spring 2000). See <www.globalexchange.com> for more information.

The second aspect of socially responsible investing is direct dialogue. You can leverage your ownership of a piece of a business to gain a place at the table and to raise a broad range of issues. Direct dialogue between caring investors and corporate management teams has been responsible for the dismantling of apartheid in South Africa, for the development of codes of conduct in sourcing from suppliers (read: sweatshops), for consistent environmental reporting, and for a host of other progressive impacts. This dialogue takes many forms. Delivering a social audit to a company for enrichment and comment is a way of alerting corporate management to issues. Letters written to gain clarification or to express either concern over or thanks for a position the company has taken can lead to good results. Consumer boycotts, selective purchase campaigns, and even lying down in front of bulldozers have been used. But the most structured and widely used form of direct dialogue with corporate management teams is the voting and filing of shareholder resolutions.

Owners of a company's stock have the right to attend the annual meeting of the company and ask questions of management. Through this right, owners and management frequently come to the negotiating table on emerging issues. When you learn what shareholder activists have done to raise awareness on heretofore overlooked corporate behavior, you wonder why activism is not better known. Awareness building is going on today over the depiction of Native Americans. Several companies, including CBS (owned by Viacom (VIA)), Gannett (GCI), Knight Ridder (KRI), and PepsiCo (PEP), have been approached. Persuading corporations to discontinue the use of caricatures of Native Americans as logos and mascots has been at the core of the conversations. The negative images of American Indians create a negative social, educational, and working environment for them.[6]

Another example of direct dialogue as a means of raising awareness is taking place over global debt and human suffering. J.P. Morgan (JPM) agreed to go on record supporting debt cancellation legislation. This came as the result of discussing with activists the human cost to already poor people living in emerging economies as their governments cut school and food budgets to repay foreign lenders. The problem results from the enormous debt incurred by nations with loans from the International Monetary Fund and the World Bank. Activist Joseph La Mar of the Maryknoll Fathers and Brothers has noted, "In order to repay foreign debts, many poor countries are being forced to divert scarce government resources away from health care, education, and other vital services." Countries such as Mozambique, Ghana, and Zambia spend more on debt repayment than on social programs.[7]

Why Social Investors Avoid Bonds Issued by the World Bank

Structural adjustment—the standard International Monetary Fund/World Bank policy package that calls for slashing government spending, privatization, and opening up countries to exploitative foreign investment—has deepened poverty around the world. In the two regions with the most structural adjustment experience, per capita income has stagnated (Latin America) or plummeted (Africa).

Many poor countries must devote huge portions of their national budgets to paying back foreign creditors, subtracting from essential expenditures on health, education, and infrastructure. The IMF/World Bank plan for relieving the debt burden is conditioned on years of closely monitored structural adjustment and will do little to decrease what poor countries are currently paying.

When the Asian crisis hit, the IMF made things worse by requiring structural adjustment as a condition for IMF loans. The result was a surge in bankruptcies, layoffs, and poverty. In Indonesia, poverty rates rose from an official level of 11 percent to 40 to 60 percent. At one point the country's food shortage became so severe that then President Habibie implored citizens to fast twice a week. Many had no choice.

Source: Russell Mokhiber and Robert Weissman, "A Dozen Reasons to Come to DC for April 16," *Focus on the Corporation*, 5 April 2000. © Russell Mokhiber and Robert Weissman.

Successful dialogues take place each year. Some recent examples follow. Bell Atlantic (now Verizon Communications (VZ)) confirmed that its operations in Belfast are consistent with the McBride Principles of fair employment in Northern Ireland. Coca-Cola (KO) boosted the recycled content of its plastic bottles. Management at Winn-Dixie Stores (WIN) committed to releasing equal employment data. Twenty years ago, dialogue centered on the corporation's role in South Africa. The most discussed issues in recent years have largely related to environmental codes of conduct, sweatshop concerns, and diversity records. This is the aspect of social investing within which most emerging issues first surface.

By addressing issues with management, socially responsible investors are able to directly help those in need. The impact is frequently immediate and quite tangible. While screening has long-term structural aspects, direct dialogue is tactical in its impact. We know that the question was heard because we receive a response. We can gain a promise to provide an annual report on environmental impact or on diversity initiatives. These are exciting results and can be shared both by the activist who initiates the dialogue and by the many other responsible investors who vote to support the question when raised.

The third leg to the stool of socially responsible investing is support of community development financial institutions. You can work outside the dominant system and seek out alternative models of finance. Through microlending pools, community development financial institutions, and other alternative structures, the responsible investor is the primary source of seed capital for borrowers who otherwise would have no access to the means to own a home or start a business of their own. We do this in recognition of populations for whom the "capitalist miracle" has not worked. The blight in our inner cities, the abject poverty in our Native American reservations, and the starvation and human suffering in emerging and pre-emerging economies all attest to the need for alternative economic models.

Grassroots financial intermediaries that address these needs do so through microlending, through partnering with social service agencies, through training and oversight, and through sharing risks and rewards in nontraditional ways. In many ways, these are the oldest and most common forms of socially responsible investing. Lending circles have ancient roots. Savings banks were originally chartered for exactly the purposes that the community development financial institutions now serve: to teach the poor how to save, how to buy a home, and how to start a business.

How Do I Begin Saving?

The simplest way to build assets is to view savings as an expense in the same way that you view your phone bill as an expense. This means that in planning your budget, you must consider putting money aside in the same way that you consider how much your other expenses are. Generally speaking, beginning savers first work to build up a nest egg that is big enough so that they can survive a severe economic crisis in their life. Depending on your job security, this might be anything between two months' and a year's worth of expenditures (what it would take to keep you going) in very safe investments such as bank certificates of deposit. Once the beginning investor has that much put aside, the same amount can be put aside each month, but probably into a mutual fund. In this way, saving and investing become life-long habits.

The old adage is true: "A penny saved [not spent] is a penny earned." The easiest way to build up assets is to spend less.

Source: Economic Policy Institute, January 2000.

How does it work? Sometimes a simple skill, such as learning how to save, is all the help a person needs. Melvonne Brooks, a single mother making $32,000 a year and supporting two children has realized her dream of home ownership. She has moved into her own three-bedroom house thanks to a savings training program developed by the Shorebank Neighborhood Institute, an affiliate of the South Shore Bank of Chicago. "It's changed my whole outlook. My sons, they saw that I was saving. I had to sit down and explain why I had to stop the fast-food treats every Friday, why Mama wasn't getting her hair done every two weeks, why we couldn't go to a movie." Melvonne Brooks was able to save the $1,800 she needed as a down payment on a home of her own.[8] The money to finance the mortgage was made available because investors of goodwill bank at banks like hers.

The social investor will generally keep a portion of his or her investment portfolio in deposits with or loans to community-based financial institutions that are in the business of meeting the needs of populations underserved by conventional banks or lending agencies. By keeping deposits at a community development bank, the investor is enabling that bank to lend out almost 20 times more money than he or she has deposited. These loans to at-risk and deserving borrowers have the effect of completely transforming the fortunes of families, neighborhoods, or communities.

Socially responsible investors use these three basic tools— screening, direct dialogue, and community development financial institutions—as the building blocks to a livable planet. By choosing to integrate goals of justice and environmental sustainability into your everyday investment decisions you become part of shaping a world in which not only your own, but all children can grow old in peace and dignity.

Spotlight on Community Lending: Cooperative Fund of New England and Equal Exchange

Equal Exchange is a long-term client of the Cooperative Fund of New England (CFNE), a community development financial institution. As an employee-owned wholesaler and marketer of coffee produced by cooperatives in less-developed countries, Equal Exchange helps farmers get fair prices for their products. "In the early years it was difficult for Equal Exchange to get capital. CFNE's loan was very important money to us," says Jonathan Rosenthal, an Equal Exchange founder. By 2000, Equal Exchange had expanded to become the largest Fair Trade certified organization in North America, selling one million pounds of coffee per year and generating more than $6 million in annual sales, thanks to early support from nontraditional lenders.

Source: "Borrower Profile," *Cooperative Fund of New England News* 5, no. 2.

Past Is Prologue 2

How the SRI Movement Started, and How It Continuously Evolves

> We ought to gain all we can gain but this it is
> certain we ought not to do; we ought not to gain money
> at the expense of life.
>
> —JOHN WESLEY

Only over the past three decades have practitioners in the field of socially responsible investing begun to think of the field as a distinct discipline, a movement to address societal issues. The debate over corporate involvement in South Africa is the best-known initiative of the field, but it is only one of numerous initiatives that led civic society itself to use investment assets and corporate practices to build a more just and humane tomorrow.

Since the dawn of humankind, societies have tried to harness the power of cooperatively undertaken commercial enterprises for the good of all. Certainly there are ancient examples of using an economic structure to create well-being for all within designated communities. Early history records seeds of social investing being planted. In 262 BC, Asoka, the most admired ruler of ancient India, renounced war and undertook extensive public works projects intended to fulfill the needs of all his subjects and institutionalize nonviolent Buddhism in his nation. Israel was founded with each citizen being granted land. By the mid-18th century, faith groups actively addressed issues we today would call human rights. In 1758, at the London and Philadelphia yearly meetings of the Society of Friends (Quakers), formal minutes urged Friends to free their slaves and prohibited those who had bought or sold slaves from engaging in the affairs of the society. One could begin the story of socially responsible investing with any one of these. But the field as we know it today primarily evolved out of faith-based investment decisions made over the past two centuries.

Faith Heritage

John Wesley (1703–1791), a founder of the Methodist Church, in his Sermon XLIV, "The Use of Money," provides a startlingly appropriate beginning point. In this remarkable document, he admonishes his flock to avoid making money or profiting "by hurting our neighbor." First, he says, do not hurt our neighbor "in his substance," specifically through gaming and harmful lending practices, as well as by engaging in unfair business practices. Second, he advises not to hurt our neighbor "in his body," specifically by profiting from the distillation of liquor. Third, he directs us not to hurt our neighbor "in his soul" by engaging in businesses that minister "either directly or indirectly . . . to his intemperance." The good master further advises avoiding work that "is attenuated with so hard or so long labour" and singles out the then nascent chemical industry as "absolutely and totally unhealthy." He urges his followers to avoid industries such as tanning that pollute the rivers and streams, as well as industries that make money by engaging in practices such as bribery. This sermon even advises the faithful to live simply and avoid an overfondness for material possessions.

How extraordinary. Here is a formula for right living that begins with identifying products that cause harm to families and avoiding profiting from them. We then consider our nearest neighbors and avoid building those businesses that would cause them harm. Next we are to look at practices that, if allowed to flourish, would tear away at the fabric of our society by undermining laws and civic structures, and we avoid profiting from these. Finally, we admit that our consumption leads to ever-refined and increased demands on the natural resources and beauty of our planet, and so we must strive to live simply.

Methodists are not the only faith group to have long avoided investments in products considered harmful. The Society of Friends has a history of avoiding profits from the sale of armaments. Members of the Nation of Islam often avoid alcohol, tobacco, pork products, and usury (interest-bearing instruments). Christian Scientists avoid health care. Many Buddhists avoid meat companies. But the most universal of these faith-based investment filters are certainly alcohol, tobacco, gaming, and weaponry. These four continue to be almost universally avoided by socially responsible investors, whether motivated by faith or not.

The older faith-based avoidance model began to evolve during the tumultuous period of the late 1960s and early 1970s and expanded to include broader ethical considerations. New ways that the investor could take a role were explored and integrated into portfolios. It was during this era that the modern form of socially responsible investing really began to take shape.

The Oneida Community

Imagine a manufacturing company where women play a key role in management, on-site childcare is free for all, and the well-being of the employees is the company's primary focus. Such a company did exist in the 19th century, in the form of the Oneida Community of Oneida, New York. Although primarily religious in nature, it placed a tremendous emphasis on communalism in life and work. The various enterprises that supported the community economically—agriculture, canning, and manufacturing—thrived under this progressive system.

Eventually, however, conflict between factions within the group and pressure from outsiders took their toll, and in 1879, members voted to reorganize the community into a joint stock company, establishing Oneida Community, Ltd. The new company operated with the same ideals of the original Oneida Community, demonstrating its commitment to its employees by offering attractive wages and safe working conditions, and weathering hard times by voluntary management pay cuts.

Though today **Oneida Ltd. (OCQ)** is much less focused on the community than in the past, the company still maintains a high level of employee loyalty, due in part to an employee stock ownership plan established in the late 1980s. Investors take note: In 1998, the company distributed its 250th consecutive cash dividend.

Source: Oneida Ltd. Web site, located at <www.oneida.com>.

The Context of the Times: 1968–1978

The late 1960s and most of the 1970s was an era of violent awakening. The United States had recently traversed through a wrenching self-assessment over racial inequities and had put into place several policies meant to address its history of racial discrimination. The Civil Rights Act of 1964 and the 1965 Voting Rights Act were enacted with a goal of allowing racial minority groups to enjoy the fruits of our national success more fully. Some funding of grassroots community development institutions began as investors of goodwill sought ways to bring minorities, especially urban African-Americans, into the mainstream.

This was also a period of war. The United States was involved in a highly controversial war against Vietnam. Feelings ran very strongly; draft cards were burned in public demonstrations and pacifists refused to invest in the armament industry. Big business was dubbed "the military-industrial complex." America went from being Europe's hero to being seen as the imperialist pig.

Baby boomers, most of whom came of age during the war, were forever scarred by it. Whether for it or against it, the war in Vietnam undermined a generation's faith in the status quo and its confidence in the voice of authority, particularly government authority.

Agribusiness: Still Creating Silent Springs

Debt-laden farmers, realizing that they will never recover from the loss of good soil, can no longer face the future and are taking their lives in a suicide epidemic sweeping through India's agricultural areas. Vast stretches of rich farmland have become poisoned and waterlogged desert. How did this agricultural disaster begin? Seed companies, selling hybrid cottonseeds locally called "white gold," lured farmers into giving up their native seeds, which the farmers could propagate themselves. The new hybrids need to be purchased every year. They also cost much more and have failed to give better crops. Worst of all, they are very vulnerable to pest attacks so pesticide usage shot up. As a result, even the trees have stopped bearing fruit since the heavy use of pesticides has killed the pollinators—the bees and butterflies. Now farmers are swallowing these same pesticides to kill themselves. What we are doing to the poor in the name of globalization is brutal and unforgivable.

***Author's Note: The major hybrid seed producers are

- **Monsanto** (currently a division of Pharmacia (PHA)),
- **Novartis** (NVS (ADR)),
- **DuPont** (DP),
- **AstraZeneca** (AZN (ADR)), and
- **Archer Daniels Midland** (ADM).

Sources: Dr. Vandana Shiva, "How Big Business Starves the Poor," *The Daily Telegraph*, 11 May 2000.

The events of the war in Vietnam underscored the fact that corporate profits were coming at the price of awful human suffering. Every American who was old enough to read during the war remembers the shock of seeing the photograph of a naked nine-year-old screaming in agony from the fire burning across her back as she ran blindly toward the camera. The photograph was taken in June 1972 shortly after the Americans dropped napalm on her village. Public outrage focused on Dow Chemical (DOW), and protests were organized across the country. What sort of monsters would manufacture and sell such a product?

This decade also witnessed rising interest in the environment. Noted marine biologist Rachel Carson set the stage in her groundbreaking book *Silent Spring* (1962), which documented the slaughter of nature resulting from pesticide use. Communes dedicated to organic farming and simple living sprang up. The first Earth Day was celebrated in 1970, and investors who cared about the environment began avoiding the stocks of companies involved with nuclear power. Emission standards for automobiles were lobbied into law and no-littering laws were passed. Early efforts to enact bottle bills mandating a deposit on soft drink bottles were supported. Macrobiotic diets became popular. In 1979, the nuclear disaster at Three Mile Island, an electric utility plant, awoke fears of massive pollution and reinforced the suspicion that nuclear power was an unproven and unsafe technology.

Against this backdrop, the issues of the nation were being forcefully carried into company boardrooms. Activists began to discover the annual meeting of corporations as a venue for bringing forth concerns over the role of the corporation in society, first with Dow and napalm manufacture, then over South Africa. In 1970, Project General Motors, the campaign launched by Ralph Nader, the famous consumer advocate and presidential candidate, managed to get two issues voted on by shareholders of General Motors (GM) at their annual meeting: reporting on efforts to diversify the Board of Directors of the corporation and on initiatives to strengthen emission standards. Although both of these votes failed, the surrounding publicity led that company to elect an African-American minister from Philadelphia, the

Reverend Leon Sullivan, to its board. Furthermore, it led the company to a policy of gradually strengthening the emission standards for its automobiles.

The Role of South Africa

The Afrikaner National Party won its electoral victory in 1948 with a slogan of "apartheid," which means "apartness" in Afrikaans. The Nationalists, who would rule until 1994, played on the white population's fear of the growing African population in an era of decolonization across the continent. In his autobiography, Nelson Mandela writes: "Apartheid was a new term, but an old idea. It represented the codification in one oppressive system of all the laws and regulations that had kept Africans in an inferior position to whites for centuries. What had been more or less *de facto* was to become *de jure*."[1] Apartheid condemned most blacks to lives of poverty and limited opportunities in the infamous homelands.

It was not until the South African state-sponsored 1960 Sharpeville Massacre that international outrage crystallized into action: The United Nations imposed a voluntary arms embargo in 1963, which became mandatory following the 1976 Soweto Uprising. These measures, however, failed to prompt regime change in South Africa, as the Afrikaner government became increasingly trenchant and brutal. The Reagan administration reversed the isolationist stance of previous administrations and attempted a "constructive engagement" to effect change through dialogue. Many U.S. citizens took a dim view of Reagan's conciliatory policy. They saw it as sanctioning racism to prop up South Africa as a bulwark against growing communism in southern Africa. Meanwhile, faith groups had found innovative new ways to address the suffering of millions of South Africans.

Each nation that the British Empire settled enjoys a vital and active branch of the Anglican Communion. Because the sun never set on the British Empire, there is a sister church in every corner of the globe. During this period of global ferment, the Anglican

Communion heard the cry of pain of her church in South Africa. As the communion struggled with the question of how to help fellow communicants in that troubled nation, the Episcopal Church in America, a member of the Anglican Communion, decided to use the approach they had observed at Project General Motors to reform the American corporate role in supporting apartheid.

In 1971, the presiding Bishop of the Episcopal Church, the Right Reverend John Hines, traveled to the annual meeting of General Motors, which was then not only the largest employer in the United States but also the largest American employer in South Africa, and asked the company to leave that troubled nation. The vote did not carry, but the company's newly elected board member, the Reverend Leon Sullivan, took a great interest in the issue. Following the Soweto Uprising in 1976, Sullivan created a code of conduct for doing business in South Africa that became known as the Sullivan Principles.

The Sullivan Principles demanded corporations conduct an audit each year on a series of indicative bellwethers and then provide detailed reports as to how they were doing. These annual reports covered such issues as nonsegregation, equal and fair employment practices, equal pay, uniform training programs, increased numbers of nonwhites in supervisory positions, and improved quality of all employees' living conditions. From this tracking system grew the conviction that American corporations operating in South Africa were not acting to dismantle racial discrimination in the workplace.

So the campaign escalated. By the mid-1980s, cities and states began refusing to purchase goods and services from corporations doing business in South Africa. Many colleges and universities, faith-based groups, and pension plans divested themselves in the stocks of American corporations doing business in South Africa as part of a deliberate campaign to ostracize and humiliate white leadership there. Still, progress was slow. In addition to general trade sanctions, the United States, the European Economic Community, and the British Commonwealth all banned new investment in South Africa in 1986. As a result, long-term capital flows into South Africa dropped dramatically.

Long-Term Capital Flows to South Africa

(In millions of U.S. dollars)

1981–1984	$422 (average)
1984	1,722
1985	−697
1986	−1,303
1987	−1,317
1988	−443
1989	−493
1990	−266

Source: *World Bank World Tables* (Baltimore: John Hopkins Press, 1995), 606–7.

In 1986, the increasingly dismal outlook for the economy prompted a group of businesses representing 75 percent of South African employers to draft a business charter calling for the end of apartheid. One of the delegates, the president of the Chamber of Mines, stated that he felt "strongly that the counter to U.S. divestment threats lies in South Africa's internal constitutional and general reform process."[2] It was a necessary step, for the country was, even at this late date, slow to respond to international pressure. By 1990, only 4 percent of managers were black at firms that had adopted the Sullivan Principles, even though blacks represented 60 percent of total employees.[3] Moreover, because American firms only employed 2 percent of black wage earners, the Sullivan Principles had a very limited sphere of impact.[4] This damning evidence led to such international pressure that the white leadership in that nation eventually called an election, one that would count the votes of all residents. The antiapartheid movement secured a sure victory in 1994, when South African citizens of every ethnic background were able to vote for the first time in nearly 50 years. At long last the apartheid regime was voted out of power.

The call to reinvest in companies doing business in South Africa came with the election. Nelson Mandela, the newly elected president of South Africa, urged cessation of sanctions and reinvestment. U.S. and European investors responded almost immediately, dropping divestment standards from investment guidelines. The leadership call had, as had the initial call to divest, come from those most affected, black leadership in South Africa.

Reinvest in South Africa

The Reinvest in South Africa (RISA) fund significantly outperformed its benchmark (and the competition) during its first six months of operation in 1999. Posting a six-month return of 16.70 percent, the new fund significantly outperformed the South African market, which returned only 10 percent. This nearly 10 percent advantage over the local market gives support to RISA's investment thesis that active management of "New South Africa Companies" will produce returns that are superior to investing in the 16 largest companies on the Johannesburg Stock Exchange (JSE).

"New South Africa Companies" are primarily small and midcap companies listed on the JSE that are in the fastest-growing sectors of the South African economy. These sectors include technology, telecommunications, financial services, and export manufacturers. Growth rates often exceed 20 percent per year. These companies must also score well on standards reflecting commitment to economic empowerment of majority South Africans. RISA criteria include encompassing diverse stakeholders, transparent governance, worker training programs, environmental responsibility, quality workplace conditions, and the creation of jobs in all business operations. RISA is a registered investment advisor based in Philadelphia and partnered with African Harvest, a multiracial firm based in South Africa. It can be viewed at <www.risafund.com>.

Source: O. Sam Folin, "RISA Fund Outperforms," *RISA Newsletter* (Spring 2000).

The antiapartheid movement built institutions that form the backbone of the growing SRI field today. Churches of many faiths joined the Anglican Communion in asking corporations to shun South Africa, or at least to sign the Sullivan Principles. Out of this coalition grew the most vital resource for shareholder activism to this day, the Interfaith Center on Corporate Responsibility (ICCR). Virtually every shareholder resolution addressing a social or environmental issue since 1972 has relied upon the seasoned faith-based advocates through the network of ICCR to bring about active dialogue. This coalition carried the cry for human dignity from a dream to reality for millions of South Africans.

The dialogue over the appropriate role of the American corporation doing business in South Africa led to a vast transformation of the understanding of the role of the corporation in society. Library board after library board, school endowment after school endowment, and pension trustee after pension trustee debated over the stand to take on the issue of South Africa. Board committees with names like Social Responsibility in Investments were set up to evaluate the issue and to make recommendations to the full boards. Many of these committees still exist today, advising on the broad range of positions that the trustees of their institutions might take on social responsibility issues presented to shareholders.

With the South African campaign came a change in vocabulary and emphasis. What had been known as ethical investing began to encompass both the making of investment decisions based on ethical or mission-centered criteria and the engagement of corporations in a direct dialogue about issues of concern such as environmental or employment policies. It began to be called socially responsible investing, and grew to encompass concerns regarding the corporate impact on several stakeholders in the company: employees, communities, suppliers, consumers, and the natural environment. Traditional negative screens were joined with positive investments in companies that performed at the top of their industry on social criteria.

The Top 14 SRI Mutual Funds

Of the 68 SRI funds tracked by the Social Investment Forum as of April 30, 2000, the top 14 in terms of net assets are listed below. These funds generally appeal to a wide range of socially responsible investors and are among the most visible funds on the market, but dozens of smaller funds also serve social investors, including funds with a specific religious orientation or that target other issues such as the environment.

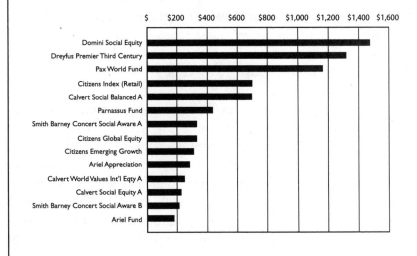

Source: The Social Investment Forum Web site, located at <www.socialinvest.org>.

By the early 1980s, several mutual funds had been founded to meet the needs of the ethical investor. Pax World Fund (PAXWX), Dreyfus Third Century (DRTHX), Parnassus (PARNX), New Alternatives, and Calvert Social Balanced Fund (CSIFX) all took both a negative and positive screening approach. Not only did they generally avoid alcohol, tobacco, gambling, nuclear power, military weapons, and American corporations doing business in South Africa, they also looked at the impact the company had on other stakeholders and tried to invest in the more responsible corporate citizens.

The way to document corporate impact to inform civic society and move it to action was discovered through the success of the Sullivan Principles. Using ascertainable data points to track impact underpins corporate social research work to this day. Where there is progress, companies can be complimented and rewarded by increased shareholder investment. Where there is a lack of progress, civic society will have the proof needed to take corrective action through shareholder activism or other means. Data collection leads to knowledge, which leads to action. That is what the South African debate taught the world.

Building Healthy Communities

The late 1960s and early 1970s were also the formative years for the modern structure of community development financial institutions. On a somewhat separate track from corporate social responsibility work but parallel to it, community initiatives were springing up, largely in response to increased awareness of racial inequity. In 1973, Milton Davis, James Fletcher, Ronald Grzywinski, and Mary Houghton founded the first bank dedicated solely to community development, the South Shore Bank of Chicago, to link their common belief in social justice to practical action that would serve the community.[5] Like many urban neighborhoods, the South Shore of Chicago area had experienced both white flight, as whites moved to the suburbs or other parts of the city, and the accompanying fleeing of retail stores in the 1950s and 1960s. The neighborhood was at risk of deteriorating into an immense crime-ridden ghetto.

The South Shore Bank was founded largely as a social experiment to see if lending to the neighborhood could stabilize it. But the needs of the South Shore area far surpassed the capacity of the bank to lend. This was largely due not to the bank's lack of capitalization, but to its lack of deposits. The bank was unable to effectively encourage local people to bank with it, and without the deposits the bank could not make loans in a cost-effective way. The lack of deposits largely resulted from the fact that the African-American community in the South Shore area remained very loyal to First Chicago, a bank that had won their loyalty by being the first Chicago bank to offer checking accounts to African-Americans but which was not lending to the community. South Shore Bank turned to a national audience and asked for deposit dollars so that it could, in turn, lend to an at-risk community in Chicago.

Today, 30 years after the founding of the bank, the South Shore area of Chicago is a socioeconomically diverse, predominately African-American, and pleasant residential community. Although it has never been able to replace its retail businesses effectively, the neighborhood was certainly stabilized and has become vibrant. The experiment worked: Loans to poor people did build their wealth and helped build a healthy community. To the surprise of many, the loans were even repaid at a higher rate than national averages. South Shore Bank has been profitable every year since 1975, thus establishing the community development financial institution as a viable business opportunity.

This model has inspired the creation of similar institutions in the United States, Europe, and developing nations with emerging economies, including Pakistan, Kenya, and Bangladesh. Credit Populaire Zairos is one such institution. Begun in 1987 by consumer cooperatives in the North Kivu region of the Congo, with financing from the Bank of Zaire provided in 1989, its stated goal is to support industry, agriculture, and other enterprises that benefit social economy. Working in much the same way as a credit union, Credit Populaire Zairos makes loans to member cooperatives for housing, reforestation programs, women's collectives, nutritional centers, and old people's homes. Recently, it has worked in partnership with Habitat for Humanity and has built or repaired 1,600 homes.[6]

Returning to the early 1980s, Social Responsibility in Investments committees, put in place over the South African debate, learned of the experiment in Chicago and recommended that commitments to communities be incorporated into their portfolios. Many were familiar with older efforts that their endowments had participated in during the Civil Rights struggle. One such fund, the Ghetto Seed Loan Fund, created in 1968 by the national Episcopal Church, was incorporated into a larger community investment portfolio in the late 1980s. New nonprofit entities, like Boston Community Capital, a loan fund originally funded by the Housing Committee of the South End Meeting House, were created. Socially responsible investing, begun as a way to avoid certain investments, now became a vehicle for seeking new and innovative ways to meet the needs of those less fortunate.

Today, social investors continue to feel a kinship with community economic development initiatives and frequently hold a portion of their portfolio in institutions like South Shore Bank. Community development financial institutions (CDFI) afford investors access to grassroots activists who can articulate the impact of corporate behavior on the nation's most severely disenfranchised populations. This both enriches the screening process and opens new avenues of inquiry in shareholder activism.

Business Practices That Create Sweatshops

Since 1986, **General Electric (GE)** has slashed its U.S. workforce by almost half and has globalized its operations by shifting production to low-wage countries. And even in these countries, the jobs remain precarious: GE recently shuttered a factory in Turkey to move it to lower-wage Hungary—and it has threatened to close a factory in Hungary and move it to India. Not satisfied to close its own plants, GE has made moves to shut down those of suppliers, too. In a startling memo, GE's hugely profitable aircraft engines division told suppliers that they would have to move to Mexico if they hoped to continue their relationship with GE. The company even holds what it calls "supplier migration" conferences. An internal

report on a meeting with suppliers says, "GE set the tone early
and succinctly: Migrate or be out of business; not a matter of if,
just when. This is not a seminar to provide you information. We
expect you to move and move quickly."

Source: Russell Mokhiber and Robert Weissman, "GE: Every Plant on A Barge,"
Focus on the Corporation, 17 May 2000. © Russell Mokhiber and Robert Weissman.

A Case Study on the Evolution of Social Investing

The socially responsible investment industry now stands
firmly on a three-legged stool: screened portfolios, shareholder
activism, and community development financial institutions.
Each of these three strengthens and deepens the other two. Each
has strengths and weaknesses. One could argue that screens do
nothing, that the creation of a corporate accountability infrastructure and knowledge base is too theoretical. One could argue that
activism does too little, that a couple of dozen companies signing
an environmental code of conduct is a drop in the bucket when
considering all that needs to be done. One could argue that community development is nice, but improving the lives of some
people means nothing in the face of a billion people living in
poverty globally. However, together, the three accomplish much.
What socially responsible investors share with each other is a
commitment to do what can be done at the scale at which it can
be done—that, and a conviction that it is important to do what
each of us can to save one life at a time. The current debate over
sweatshops shows how.

One of the fastest-growing areas of concern for socially responsible investors is the one commonly referred to as the sweatshop,
or supplier, issue. The sweatshop of today is the result of changes
in manufacturing that have taken place over the past few
decades. When the debate raged in South Africa, it concerned
corporations that owned and operated manufacturing facilities in
the country. Today corporations buy from suppliers they do not

own, but do have tremendous influence over. How accountable is a corporation for working conditions when it does not own and operate the manufacturing facilities that produce its goods? Suppose a company requests bids on supplying 10,000 T-shirts and awards the contract to a manufacturer operating in Haiti. Even the most humane purchasing agent sitting in her New York City office is unlikely to notice the human rights implications of what appears to be a perfectly straightforward economic decision.

Child Labor

The International Labour Organization estimates 250 million children between the ages of 5 and 14 work in developing countries; of that number, 120 million children work full-time. Asia is home to 61 percent of child workers, Africa, 32 percent, and Latin America, 7 percent. The Associated Press identifies child labor as a continuing presence and problem in some U.S. industries, particularly agriculture, and estimated that the number of children working illegally in the United States to be 290,000. In addition, the AP linked these illegal and unethical practices to high-profile, mainstream companies, including **Costco (COST), Heinz (HNZ), Newman's Own, J.C. Penney (JCP), Pillsbury (owned by Diageo (DEO)), Sears (S), Wal-Mart (WMT), and Campbell Soup Co. (CPB)**. When confronted with the information that their suppliers were using child labor, the majority of these companies condemned the practice and switched suppliers.

Source: The *Quality Digest* Web site, located at <www.quality digest.com>.

The current campaign over the sourcing of goods can probably best be traced to a Catholic congregation of Oblate missionaries working in Haiti. They first raised the question of human rights in shops manufacturing baseballs. Factory conditions in

Haiti can be inhumane, unhealthy, and dangerous. Furthermore, the winding of a string ball continuously for hours is a strenuous physical activity. Tax incentives and low wages attracted foreign-owned manufacturing plants that produce electronics, clothing, and sporting goods like baseballs for sale abroad, mostly in the United States. In 1990, women made up about 75 percent of the factory workers, and were paid only $3.20 a day.[7] Most work under conditions unimaginable to the end purchaser of the product.

Alternatives for Haitian Youth: Spotlight on Group Kreyol Community Development Lending at Work— Project of SEED

Group Kreyol is one of the many projects that **SEED: Haiti Community Development Loan Fund** is undertaking in 2000. Concerned with the problems of unemployment and accompanying emigration by Haitian youth, Group Kreyol has been working to develop a profitable business. The 95-member youth cooperative has moved into three forms of production: Kreyol Kitchen (producing candy, jam, juices from local agricultural products), Kreyol Couture (producing special indigenous embroidered shirts), and Boutique Kreyol (a merchandise outlet where products of Group Kreyol and other co-ops will be sold). All three are owned and controlled by the co-op. With the help of SEED, these Haitian youth have a better chance of making a living in their homeland.

Source: *SEED: Projects 2000*, a publication of SEED: Haiti Community Development Loan Fund.

The baseball campaign was not well covered in the popular press, but among Catholic congregations of religious men and women doing missionary and charity work around the world, it struck a chord. This was not an issue unique to Haiti; sweat-shops had taken root throughout most emerging economies. Other sporadic campaigns run by missionary groups working in Guatemala, Mexico, and El Salvador sprang up. Some of these campaigns targeted companies that owned the manufacturing facilities, while others went beyond ownership to sourcing.

When labor unions began raising the issue, the U.S. Department of Labor, under Secretary Robert Reich, undertook sweeping investigations. Mainstream Americans learned of the issue when talk show celebrity Kathy Lee Gifford, on a live tele-vision broadcast, tearfully confessed her own culpability in out-sourcing her clothing line's production to a sweatshop in Asia. These events forced the American public to recognize the wide-spread involvement of sweatshop labor in imported goods.

Nike (NKE) landed at the center of the sweatshop debate after the CBS news program *48 Hours* ran a segment detailing the abuse of Nike workers in Vietnam, and a boycott began in October 1996. A group of grassroots volunteers, deeply dis-turbed by the report, decided to contact labor groups and jour-nalists in Vietnam to verify the report. They met with Nike offi-cials to discuss the problems and organized a group called Vietnam Labor Watch (VLW) to monitor the issue on an ongoing basis. At Nike's invitation, (VLW) traveled in Vietnam March 2–18, 1997, to visit the factories and investigate labor law viola-tions, wages, working conditions, health and safety practices, and sexual harassment. The injustices they uncovered prompted a massive anti-Nike boycott, including 53 members of Congress, writer Alice Walker, and a host of public interest groups.[8] The company became almost a symbol of the sweatshop controver-sy; the consumer boycott caused most mutual funds that serve social investors to divest the stock.

How should the socially responsible investor respond to the sweatshop issue? In a survey conducted by Domini Social Investments, avoiding companies that utilize sweatshops ranked as the number two concern of social investors. Only the environment drew greater concern ratings. But screening out companies that manufacture in sweatshops is virtually impossible today. No good data are available yet. As in formulating a response to South Africa, we must gradually feel our way forward.

More Women Invest Responsibly

Of 800 adults surveyed regarding their investment attitudes, women showed more commitment to investing in companies screened for different criteria, including:

Criterion	Women	Men
Environmental practices	73%	67%
Hiring and promoting women	69	56
Hiring and promoting minorities	69	55
Labor practices	62	51
Tobacco manufacture	54	45

Source: 1999 Yankelovich Partners survey.

The social investment industry seeks advice from on-the-ground activists on an emerging issue. It was only after black South African leadership asked Americans to step up the campaign by selling companies tainted by factories in South Africa that the divestment campaign began. But no such call for divestment over sweatshops is being raised since leadership is diffuse. The nature of sweatshops is such that no governing voice exists. Human rights activists such as Human Rights Watch or Coalition for Justice in the Maquiladoras have urged responsible investment fund managers to enter into dialogue with companies about sourcing codes of conduct, which can free workers from inhumane working conditions while protecting their jobs. Furthermore, as the South African debate taught us, codes of conduct will provide the data needed to move civic society from lethargy to action.

Today, increasing shareholder activism on the sweatshop issue forces investment managers and corporations to consider issues of basic human dignity as part of their mainstream business. In 2000, 17 leading U.S. clothing retailers, including Calvin Klein, Liz Claiborne (LIZ), Sears (S), and Tommy Hilfiger (TOM), agreed to settle claims against them in a federal class-action lawsuit alleging sweatshop conditions in the garment industry on the Western Pacific island of Saipan. The plaintiffs included human rights organizations and garment unions, and the $8 million settlement will provide for independent monitoring, payment of back wages to workers, safe food and water, and public education.[9]

The sweatshop dialogue has led to the development of standards. Over time, a more sophisticated assessment of corporate adherence to these standards will develop, and the tools for deciding which companies are more responsible, and which are less, will evolve. At that point, real screening can take place, but to date only Nike (NKE) has become a boycott target and therefore a divestment target. Corporate responsibility for the existence of sweatshops is only just beginning to be understood. The evolution of socially responsible investing will be profoundly affected by this debate, which is perhaps the most complex issue the field has faced since South Africa.

Screening Your Investments 3

A Look under the Hood

She would rather light candles than
curse in the darkness and her glow warmed the world.

—ADLAI STEVENSON, IN

HIS EULOGY FOR ELEANOR ROOSEVELT

.

When you invest in companies that meet certain social or ethical criteria, you reconcile your investment decisions with your personal values and reintroduce human dignity and environmental sustainability as goals of equal importance to profits and maximizing shareholder returns. To select the companies you invest in, you must first pass candidates through a filter called social screens. This filtering process allows you to avoid certain products or practices and to emphasize others. Through the past 20 years, these screens have evolved into a way of assessing the negative and positive effects a corporation has on its various stakeholders. This chapter goes into some detail on the "hows" and "whys" of the screening process.

As a socially responsible investor, you choose to be as deliberate with investment decisions as you are with charitable giving and lifestyle choices. This is true whether you can screen the stocks and bonds you own or decide to invest in an SRI mutual fund. When you invest in a mutual fund that files shareholder resolutions and invests in community development financial institutions, you are likely to achieve a greater impact than would be possible acting on your own, but you may feel that you lose a sense of personal involvement. Whether you want to choose your own portfolio of stocks or simply want to understand the screening at a fund you are considering investing in, it all begins with the decision to be deliberate.

What Is a Stakeholder?

A stakeholder is a party who is strongly affected by the policy and practices of the corporation.

My own list follows:

- **Communities**—people in places where the corporation has operations; these stakeholders generally care whether the company pays local taxes, provides jobs across a broad socio-economic spectrum, has charitable giving programs that support public institutions in their geographic region, and builds attractive and human-scale facilities.
- **Customers**—those who purchase from the corporation; these stakeholders particularly care about receiving a safe and useful product.
- **Employees**—those who work for the company; these stakeholders particularly care about the programs specifically geared toward job protection, safety, job enhancement, pay, equal access to opportunity, ongoing education, and recognition that the employee has a family.
- **Lenders**—individuals, banks, and other institutions lending to the corporation; these stakeholders particularly care about the cash flow the company generates from its operations.
- **Shareholders**—the owners of the company; these stakeholders particularly care about seeing a constantly higher

stock price and are also concerned about the way in which a company governs itself.

- **The Natural Environment**—our world; this stakeholder would prefer to be left in better condition as a result of the corporation's existence and is concerned both with pollution and with efforts to create a cleaner and pleasanter environment.
- **Vendors or Suppliers**—those who sell to the corporation; these stakeholders want to understand the rules by which a company makes decisions about the source of materials.

A special note on **diversity**: In recognition that the United States is a particularly diverse nation, diversity is frequently cited as a stakeholder. Another approach is to say that corporations are strengthened by diversity when they have solid relationships with certain other stakeholders. For instance, specific programs encouraging diversity in the workplace might come under employees. Programs to purchase a certain amount from women and/or minority-owned suppliers might come under suppliers.

What Is a Mutual Fund?

A mutual fund is a portfolio of (or holding place for) stocks and/or bonds. The portfolio is managed according to a specific philosophy spelled out in the fund's prospectus. The purchaser of shares in a mutual fund is, generally speaking, buying that particular fund because he wishes to invest in a portfolio with a proven track record and a stated philosophy. For most investors, this is a more efficient and effective way of investing than selecting individual stocks or bonds.

Almost all mutual funds are "open-ended," which means that there is no fixed number of shares available, as there is for a corporation. Open-ended mutual funds are priced based on what the stocks of the companies the fund portfolio invested in are worth. This means that if your mutual fund owns shares in XYZ Corp., and XYZ Corp.'s stock goes up in price, then your mutual fund's value will be adjusted for that price rise. This is good. When you buy a table at a flea market, you have to haggle (bid against all the other buyers and sellers) over price. When you buy stock in XYZ, you have to haggle over price. When you buy shares in an open-ended mutual fund, you get a fair price for that day.

The Importance of Negative Screens

Socially responsible investors around the world avoid manufacturers of alcohol, tobacco, and firearms, along with the providers of power generated from nuclear sources and managers of gambling casinos or manufacturers of the equipment for the gambling industry. Even these relatively simple avoidance screens are more complicated than they appear to be at first glance. For instance, in the United States, the standard is to consider the leafy substance to be tobacco but not to consider the store that sells the leafy substance to be tobacco. Nonetheless, most social investors avoid the store that receives an inordinate amount of its profits from the leafy product since such an investment seems inconsistent with the goals of the screen. This thinking is applied to all the negative screens.

As an example, the Domini Social Equity Fund (DSEFX) screen that excludes alcoholic beverage manufacturers also excludes companies that derive more than 15 percent of their revenues from the retail sale of alcoholic beverages. This eliminates some restaurant chains and convenience stores. The screen also excludes a number of agricultural companies that sell products used in the production of alcoholic beverages, such as distilled corn spirits. Suppliers of unprocessed agricultural goods, such as barley or grapes, are informally excluded if the volume of sales to alcohol producers exceeds 15 percent of the company's revenues.[1]

The 25 Largest Gambling Companies Worldwide

Company Name	Country
Namco Ltd. (9752)	Japan
Round One Corp. (4680)	Japan
Genting Berhad (GENT)	Malaysia
Jaleco Ltd. (7954)	Japan
MGM Mirage (MGG)	United States
Hilton Group PLC-Sp Adr (HLTGY)	Britain
Park Place Entertainment (PPE)	United States
Tabcorp Holdings Ltd. (TAH)	Australia
Tanjong PLC (TJN)	Malaysia
Magnum Corp. Berhad (MNM)	Malaysia
Hilton Group PLC (HG/)	Britain
Berjaya Sports Toto Berhad (BST)	Malaysia
Harrah's Entertainment Inc (HET)	United States
Kersaf Investments Ltd. (KER)	South Africa
Aristocrat Leisure Ltd. (ALL)	Australia
International Game Technology (IGT)	United States
Mandalay Resort Group (MBG)	United States
Sun International (South Africa) Ltd. (SIS)	South Africa
Prime Gaming Philippines Inc (PGMC)	Philippines
Tab Ltd. (TAB)	Australia
Berjaya Land Bhd. (BL)	Malaysia
Sky City Ltd. (SKC)	New Zealand
Berjaya Group Berhad (BG)	Malaysia
Station Casinos Inc (STN)	United States
Wah Yik Holdings Co. Ltd. (862)	Hong Kong

Sorted by Market Capitalization as of July 30, 2000

Source: Bloomberg.

The Calvert social funds employ similar thinking with their screen for the weapons industry. Calvert will not invest in companies significantly involved in weapons production. They avoid companies that have weapons contracts exceeding 10 percent of gross annual sales. Specifically, Calvert's social funds do not invest in companies that comprise the top 85 percent of the total market for weapons contracts with the U.S. Department of Defense, or the top 90 percent of the total market for nuclear weapons contractors. The top 40 weapons contractors were excluded as a result of applying the 85 percent market threshold standard. In 1996, the top 25 nuclear weapons contractors were excluded as a result of applying the 90 percent market threshold standard.[2] By setting a percentage limit of acceptable involvement in an unacceptable industry, social investors limit their involvement in products and services such as alcohol, tobacco, gambling, and weapons. It is hoped that this will highlight the particularly troubling aspects of these industries.

Not every social investor cares about every negative screen. Some feel that a strong military is a good and necessary thing. Others view alcohol consumption as a personal choice that is relatively benign. However, you don't need to avoid alcohol to see that the product is addictive, probably shouldn't be advertised, and has led to a great deal of suffering on the part of millions. You don't need to be a pacifist to feel that weapons are in too many hands. The simple answer to why these are the industries eliminated is that they always have been, but there are more complex reasons as well.

Avoidance screens may have developed earliest, but they are by no means old-fashioned. Consider the more political interpretation. When one considers the best use of the for-profit system, it is to distribute a product to as many people as possible at the lowest possible price. Capitalism has been an effective means of delivering desired goods and services to vast numbers of people. Are you willing to state that it is in society's best interest to deliver alcohol, tobacco, gambling, or weapons as cheaply and broadly as possible?

The 25 Companies from around the World with the Largest Percent of Revenues Coming from Sales to the Military

Company	Country	Percent of Revenues from Military
Elbit Systems Ltd. (ESLT)	Israel	99.9
Vosper Thornycroft (VSP)	United Kingdom	99.9
BVR Systems Ltd. (BVRS)	Israel	99.0
Alvis PLC (ALV)	United Kingdom	99.0
Avimo Group Ltd. (@AV)	Singapore	94.0
DY 4 Systems Inc. (DYF)	Canada	90.0
PSC Industries BHD (PSC)	Malaysia	83.0
BAE Systems PLC (BAE)	United Kingdom	73.0
Radamec Group PLC (RDM)	United Kingdom	65.0
Precision Standard Inc. (PCSN)	United States	63.7
Singapore Tech. Engineering (STE)	Singapore	60.0
Thomson-CSF SA (HO)	France	57.0
Dassault Aviation SA (@AM)	France	55.0
Dyno Industrier SA (DYN)	Norway	55.0
Korean Air Lines (0349)	South Korea	51.0
Hunting PLC (HTG)	United Kingdom	51.0
Rada Electronic Industries Ltd. (RADIF)	Israel	50.0
Saab AB (SAABB)	Sweden	50.0
BAE Systems Canada, Inc. (BAE)	Canada	43.0
ShinMaywa Industries Ltd. (7224)	Japan	43.0
General Dynamics Corp. (GD)	United States	41.9
Spar Aerospace Ltd. (SPZ)	Canada	39.0
Akzo Nobel NV (AKZO)	Netherlands	39.0
Racal Electronics PLC (RCAL)	United Kingdom	38.0
Newport News Shipbuilding, Inc. (NNS)	United States	35.2

Source: Kinder, Lydenberg, Domini & Co., Inc. Socrates database <www.kld.com>.

Negative screens grew out of a deeply personal conviction that it would be wrong to make money from certain industries, but it is also arguable that these industries, if allowed to benefit from unfettered for-profit management, would benefit to the detriment of civic society. In fact, in most nations alcohol, tobacco, gambling, and weapons manufacturing facilities were owned and managed by government until quite recently, and in many places still are. In India, for instance, there is only one privately held factory licensed to produce weapons, and these are sold solely to the Indian government. Government ownership may not be perfect, but it at least clearly states that some products must be made available only in a manner that serves society as a whole.

Several other industries are troublesome in a for-profit environment and are avoided by socially responsible investors. For-profit correctional institutions, managers of public schools, and health care facilities are among generally avoided industries, though not enumerated in most literature about SRI. A common thread that runs through these industries is that their immediate clients (prisoners, sick people, and preschool children) are at a particular disadvantage as consumers of the services being offered. One could argue that, ultimately, the clients of these corporations are sophisticated and well-informed consumers (government or parents), but their connection to the services rendered is at one level removed. It is quite possible that the structure will allow and even encourage abuses to go unchecked.[3]

An Example of a Negative Screen: For-Profit Prisons

Few people are more qualified to comment on the tragedy of for-profit prisons than Ted Strickland. A U.S. representative from Ohio, Strickland worked as a psychologist at the Southern Ohio Correctional Facility, a maximum-security prison. We share his thoughts here.

"A public prison is obligated to maintain a safe and secure environment for the corrections staff, the inmates, and the surround-

ing community. A private prison, on the other hand, is obligated
to its corporate shareholders. The raison d'être of a private prison
is profit, not protection ....

"The trend toward prison privatization is disturbing in another
way—because of its potentially corrupting effects on public policy.
Prison corporations like CCA [**Corrections Corp. of America**] have
hired politically well-connected lobbyists to advocate for their
cause. The profit motive is also an incentive for private prison advocates to begin lobbying for long-term and mandatory sentences
that would keep their beds filled, their profits flowing, and their
investors happy.... Correctional staff can influence parole decisions.
For example, consider a prisoner who receives a 15- to 45-year sen-
tence. What happens within the prison walls—the relationship
between the prisoner and the correctional staff and the disciplinary
record established—can lead to the early release of that prisoner or
his or her continued incarceration for the entire 45 years. But when
private prison employees receive part of their compensation based
on the company's stock value, those employees benefit personally
from the continued incarceration of their charges ....

"Ultimately, private prisons are tempted to do whatever it takes to
keep costs down and keep their beds filled, since, like a hotel, a private prison makes more money at full capacity. This may be acceptable when we are talking about hotel/motel management, but it is
absolutely intolerable when we are talking about public safety."

Source: Ted Strickland, "Private Prisons: The Bottom Line," *The Washington Post*, 13
June 1999, final, B01.

Responsible investors struggle with how best to deal with
these and a number of other troubling industries. Many have
come down on the side of avoiding problematic industries completely. Others decide to underweight some industries while
avoiding others. Consider the petroleum industry, for instance.
Humankind has, quite possibly, placed the ultimate bet by using

petroleum as our primary energy source. It now seems almost certain that the use of petroleum as a fuel has had an extremely detrimental impact on our natural environment and that emissions and the greenhouse effect may in fact lead to an environment in which life as we know it cannot exist. Nonetheless, consumption continues to rise every year and no meaningful alternatives have emerged. This conundrum leads some socially responsible investors to avoid the petroleum industry altogether and others to vastly de-emphasize the industry, whether they drive cars or not.

Biotech Controversy Failing to Feed the Starving Masses

Global biotech companies, including **Monsanto** (currently owned by **Pharmacia (PHA)** which has plans to spin it off), feature starving masses in their advertisements to bolster claims of fighting world hunger. But in July 1999, the USDA revealed that biotech crops had not improved yields or decreased pesticide costs for soybean and cotton growers. In fact, a 1998 study of 8,200 soybean varietal trials by Charles Benbrook, Ph.D., found that Roundup Ready soybeans, bioengineered to resist Monsanto's Roundup herbicide, actually produce lower yields than comparable, nonengineered soy under most conditions.

It's hard to argue that bioengineered crops will assuage world hunger when more than 90 percent of America's soy and 80 percent of its corn goes to livestock feed, not hungry humans. None of the other transgenic crops—soy, corn, potatoes, papayas, squash, canola, or cotton—are dietary staples of the poor in most developing countries. What's worse is that genetically engineered seeds are much more expensive for all but the largest third-world farmers.

Source: A. Ikramuddin, "Far Afield: Biotech Propaganda and the Truth," *The Green Guide* 72 (October 1999).

The same can also be said of meat production, another business that has a disastrous environmental impact. The Center for a Livable Future at the Johns Hopkins School of Public Health launched a project to coordinate research and discussion on all aspects of industrial animal production (IAP), including its effects on human health, the environment, and the animals. Project director David Brubaker, Ph.D., asserts, "The way that we breed animals for food is a threat to the planet. It pollutes our environment while consuming huge amounts of water, grain, petroleum, pesticides, and drugs. The results are disastrous." He estimates that a hog farm with 5,000 animals produces as much fecal waste as a city with 50,000 people, yet the disposal methods are far more primitive.[4] As with petroleum, meat producers tend to be either completely avoided or very underweighted by social investors.

There are some unpopular industries that are not avoided by social investors. The huge, box-like superstore is here to stay despite the fact that the public finds it so offensive. We find a complete lack of humanity there. The parking lots have no benches, no garden areas; there is no pleasantness to the facade, no playground, no outdoor art. Inside are no pleasant sitting areas and no way to get information; finally, there is no relief from the continuous assault of advertisements. If corporations and society had standards for new construction (or any other action affecting stakeholders) that integrated the long-term, most pleasant life goals into behavior, what a different world we would see. Too often, permits are granted and impact fees or local regulations waived because of a hope that the store will bring jobs. But these are minimum wage jobs and not living wage jobs, so the local economy is not meaningfully helped. For these types of reasons, many social investors are uncomfortable investing in chains of superstores. The dominant response, however, is to hold a few and continuously work with their management, through shareholder dialogue, to strive for more responsible and caring practices. This is because it is not the nature of the product, but rather the role of society, that is raised by big boxes. Society needs to create rules.

Negative screens apply to bonds as well as stocks. There are bonds of entities that do not have stock, such as municipalities and the government, and these are evaluated just as companies would be. Socially responsible investors have chosen to avoid investments in certain government-sponsored debt securities. The U.S. Treasury is so general in its purpose, and so much of the U.S. budget goes to the military, that Treasury bonds are not bought by most social investors.

Why Social Investors Avoid Bonds Issued by the World Bank: Environmental Ineffectiveness

Heavily in-debt nations are forced to increase their exports to repay foreign debt. As a result, explains Friends of the Earth, "Countries often over-exploit their resources through unsustainable forestry, mining, and agricultural practices that generate pollution and environmental destruction." World Bank forest sector loans to countries around the world have done nothing to improve the situation. In November 1999 the World Bank's own Operations Evaluation Department said, "Bank influence on containing rates of deforestation of tropical moist forests has been negligible in the 20 countries with the most threatened tropical moist forests."

Source: Russell Mokhiber and Robert Weissman, "A Dozen Reasons to Come to DC for April 16," *Focus on the Corporation,* 5 April 2000. © Russell Mokhiber and Robert Weissman.

Most socially responsible investors avoid bonds issued by the World Bank since the projects they sponsor seem to create hardships on the very people they are supposed to help. Ever since 1982, when Mexico stunned the world by announcing that it could no longer service its foreign debt, many poor countries have been forced to borrow from the bank in exchange for repayment relief. Remember that the poor did not borrow the money originally. Often a corrupt leader or inept businessman drew up a business plan and then simply banked the money or failed, leaving the nation to hold the bag. The World Bank demands that the already desperately poor nation repay a loan a responsible lender never would have made. Between 1996 and 1999, the debt of heavily indebted poor countries (HIPC) increased by 10.6 percent. Debt relief for the 20 most affected nations would amount to less that $7 billion—less than the cost of one Stealth bomber.[5] And yet the wealthy nations of the world refuse to grant full relief.

The result of filtering out the most harmful products and services is that most social portfolios, whether individual stocks or mutual funds, greatly underemphasize some things that traditional investors would buy. But socially responsible investing is not simply ecofundamentalism at work. The field is complex and strives to steer for-profit systems toward creating a world where human dignity and environmental sustainability can survive. It would be illogical to emphasize avoiding an ever-increasing laundry list of products and services. Rather, the trend in SRI has been to emphasize positive stakeholder impact while recognizing that stressing positives implies avoiding negatives.

Weeding out some companies and industries is an important first step, not only because it is so central to socially responsible investing, but also because it emphasizes both the role that corporations should play in society and the role that society probably should assume—in another manner, such as through civic institutions and government.

Qualitative or Positive Screening

Probably the most misunderstood aspect of socially responsible investing is the extent to which the qualitative, or positive, screens are based on cold, hard facts. Again, to understand how these screens evolved, we look to history.

In the past, those who studied corporate impact did so from the perspective of only one stakeholder at a time. Consumer rights groups would follow and publicize product safety issues or pricing issues; environmentalists would study and expose harmful environmental practices, and labor unions would focus on workers' rights. The entire corporate social research industry depended on either philanthropy or government for funding. This made ongoing research unlikely.

Foundations and government generally prefer to provide funding for studying an issue if there is a goal of using the data to create an action plan. They have their own purposes, and providing continuous funding of a study that never ends doesn't fit. So the collection of data would take place for a few years in one area and then halt. This had the effect of undermining the potential longer-term impact of important ground-laying work for continuous surveillance and evaluation. A foundation that cares about the environment, for instance, is so committed to that research that it sees each decision through the lens of environmental impact. The attachment of special purpose funds to its primary issue precludes the creation of a comprehensive context, one that evaluates overall corporate impact.

Socially responsible investors bring all these threads together by collecting data generated by those who look at a company through the eyes of one constituency only and then integrate it all into a corporate social responsibility profile.

The unique perspective investors bring is a more holistic interest in a company. You invest in the entire company, not just one aspect of it, so you quite naturally take a more comprehensive approach to the evaluative process than an environmental advocacy group or labor union would. This big-picture approach leads investors to assimilate important information from various corporate social responsibility watchdogs and from corporations themselves. From the data we can make an informed assessment of a company's overall record. It is a nice partnership. Watchdogs have a good handle on a particular issue, while as investors, we research the complex influence companies have on a multitude of stakeholders.

Steve's Stakeholder Story Stocks: Corporations and Civic Values Community—Infrastructure and Empowerment

Steven D. Lydenberg, research director at KLD chose these examples of companies that work to develop and support the infrastructure of small businesses, affordable housing, diverse media, and education.

- **Allied Capital Corp.** is a business development corporation concentrating on small business lending, a vital service for community economic development. Joan M. Sweeney is the company's managing director and second highest-paid officer.
- **DeVry Inc. (DV)** is a provider of career-oriented postsecondary education. Minorities account for 45 percent and women for 25 percent of student enrollment.
- **Fannie Mae (FNM)** is a financial institution providing liquidity to the secondary market for affordable housing. As of December 1998, the company's foundation had approximately $15.5 million in below-market loans outstanding to community development organizations across the country.
- **Radio One (ROIA)** is an African-American-owned and operated network of radio stations serving and supporting the African-American community. In addition, the company regularly sponsors events aimed at addressing issues of concern to these communities. For example, it supports events that raise awareness about diseases disproportionately affecting African-Americans and engages in fundraising aimed at supporting African-American single mothers with substantial day care expenses and African-American churches hit by arsonists.
- **St. Paul Companies (SPC)** is an insurance company with a generous charitable giving program targeted to a diverse array of neighborhood groups. Gifts include support for local artists and for a broad range of housing initiatives.

- **Wainwright Bank and Trust (WAIN)** has, since its founding in the mid-1980s, made an exceptional commitment to providing lending to the nonprofit community in Boston. It is one of the most active lenders to affordable housing, hunger, and AIDS-related organizations in the city. It also offers a certificate of deposit program that targets lending to urban revitalization programs. It offers a community credit card that donates 1 percent of purchases to AIDS work and homeless groups.

Source: You can reach Steve at stevel@kld.com or visit his Web site <www.kld.com>.

For instance, in the United States, the Environmental Protection Agency mandates that corporations report on emissions of certain toxic chemicals. This law does not exist in other countries, but most nations do have some public access to certain environmental impact information that allows social analysts there to view the corporation though the eyes of the natural environment. Once separate analysis takes place, it is compiled into the comprehensive social profile.

Here in America, most companies are proud of any charitable giving they do and so report it. This is picked up and circulated by various third-party sources. Most European companies report on their social responsibility to communities as well, though not with as much specificity as American companies do. The laws may vary but the ability to look at the company through the eyes of the community remains.

Bobby's Best New Energy Picks

Bobby Julian is finance director at Preferred Energy, Inc., a Manila, Philippines-based nongovernmental organization with direct investments in renewable energy enterprises. He also develops projects in other areas of the environmental infrastructure space—e.g., water and waste. His main interest is in technology that provides access to new or improved basic services for the many, which ironically in this day and age means his choice investments lean toward the speculative.

- **Capstone Turbine Corp. (CPST)** makes the Capstone MicroTurbine, a power-generating system that produces environmentally friendly electricity and heat. Microturbines can run on a variety of liquid and gaseous fuels, making it ideal for use in resource recovery (burning oil and gas production by-products), space heating, backup power supply, and hybrid electric vehicles. Its greatest potential, however, is in providing electricity to the unserved in developing countries lacking the energy infrastructure. To increase its reach, the company has entered into marketing alliances worldwide.
- **GreenMountain.com** is a green power e-tailer. It buys electricity from renewable-based power producers and resells it to retail customers in deregulated markets through the Internet. GreenMountain.com is currently building its own green power plants to secure the supply for its markets. The business model is compelling as it puts the Internet in the service of social objectives.
- **Plug Power Inc. (PLUG)** is a designer and developer of fuel cells for residential applications. Fuel cells are on-site power generation devices that produce electricity through an electrochemical reaction (rather than combustion) and therefore operate both more efficiently and reliably. Further, they produce near-zero emission of pollutants. PLUG will thrive where the gas and electric utilities are being deregulated and when there is a heightened awareness of climate change. The company, together with GE MicroGen, recently entered an agreement with Joh. Vaillant GmBH u. Co. of Remscheid, Germany, to develop a combination furnace, hot water heater, and fuel cell system that will provide both heat and electricity for the home.

Source: You can write to Bobby at Preferred Energy, Inc., 10th Floor, Strata 100 Building; Emerald Avenue, Ortigas Center; Pasig City, Philippines 1605. You can also reach him by telephone at 632-631-2826 or fax at 632-632-7097. His e-mail address is pei@info.com.ph.

Consumer watchdog groups evaluate product safety in most countries. Whether through a voluntary recall a company might issue, a write-up in *Consumer Reports,* or through an exposé on the front page of *The Paris Match*, it is relatively simple to collect data about a company's product safety record. This provides a way to look at the company through the eyes of the consumer.

Before I turn to the present approach to qualitative research, I first review some basic points about the process. The important thing to remember about research is that the information should (at least ideally) be available without the company's assistance; it is best if you can find data points that can be counted numerically (so as not to be influenced by writing style); the information should offer a significant insight. While this may seem like a challenge when talking about the environment, employment practices, or community relations, it is a challenge that has largely been met by corporate social research firms.

The process is complex for a number of reasons. Reliable stakeholder impact data are not only difficult to find but also difficult to quantify. Certain corporate actions can be viewed as positive by one stakeholder and negative by another, so the investor is placed in the unenviable position of weighing the relative importance of competing stakeholder benefits.

An Industry Takes a Stand for Diversity

In early 2000 the nation's three largest automakers, **Ford Motor Co. (F), DaimlerChrysler (DCX),** and **General Motors (GM),** announced they would extend domestic-partner benefits to same-sex employees and their children. "The coverage follows a commitment we, the three companies, made to study the subject as part of our current UAW contract," said GM spokesman Tom Wickham. He said the benefits will not extend to opposite-sex domestic partners because they have the legal right in this country to get married. The companies will offer health, vision, and dental benefits to the same-sex partners of employees and their children. Most corporate estimates are that only about 1 percent of employees applies for these benefits when they are offered.

About 3,400 companies now offer these benefits. A Society for Human Resources Management benefits survey conducted earlier this year found domestic partner benefits at 21 percent of companies with more than 5,000 employees. Some of the larger companies to offer this benefit include **American Express (AXP), Walt Disney Co. (DIS), United Airlines (UAL), American Airlines (AMR), US Airways (U), Microsoft (MSFT), IBM, Levi-Strauss, Tower Records, Honeywell (HON), and Xerox (XRX).**

This marks the first time major companies in an industry have granted same-sex partners of employees health benefits simultaneously. "This is really a landmark," Kim Mills, education director of the Human Rights Campaign in Washington, D.C., told the Associated Press. The three automakers said they hope the new benefits will encourage gays and lesbians to join and stay with their companies.

Source: Barbara Frankle, "Big Three Automakers Offering Same-Sex Benefits," <*www.diversityinc.com*>, 8 June 2000. © 2000 <www.diversity.com>.

Some desired information is simply not available. For instance, companies do not keep detailed records of environmental or diversity statistics that might be of interest to the SRI industry if it is not required by law. Companies are able, by law, to keep certain other information confidential. But where civic society has focused on protecting a particular stakeholder, there are more data. For instance, employees subjected to unfair conditions or prejudice in the workplace have legal resource. Legal actions are a matter that is publicly disclosed so class-action suits can be found by searching legal databases.

In the last chapter, I reviewed the sweatshop issue. Suppliers to a corporation have traditionally not been a protected class, so no robust source of data collection that traces the positive or negative aspects corporate actions have on suppliers exists.

But the concerns that products are being made under crushingly inhumane conditions led to shareholder actions, codes of conducts, and internal company audits. Hopefully this will lead to more consistent and comprehensive data on suppliers.

Working Mother's *Top Ten Companies for Working Mothers, 1999*

Company	Years on the List
Bank of America (BAC)	1
CIGNA (CI)	8
Deutsche Bank (DTBKY (ADR))	4
Fannie Mae (FNM)	6
First Tennessee (FTN)	5
IBM (IBM)	14
Eli Lilly (LLY)	5
Lincoln Financial (LNC)	13
Lotus Development (a division of IBM)	9
Prudential	10

Source: First appeared in *Working Mother*, October 1999. Reprinted with the permission of MacDonald Communications Corp. Copyright © 1999 by MacDonald Communications Corp. <www.workingmother.com>. For subscriptions call 1-800-627-0690.

Having covered some general social research issues, I now turn to the nitty-gritty. In this section I talk about what the professional researcher does. I'll try to include information about sources of data as I go along. Most investors are not going to want to take quite such a detailed approach, so toward the end of this chapter, I'll also talk about some easy steps the individual can take.

Fortune's *Top Five Companies for Hispanics*

- Public Service Co. of New Mexico (PNM)
- Sempra Energy (SRE)
- Darden Restaurants (DRI)
- US West (now Qwest Communications (Q))
- Southern California Edison (SCE)

Source: "The Diversity Elite," *Fortune*, 2 August 1999, 28.

To illustrate the way that research on qualitative issues is carried out, I rely heavily on the approach taken to maintain research for the Domini 400 Social Index. Kinder, Lydenberg, Domini & Co., Inc. (KLD), has developed this approach over the last ten years. Research is primarily based on information that is:

1. available to the public,
2. quantifiable, and
3. significant in understanding the company.

The research process is far more scientific than most people believe. What follows are several examples. You can find a complete social audit on Johnson & Johnson (JNJ) at Appendix A. A list of the questions that are answered before a company is considered for inclusion on the Domini 400 Social Index can be found in Appendix D.

Publicly available data for social research exist in large part due to past wrongs. After the great crash of 1929 and the depression years, new laws and institutions were designed to protect small investors from the sorts of abuses that contributed to the collapse. Prior to 1932 the management at corporations engaged fairly freely in practices that today would be considered self-dealing or fraud. Compounding the problem, brokers and bankers acted in collusion with corporations to circulate false reports of good earnings or big contracts. Standards of fair practice were constructed and a watchdog federal agency—the Securities and Exchange Commission (SEC)—was created to protect investors under securities acts signed into law in 1933 and expanded in 1934. These laws make data available on American companies that might not be available on foreign ones.

Law now mandates a certain transparency on the part of corporate management teams. Most of the disclosed information is published in three important documents: the annual report to the public, one prepared for the SEC (called Form 10-K), and the shareholder proxy statement, which gives investors information in preparation for the annual meeting of the company. Today it is common to find the 10-K integrated into the annual report the public receives.

Fortune's *Top Five Companies for African-Americans*

- Fannie Mae (FNM)
- Advantica (DINE)
- Allstate (ALL)
- Shoney's (SHOY)
- Sempra Energy (SRE)

Source: "The Diversity Elite," *Fortune*, 2 August 1999, 28.

We have the right to review management compensation annually as a part of U.S. investor protections. Each year the proxy statement provides shareholders with this information. This helps us review employee benefits. Top managers will benefit from retirement, savings, or bonus plans that all other employees benefit from, so one can review the proxy statement and discover therein several programs that benefit all of the company's employees. For instance, if the corporation matches employee contributions to its retirement plan (generally a 401(k) plan), the plan will be discussed in detail in the proxy statement. Corporate social researchers can evaluate the plan and compare it to those offered by other companies. These data are available and quantifiable.

In evaluating the 401(k) plan, KLD searches for a level that can be considered an indication of significant commitment to the employees. Studying the data taught us that a match of 6 percent of an employee's salary meant that a corporation is among the best 8 percent of the companies tracked by KLD. To be among the best 8 percent would imply that the company has made a decision to have particularly rewarding programs in place for the future retirement benefits of its employees. This in and of itself makes the information significant and worth highlighting as an aspect of the social profile of the corporation. Several other examples follow.

The proxy statement also contains any cash profit-sharing bonuses to a class of employees that includes management. Again, this is due to the SEC oversight discussed above. In research done in 1999, KLD found that if a cash profit-sharing plan paid bonuses to at least 50 percent of employees within the past two years, then the company was among the best 19 percent of companies evaluated by KLD that year. It is also significant since it indicates that the management team has made a deliberate decision to benefit a broad range of employees whenever the company has achieved its own goals, building a strong stakeholder sense among employees, which probably also helps make it possible to achieve those corporate goals.

It is fairly easy to find photographs of the board of directors of a company. These are often published in both the annual report and the shareholder proxy statement. If there are four women or minorities (without double counting) on the board, then the company is among the best 13.6 percent of companies KLD evaluated in 1999. This information meets the needs of good research. It is ascertainable, quantifiable, and significant.

Business Week's *Top Ten Companies for Women*

Company	Women/ Total Officers	Percent Women Officers
US West (now Qwest Communications (Q))	6/14	42.9%
PacifiCare Health Systems (PHSY)	15/35	42.9
Lincoln National (LNC)	6/14	42.9
Avon Products (AVP)	9/21	42.9
Nordstrom (JWN)	15/36	41.7
Fannie Mae (FNM)	61/158	38.6
Washington Mutual (WM)	3/8	37.5
Times Mirror (TME)	11/31	35.5
Dayton Hudson (now Target Corp. (TGT))	8/23	34.8
Venator (Z)	8/23	34.8

The top ten are selected based on women in management. Data are from information reported by the 500 largest public corporations, based on revenue, in 1998 annual reports, proxy statements, and 10-K statements. Reflects officers as of March 31, 1999, or earlier.

Source: Reprinted from the November 22, 1999 issue of *Business Week* by special permission, copyright ©1999 by the McGraw-Hill Companies, Inc.

You also find good data by searching third-party resources and not mandatory disclosure documents. Awards, like those offered each year by *Working Woman* magazine for friendly workplace environments for women, are important third-party validations of a company's commitment to employees. One, the Malcolm Baldrige National Quality Award in manufacturing, is a widely publicized and much coveted award for achieving excellence. A nationally recognized award is given to about 10 percent of the companies KLD follows, which would indicate that such an award signifies a particular strength on the part of the company.

Fortune's *Top Five Companies for Asian Americans*

- Applied Materials (AMAT)
- Computer Associates (CA)
- Texas Instruments (TXN)
- Toyota Motor Sales
- Union Bank of California (UB)

Source: "The Diversity Elite," *Fortune*, 2 August 1999, 28.

What about negative indicators for each stakeholder? Using 1999 figures, if there are no women on the board of directors or among the top line (as opposed to staff) management of a U.S.-based corporation, then the corporation is among the bottom 16 percent of companies KLD evaluated that year. It therefore seems likely that the corporation neither has made an attempt to hire or appoint women to positions of responsibility nor has built an environment within which they can rise to the top. While I do not argue that a leadership group composed of only males would be incapable of managing a company, it is a fact that the world is made up of more than one gender. The inability of a corporation to explicitly recognize this in its leadership would seem to indicate failure to be aggressive about drawing upon the best and the brightest no matter what package they come in. It also probably has implications for management's relationship with employees and customers in general.

Communities are stakeholders and charitable giving is generally disclosed. A company that has given 1.5 percent of pretax profits to charities each year for the past three is among the best 8 percent of companies within KLD's universe. Being in the best

8 percent implies that the company has made a decision to be involved in its communities and has created a policy that it follows through on each year, making it a significant piece of information to collect.

This smattering of examples is meant to give a sense of how the methodology is created for evaluating qualitative issues: standards must shift through the years. New information becomes available, data sources dry up, and experience informs us. For instance, KLD used to "draw the line" at 20 or more Superfund sites, which are federally designated polluted sites. While this level was fairly successful, it did often mean that insurance companies and banks were being highlighted for their negative environmental impact. Since the purpose of the screen is to discover that a company is in a dirty business, the acquisition of the hazardous waste site through investment banking did not seem to be on the point. The threshold level was therefore raised to 30 or more Superfund sites, a level at which the result is more consistent with the purpose of the screen.

Carsten and Leslie's Picks

Carsten Henningston and **Leslie Christian** are founders of Portfolio 21, a global mutual fund investing in a sustainable future. They want to share the following company stories with social investors.

- **AssiDomän** is one of Europe's leading forest products companies and is making great strides in an industry that has traditionally been detrimental to the environment. All of the company's forest holdings meet Forest Stewardship Council (FSC) certification and provide approximately one-third of the company's timber inputs. The company has green products ranging from FSC-labeled joinery timber to paper and paperboard products with recycled content. AssiDomän's environmental leadership is clearly illustrated by its three-year project with the World Wide Fund for Nature, aiming to promote long-term sustainable forestry.

- **AstroPower (APWR)** is making a significant contribution to the alternative energy industry. The company's proprietary technology has both reduced the cost and increased the efficiency of solar energy cells. By using recycled semiconductor wafers as a raw material, AstroPower has been able to reduce the energy payback period of its cells from the industry standard of three years to approximately one month.
- **Interface (IFSIA)** was one of the first companies in the United States to adopt the Natural Step principles; Interface has become an outstanding role model through its efforts to radically reduce its environmental impact. The company has installed photovoltaics to power its Los Angeles factory with solar energy. The company is now developing carpet made from renewable natural materials that can be composted or recycled back into the same product. Interface aims to have zero waste and closed loop production, the ultimate goals of a sustainable business.

Source: You can reach Carsten at carsten@portfolio21.com or check out the fund's Web site at <www.portfolio21.com>.

Shareholders are stakeholders who want to know that their interests are protected. One concern is a CEO who earns too much. How much is the right amount? If the top 10 percent is a sign of too much, then the cash threshold level would have to be raised every year to keep pace with the extraordinary pay some CEOs are taking home. This approach is workable, but is bloated CEO pay a healthy trend for society? KLD took the approach of readjusting the threshold level every few years to highlight the question of whether one person should make 20 or 30 times more than middle-tier management in the same company, 200 times more than the lowest-paid employees, and 2,000 times more than the lowest-paid employee of its suppliers.

To choose just one example, the former CEO of Toys "R" Us (TOY), Robert Nakasone, received a compensation package that the company valued at approximately $11.1 million, including a non-cash component consisting primarily of stock options that the company valued at approximately $5.3 million, over $200,000 a day.[6] The company is a major purchaser of toys manufactured by contract suppliers, where employees might earn $8 a day.

Sometimes Only the Top Five Executives Benefit from Stock Benefits

Stock Options Granted to Top Five Executives

Company	Percent of option to top 5	Worth at expiration if 5% annual growth
Aetna (AET)	14.90%	$22,864,495
Archer Daniels Midland	10.46	2,267,224
Bank of America (BAM)	3.12	40,218,063
Duke Energy	40.80	53,744,942
General Motors (GM)	4.91	24,432,556
International Paper (IP)	8.00	7,432,888
JC Penney	11.90	8,651,874
Johnson & Johnson (JNJ)	3.20	16,162,089
Kmart	23.69	10,962,802
Lockheed Martin	11.50	18,967,462

Source: Financial Markets Center, <www.fmcenter.org>. *FOMC Alert* is a publication of the Financial Markets Center, an independent, nonprofit institute that provides research and education resources to grassroots groups, unions, policymakers, and journalists interested in the Federal Reserve System and financial markets.

The above discussion is meant to show how professional corporate social accountability research is based on information that is ascertainable, quantifiable, and significant. Generally, particular tidbits of information are not enough to either guarantee a company's inclusion in an SRI portfolio or to guarantee its exclusion. Each tidbit of information is only one of many indicators of a corporate culture and commitment. Only after the various pieces of information are systematically gathered and corporations compared one to another with the information in hand can a decision to purchase be made.

One underrecognized benefit to this approach is that through the qualitative social-screening process, the corporate social researcher has developed a formidable tool for evaluating the quality of a management team at the helm of a corporation. Furthermore, it is increasingly apparent that the analysis exposes the corporate culture in a particularly thorough and revealing way. This will be further examined in Chapter 8. Now let's look at some simple steps the individual can take to screen a portfolio.

Screening Made Easy (or Easier)

Complex as the assessment of a corporation's interaction with society is, you can get pretty far down the path of a reasonable analysis on your own. This section is designed to help you find stocks you want to own. Most of us start by having an idea and wanting to investigate that idea further. Some of us start by having no idea of what stocks we'd like to buy and need a source list. Either way, there are some simple steps you can take to be sure you have a pretty good social portfolio.

If you are interested in a company and want to know more about its social profile, a pretty good place to start is the annual report, 10-K, and proxy report. Today, most companies make these available on their Web sites but you probably want to phone the company's investor relations department and get hard copies.

The annual report contains mainly photographs and an introduction to the company's major business lines. The numbers are at the back and the letter from the chief executive officer is at the front. Looking through the annual report will tell you a lot about what the company makes. Reading the letter from the CEO will tell you what the vision for future growth is. Either this letter or a statement in the inside cover will tell you whether the company has a strong mission statement. The rear cover often carries a nondiscrimination statement, and often the page between the pictures and the numbers frequently talks about the company's commitment to communities in which it operates.

The 10-K is sometimes more specific about the lines of business; it is often actually bound into the annual report. One important extra carried in the 10-K is disclosure about any potential liabilities of more than a routine nature. If, as an example, three widows of three former workers are suing over unsafe working conditions, that will be found in the 10-K, but not necessarily in the annual report.

Ben & Jerry's: Selling Out or Being Brought In?

In spring 2000, Ben & Jerry's Homemade was acquired by **Unilever (UN, UL (ADRs))** for $326 million, thwarting a counter-offer by socially responsible investors. But those making the counter-offer stayed in the negotiations in an attempt to preserve social responsibility leverage for Ben & Jerry's within Unilever. The result: Unilever agreed to continue purchasing local, hormone-free dairy products, to increase the purchase of organic milk, and to contribute approximately 7.5 percent of Ben & Jerry's pretax profits to charity. Workers got a guarantee of five years employment with full benefits. Most significantly, Unilever committed to a social and environmental audit for its entire worldwide operations. Time will tell how this David and Goliath story pans out. Founder Ben Cohen said, "I hope this isn't selling out, but being brought in."

Source: "Ben & Jerry's: A New Chapter," *Connections Networking for Responsible Business and Investing* 30 (Spring 2000).

The proxy report will carry information about who the board is, who top management is, how much the board and top management earn for their jobs, and other issues that need to be voted on at the annual meeting. Remember, this is where shareholders raising social issues will have their say. Just because there is a shareholder issue on the ballot, don't think you don't want to own the company. As many shareholder resolutions are filed at companies you want to own as at those you don't want to own. You do, however, want to read the issues and management's response so that you can draw your own conclusions as to the merit of the resolution and as to management's thoughtfulness.

The next step in your investigation is to go to a place you can get Internet access and do a search on news stories for the company. Use both the popular press and the business press search functions. Even if all you do is read the headlines, you will get a good sense of the company's personality from these. Negative press is not meaningful in and of itself, but a landslide of negative press on an issue you care about will most certainly tip the scales.

If you have done the above, you will have done more than practically any individual investor in the company. You can, however, go another step. Mutual funds publish their holdings twice a year. Some only give you a list of their holdings when you ask for it, but most publish them in their routine reports and most can be found at the mutual fund's Web site. If the company is a well-known one, you could look at the holdings of the socially managed mutual funds to see if they are held.

This is also the best starting point for investors who want ideas of stocks to buy. By going to a local library or through your own Internet access, you can visit <www.socialinvest.org> and <www.socialfunds.com>. These two Web sites link you to every mutual fund in the United States that is run with social criteria. Through the links you find easy access to many fund holdings. Most of the funds provide some brief information about what they like about some or all of their holdings. For connections to European funds, <www.uksif.org> connects to the fund managers and from there you can get to the funds. Some of the boxes in this book have stock picks from managers of social mutual funds. I have tried to give contact information in each box so that you can follow their recommendations.

Even conventional investors do best when they invest in something they know. Start looking at your shopping purchases as investigative research for stock ideas. If you shop at Whole Foods Markets (WFMI), maybe you'd like to invest in their stock. If you like the Scholastic (SCHL) children's books, maybe you'd like to invest in their stock. If you are buying a Zap (ZAPP) bike, maybe you should consider investing in their stock. Some of the smartest investors find ideas by watching trends that they themselves are a part of.

What Social Screening Cannot Do

Social screening is not very effective at dealing with issues that lie at the core of the for-profit system such as monopolistic tendencies, aggressive marketing practices, and the like. Such issues are probably better left in the hands of government and communities. The government case against Microsoft (MSFT) raised this issue for social investors. A company found guilty of acting in a monopolistic way would certainly have been evaluated with that fact in mind, but prior to the Microsoft case, the great majority of these were completely different in impact. The Microsoft case raises the issue of scale and of the strategic nature of the harm to society that a monopoly over computers and the Internet might carry.

Social mutual funds and other portfolios did not move to divest Microsoft from their portfolios, even after a guilty finding. Why this is the case is hard to see at first glance. The decision rested largely on the sense that a guilty finding was good. It meant that the checks and balances in the system that civic society has put into place still function. It is possible, however, that a point will come when social investors may feel it is important to point out a breakdown in normal remedies and divest Microsoft as a protest statement.

Screening has not yet developed a response to dealing with the company that succeeds too well at ordinary business practices. We may be personally distressed by the arrival of Home Depot (HD) and the loss of a corner hardware store but these are the success stories of capitalism. Home Depot is succeeding with a tactic that Ames (AMES) or Woolworth (now Venator Group (Z)) tried in earlier years with less success. The same can be said for Wal-Mart (WMT), Starbucks (SBUX), and Staples (SPLS). What socially responsible investors can do and have done is hold these successful companies to higher standards of commitment to the local community; to sourcing goods; to hiring, training, and promoting minorities; and to protecting our planet's natural resources.

Screening a portfolio does much. It creates market demand for corporate accountability information and thereby creates ongoing, baseline research on corporate impact. It brings the investor into closer alignment with her personal values. Screening creates a context for dialogue between corporations and society on the many problems we must face together. As of 1999, $1.49 trillion in the United States was being managed with social screens.[7] Social screening does not generally deliver immediate positive social change results, but is nonetheless extremely powerful due to its subtle and strategic nature.

Screening the investment portfolio is an important aspect of building a better tomorrow. The process itself creates ongoing dialogue between companies, communities, activists, and researchers. It also constitutes a basis upon which global corporate social research rests, allowing the sort of data collection that led civic society to take action in the South African debate. Screening is far more complex and specific than is widely understood. It causes us to grapple with the larger issues of the role of government, society, and corporations. For most socially responsible investors, screening the portfolio is the bedrock upon which all else rests. By screening, we have created a new way that corporations and their various stakeholders are able to enter into conversation with each other. These conversations are central to our efforts at building a more livable world.

Screening has had an unanticipated long-term strategic impact that is powerful beyond all expectations. This is so because it demands data and information, which in turn has led to corporate social research. Socially responsible investors have created a demand for the ongoing collection and assessment of systemwide corporate social impact data.

Why Agribusiness Is Underweighted in Most Social Portfolios: The Way We Count Doesn't Tell the Whole Story

Who feeds the world? It is small farmers who are the primary food providers in the third world. Their small farms are more productive than industrial monocultures. These rich and sustainable systems of food production are being destroyed in the name of increasing food production. However, the numbers don't tell a true story. For example, the Mayan peasants in the Chiapas are characterized as unproductive because they produce only 2 tons of corn per acre. Yet the overall food output is 20 tons per acre when their beans, squashes, and fruit trees are taken into account. This is how the numbers are used to prove the case for agribusiness.

Source: Dr. Vandana Shiva, "How Big Business Starves the Poor," *The Daily Telegraph,* 11 May 2000.

Direct Dialogue 4

Speaking Up as an Investor to Make a Difference

In Germany, they first came for the communists,

and I didn't speak up because I wasn't a communist.

Then they came for the Jews, and I didn't speak up

because I wasn't a Jew. Then they came for trade union-

ists, and I didn't speak up because I wasn't a trade

unionist. Then they came for the Catholics, and I didn't

speak up because I wasn't a Catholic. Then they came for

me—and by that time there was nobody left to speak up.

—PASTOR MARTIN NEIMÖLLER

AT THE NUREMBERG TRIALS

When you enter into structured dialogue with the management of a company, you have an opportunity to influence directly the manner in which that company does business and you are able to see immediately the sometimes truly extraordinary difference you are making. Efforts to build a world where justice and human dignity hold equal weight with profits and maximizing shareholders' returns are at their most intimate when you engage directly in dialogues with corporations and their management teams.

Let's begin with a story of how it works. During the war years in El Salvador, a coffee boycott raised general awareness of the brutal military suppression of coffee growers by cartels that bought their coffee at prices the farmers could barely survive on. A young man who happened to be the great-great grandson of the cofounder of Procter & Gamble (PG) was concerned and in 1990 filed a shareholder resolution calling for an end to Salvadoran bean purchases by Folgers Coffee, a Procter & Gamble subsidiary. He argued that such purchases funded the country's largest growers who had been connected with "death squad" killings of workers for years.[1] Even though his resolution achieved only 2.7 percent of the vote, less than the 3 percent then needed to keep the resolution on the ballot, his efforts heightened awareness and thereby contributed to a California ban on Salvadoran beans, thus giving the company an incentive to seek other sources of beans. This is shareholder activism in action.

Shareholder activism is possible because as the owner of a stock you are a part owner of a corporation. In the United States, this gives you certain rights and, arguably, responsibilities. These rights are largely the result of the same legislation that created the Securities and Exchange Commission (SEC) and other shareholder protections mentioned in the last chapter. This legislation gives you, as an investor, the right to receive financial information quarterly in unaudited form, as well as an audited annual report, which we use as the basis for much of our social research.

Patrick's Picks

Patrick McVeigh is a portfolio manager and senior vice president of Trillium Asset Management, a firm that specializes in socially responsible investments and manages the Advocacy Fund, a mutual fund. Patrick thinks these three companies are ones to follow. He tells their stories in his own voice:

- **Green Mountain Coffee Roasters (GMCR)** is one of my favorites even though I don't drink coffee. I love well-managed companies and this Vermont-based coffee company has a superlative record on corporate social responsibility. Check out its Web site <www.greenmountaincoffee.com> to see what makes it such a leader in fair trade, environmental, and community relations issues.
- **Lifeline Systems (LIFE)**, another superbly managed company with lots of growth potential, is the market leader in providing personal response monitors to the elderly. These low-cost devices, which provide a direct communication link to emergency care, allow seniors to live at home rather than in nursing homes. As the population ages and more medical care can be provided over telephone lines, Lifeline's growth rate should accelerate.
- **Medtronic (MDT)** is about the best-managed company I know. This medical technology company is the market leader in pacemakers, defibrillators, and other products for the heart and back. Since growth has been so consistent in the 20 percent range, this large company usually costs more than I normally would like to pay. But a new technology called the Chronicle that will allow doctors to monitor heart failure patients out of the hospital should be a blockbuster that will drive the growth rate even higher over the next decade.

Source: You can reach Patrick at pmcveigh@trilliuminvest.com or check out his Web site, <www.trilliuminvest.com>.

We have other rights as well. Investors also have the right to participate in profits to the extent of our proportional ownership. These profits may come in the form of dividends paid, or they may come in the form of growth of valuation in the underlying corporation. Management cannot distribute the benefits of a successful enterprise unfairly. Investors have the right to sell, transfer, or assign their stocks to another. We do not have to go to the company's management to receive permission to sell shares.

But of greatest interest to shareholder activists are the rights pertaining to how a company is governed. Because we are owners, we have the right to vote to approve the selection of an auditor of the books of the corporation and to approve the board of directors who will oversee the corporation. We have the right to annually review senior management's pay and that of the board of directors. Furthermore, of special interest to responsible investors is the fact that ownership of a corporation's stock gives us the right to attend the company's annual meeting at which various shareholder votes take place. If a mutual fund is the owner, then the mutual fund has this right.

Because most people do not actually attend the meeting but rather send a card as their proxy indicating how they choose to vote, voting on issues is known as proxy voting. Technically, it is not the proxy but the question up for vote on the proxy that we are referring to. Most of the time the votes you, as a shareholder, are asked to cast relate to issues management has placed before you. These include the approval of the auditor and the board slate. Management may ask you to consider adopting a shift in the way the bonuses paid to the CEO are calculated or a plan for making a hostile takeover of the company more difficult. Sometimes it is not management but shareholders themselves who place an issue on the ballot. When they do, management usually urges other shareholders to vote against the matter.

These questions, whether asked by management or by shareholders, are framed in a formulaic way. They recite several clauses beginning with the word "whereas" and then have a paragraph that begins with the phrase "Therefore be it resolved." While the "whereas" section may help shape the issue, it is the "resolved" section that you are casting a vote on. For this reason these questions are called resolutions. Appendix C contains a sample shareholder resolution. This one was filed by United for a Fair Economy at Raytheon (RTN) in 1999. That year, similar resolutions were filed with AT&T (T), Fleet Financial (FLEW), and Huffy Corp. (HUF).

Shareholder resolutions generally raise issues that management would rather not see discussed. So activists will try to educate other shareholders about the issue they are bringing up. These are called shareholder proxy campaigns. They result when concerned shareholders, like you, add questions to the annual meeting's agenda.

Not every question can get placed on the ballot. You must file the resolution in a strictly constructed format. There are rules, which can be found in Appendix B at the end of the book. But properly framed, most relevant issues can be filed and raised at the annual meeting of the company to be voted on (through proxy cards—either e-mailed or "snail-mailed") by other shareholders.

Shareholder Activism Victory: General Electric Adopts Stricter Standards for Clothes Washers

Stricter water and efficiency standards for washers may mean big savings for consumers and the environment, but they also mean high reengineering costs for **General Electric (GE)**. The corporate giant vigorously fought tighter standards until a number of activist organizations, including Calvert Group, Interfaith Center on Corporate Responsibility, Corporate Governance, and Friends of the Earth, appealed to GE shareholders. Their efforts were successful. The company agreed to meet with environmentalists, and as a result all new clothes washers will be 20 percent more efficient in 2004, increasing to 35 percent by 2007.

This is a huge victory for consumers and the environment. Over the next 30 years, consumers will save $30 billion, preserve 11 trillion gallons of water, conserve more than 4 quadrillion BTUs of energy (equivalent to the annual energy use of about 21 million households), and eliminate 310 million metric tons of carbon dioxide.

Source: Michele Chan-Fishel, Friends of the Earth, <www.foe.org>.

Concerned shareholders tend to be divided into two camps. One camp files resolutions intended to maximize the potential for financial well-being of the investors, frequently at the cost of other stakeholders. An example would be a resolution that makes it easier for the company to be bought by another company. The shareholder might benefit, but the employee, the taxpayer, the community, and perhaps the consumer will not. Ironically, the same individual who is helped financially pays for it dearly in shoring up the community or paying the costs of living in a place with higher unemployment.

The other camp files resolutions that are geared to maximizing the potential for the well-being of a stakeholder, frequently not the investor, so that the investor as a living person can avoid the costs now looming large on the horizon as the result of specific corporate behavior. A resolution asking the company to sign an environmental code of conduct and to report on progress toward meeting that code each year might cost a penny to the shareholder over the years that the stock is owned. But this cost is more than made up for by the benefits gained by the living person, the shareholder, who stands a chance of growing old on a planet with a breathable atmosphere.

The popular vocabulary identifying which camp the shareholder resolution falls into is fairly misleading. When only monetary benefits to the investment side of the living person are considered, the filers of the resolution identify their work as corporate governance. When benefits to the whole person are considered, the filers tend to identify their resolution as social. In fact, both have profound corporate governance and social impact implications.

Shareholder Rights
Lead to Activism Opportunities

You can be an activist on issues in many ways. Citizens write letters, consumers launch a boycott, employees or others sue, but shareholders bring a unique capacity to raise issues in a formal, structured way through the annual meeting of the corporation. Coordinated shareholder activism began during the South African debate and was at first carried on almost exclusively by faith-based groups, but today enjoys robust support from a broad array of concerned investors.

Are Corporations Stealing from the Poor?

International Monetary Fund bailouts direct money for the purpose of paying off loans to foreign banks, which then escape significant losses for imprudent lending decisions. For example, **Citigroup (C)**, **Chase Manhattan (CMB)**, and **J.P. Morgan (JPM)** are among the beneficiaries of the Korean bailout. The World Bank's International Finance Corp. also finances and provides advice for private sector ventures and projects in developing countries in partnership with private investors such as **ExxonMobil (XOM)**, **British Petroleum** (now **BP Amoco (BPA (ADR))**, **Coca-Cola (KO)**, **Kimberly-Clark (KMB)**, and **Marriott (MAR)**. Why are public development institutions, supposedly working to fight poverty, lending money to these rich multinationals?

Source: Russell Mokhiber and Robert Weissman, "A Dozen Reasons to Come to DC for April 16," *Focus on the Corporation*, 5 April 2000. © Russell Mokhiber and Robert Weissman.

As the campaign ending apartheid in South Africa developed a momentum of its own, faith groups looked at their other mission-based concerns. An early campaign raised the questions as to whether it was right to sell infant formula to women who lacked access to clean water. This issue arose when Catholic congregations such as the Sisters of Mercy, who were working with the poor in the third world, saw more babies dying. They soon found the cause. Infant formula companies were giving free formula to new mothers. It was seen as Western and as more healthful by these unsophisticated mothers who used the formula rather than breast-feed. When a mother doesn't breast-feed continuously, her milk dries up and she no longer can. This causes dependence on formula, which many cannot afford. Formula needs to be mixed with water. Because of the cost of the formula and the fact that the mothers couldn't read, the mixture was often watered down, leading to malnutrition. Worse, however, was the water itself, which was often unclean and caused cholera, the single biggest killer of children in the third world. A campaign was launched to boycott products made by Nestlé, a Swiss manufacturer of infant formula, and shareholder activists raised the issues with infant formula manufacturers based in the United States. Finally, the World Health Organization addressed the matter and created standards for the distribution of infant formula, but the matter is far from settled.

Such human suffering caused faith groups to feel that they must use their shareholder rights as a tool in their mission to serve the poor and work toward a world of justice and human dignity. They began to raise questions over a broad range of issues, including infant formula sales, environmental responsibility, plant closings, and product safety. Through direct dialogue, particularly through shareholder filings, an effective link can be made between grassroots organizations, mainstream asset managers, management teams at corporations, and corporate boards of directors. Faith-based groups soon learned how to use their shareholder rights.

A resolution to be voted upon by shareholders at the annual meeting most certainly convinces top management to focus their attention on an issue. Even the threat of a resolution can prompt action from management, who dread standing "before testy shareholders or chanting church groups while below a row of smirking reporters scribble notes."[2] Perhaps the most powerful aspect of this kind of activism lies in the fact that because it will go into the proxy statement, the issues raised in a resolution will be taken up at the board level, causing management to feel pressure both from above and below.

Each year, several hundred conversations on a broad range of issues are carried on through the mechanism of shareholder dialogue. These range from staggering the election of the board to tying executive pay to environmental performance to reporting on the government subsidies received (corporate welfare) or developing a code of conduct for sourcing (sweatshops). Sometimes a resolution is withdrawn due to an agreement to meet halfway. Other times the resolution is voted on with enough success to raise the issue again next year and that fact leads to an agreement.

Here is a review of some of the newer, mostly still unresolved dialogues.

In 1999, Exxon acquired Mobil (creating ExxonMobil (XOM)) and replaced Mobil's Equal Employment Statement with its own, which simply stated that it would not discriminate. Mobil had had in place a fairly specific nondiscrimination policy. When the new company moved to general language, employees of Mobil became alarmed that a reversal of standards on discrimination was under way.

Employees approached management and asked that the company be made to live up to the commitments Mobil had made to them. Concern ran high. Was this the beginning of the rollback of hard-won basic workplace benefits? ExxonMobil's management refused to meet even when employee voices were joined by those of shareholders. Fed up with management's lack of willingness to address the question, The Equality Project, New York City Employees Retirement System, Trillium Asset Management, and the Unitarian Universalist Association jointly filed a shareholder resolution to be voted on at the company's annual meeting. In proxy season 2000, the resolution received a healthy 6 percent of the vote. This level is quite good for a new issue the first year on the ballot, and it was more than enough to allow the resolution to go on the following year's agenda.

The movie *Erin Brockovich* portrayed the story of a woman who led a citizen's action that culminated in a 1993 class-action lawsuit against PG&E ((PCG) formerly Pacific Gas & Electric), claiming a 30-year pattern of contamination of the groundwater in a California town. A $333 million settlement resulted. With such a record, shareholder activists approached the company in 1999 to inquire about emission standards. A number of the company's New England plants are not subject to Clean Air Act regulations, but community groups have asked the company to voluntarily meet these tougher emission standards. Their concern, in part, results from evidence that an abnormally high number of children suffering asthma attacks are being treated at local hospitals in Salem, Massachusetts, where one plant is located. Soon shareholders, including activist money manager Walden Capital, learned of the potential liability implied by these concerns and began a dialogue.

The Secret History of Lead

In 1986, leaded gasoline was banned in the United States. Added to gasoline to eliminate engine knocking, lead is now known to increase learning disabilities, hyperactivity, and behavioral problems in children, and is linked to high blood pressure, cardiovascular disease, and heart attack in adults. But few know that way back in the 1920s the major manufacturers of leaded gasoline voluntarily took it off the market.

In 1924, **DuPont (DP), General Motors (GM)**, Standard Oil (predecessor of **ExxonMobil (XOM)**), and **Ethyl Corp. (EY)** pulled leaded gasoline off the market and asked the U.S. Surgeon General to hold a hearing on its health risks. Workers were suffering from severe hallucinations, an early sign of acute lead intoxication, and soon the public was in fear of being poisoned. A study reported that while it could not, in the time allowed, confirm that leaded gasoline would not endanger human health, it could be manufactured safely. The public seemed satisfied, and lead returned to gasoline—even though the companies knew of a safe alternative—and it stayed there for another 40 years, until it was discovered that lead destroyed cars' emissions control systems.

Thus the history of leaded gasoline in the United States comes to an end. But the story continues for much of the rest of the world: Ethyl Corp. still sells lead as a gasoline additive everywhere but in the United States and Europe.

Source: Russell Mokhiber and Robert Weissman, "The House of Butterflies," *Focus on the Corporation*, 13 March 2000. © Russell Mokhiber and Robert Weissman.

Dialogue can sometimes lead to fairly immediate results. This was the case when shareholder activists met with management at Winn-Dixie Stores (WIN) to request that Equal Employment information be disclosed. The action began as the result of learning that the company had agreed in 1999 to settle for $33 million a case related to gender and race discrimination. After being approached, the company agreed to disclose the information to interested investors. It is hoped that because shareholders are receiving information on diversity efforts, management will try harder to succeed at them.

Diversity at Denny's

In the early 1990s the words "Denny's Restaurant" were virtually synonymous with discrimination. The company was pummeled in the courts and by the media for outrageous acts of discrimination committed in individual restaurants. In 1993, only one African-American owned a Denny's franchise, and only one minority sat on the board of directors. Just five years later, however, minorities owned 35 percent of the company's 737 franchised restaurants, and now minorities represent approximately one-third of the board. The parent company, **Advantica (DINE)**, saw the need for sweeping reform and acted accordingly.

In 1999, Home Depot (HD) announced that it would phase out sales of products made from woods harvested in old-growth forests. This happened after about three years of shareholder dialogue. During that time a series of meetings between environmentalists, concerned shareholders, and management took place. Selective store boycotts led by consumers and a fair amount of negative press on the practice of harvesting from these fragile ecosystems also focused public attention on the issue. Home Depot had previously enjoyed a pretty good record with environmentalists. It had been the first chain store of its type to offer a line of products that were environmentally friendly, and it decided to maintain environmental leadership in its field.

These are exciting success stories. Although coffee-growing cartels still buy roving militia, discrimination has not ended, and the harvesting of old-growth forests has not halted, conditions have improved in ways that they would not have had caring shareholders not entered the picture. Direct dialogue is tactical and immediate in its results. It creates a framework for evaluating new issues; it creates models for other companies to follow; and it makes management sit up and take notice.

Since the successful South African campaign, nothing has captured the interest and attention of the American public so much as the tobacco issue. Survey after survey of social investors indicates that tobacco avoidance is the single most commonly applied screen they use. By studying the tobacco campaign, we can see how direct dialogue can enhance a broad-based grassroots initiative.

An Economic Argument for Greater Diversity Awareness

Most people leave the couch only during commercial breaks to avoid missing their favorite shows. During the Super Bowl, however, the creative, expensive spots often are the main event. So it's surprising that only 17 of the 69 commercials aired during Super Bowl XXXIV offered closed-captioning, ignoring a consumer group of 24 million hearing-impaired people in the United States, according to <www.captions.com>, a watchdog Web site for the hearing impaired.

Many hearing-impaired people consider captions important when they choose which products to buy. About 66 percent of hearing-impaired TV viewers buy products that have captioned commercials and 35 percent switch brands, according to the **National Captioning Institute (NCI)**, a company that creates captions for television programs. "They do watch the captioned commercials and they do switch brands and buy products from advertisers that cater to their needs," Karen O'Conner, NCI's director of sales and marketing, said.

Source: T.J. DeGroat, "Missing Captions Alienate Audience," <*www.diversityinc.com*>, 8 June 2000. © 2000 www.diversity.com.

The Tobacco Campaign: Activism in Action

One of the most revolutionary changes that has taken place in American society over the past 15 years has been the shift in attitude against cigarette smoking. This shift resulted from a great many things coming together simultaneously. Americans had begun to be more health-conscious in general: The science on cigarette smoking was becoming better understood, and the costs to the health care system of tobacco-related disease was being better quantified.

When I was first pregnant, I was a stockbroker in Cambridge, Massachusetts, and smoking was the norm. The small office I worked in had four cigar smokers (this represented half our sales team) who puffed away throughout my pregnancy. In 1982, it did not occur to me or to them that it was not their absolute right to do so. Over the course of the next decade, individuals braver than I began demanding people not smoke in their presence and then began demanding environments that were smoke-free. Concerns were raised about teenage smoking problems and advertising campaigns that seemed to encourage the very young to view cigarettes as cool.

Joe Camel, the cartoon figure invented by the former RJR Nabisco (the company's tobacco operations are now R.J. Reynolds Tobacco Holdings (RJR)), became one of the most recognized characters in our culture. By 1991, 91 percent of

American six-year-olds could match Joe Camel with a picture of a cigarette, making him as well known as Mickey Mouse. Camel's share of the under-18 market soared from 0.5 percent to 32.8 percent in the first two years of the Joe Camel campaign, representing a $476 million increase in annual sales for RJR Nabisco.[3] Following Joe's introduction, the number of children who smoked Camels increased as of 1991 by a factor of 50.[4]

Despite such evidence, R.J. Reynolds argued that children were not the intended targets of such advertising. Concerned parents and activists, coordinated by INFACT, a nonprofit that began its activism during the Nestlé boycott, mounted a successful campaign demanding the retraction of Joe Camel on the grounds that intended or not, children were nonetheless still the ones responding to the advertisements in unwanted numbers. A number of shareholder activists supported the effort by filing resolutions that asked for abandonment of the "cool camel."

This was not the only way shareholder activists took the anti-smoking argument into corporate boardrooms. Most vocal were the health care chains run by Catholic congregations of women, such as the Sisters of Charity and Mercy Healthcare. Because they were in the health care business, some of these congregations didn't own tobacco stocks. Nonetheless, they found ways to carry their mission further. They filed shareholder resolutions that asked airlines and restaurants to provide smoke-free environments. They asked conglomerates to divest their tobacco businesses. They filed resolutions with insurance companies that asked whether the company's board had considered the ethics of a health or life insurer owning stock in a company that provided tobacco products.

Soon the tobacco issue was taken up by states, which sued to recover health care costs. Settlement claims reaching well into the billions of dollars cut down on the potential profitability and raised the risk of tobacco tolerance. Those that could run for the exits quickly did. Airlines and restaurants went smoke-free, as did hospitals, municipal buildings, and, finally, office buildings.

The Internet played a leading role in popularizing antismoking sentiment with sites such as Get Outraged and The Truth, written for and by a young hip audience. Antismoking groups sought to fight Big Tobacco on its own ground, Madison Avenue, by launching fresh advertising campaigns that put the cigarette companies on the defensive. The campaign infused our popular culture as mystery books, movies, and even a comic strip, *Doonesbury*, by Gary Trudeau highlighted the controversy.

Over a relatively short period of time, perhaps 10 to 15 years, the mood of the nation had shifted completely. Cigarette smoking (let alone cigar smoking) is now relegated to small designated areas, frequently on the sidewalks behind a building, to avoid creating an unpleasant appearance at the front doors of a dozen huddled smokers dropping cigarette butts on the sidewalks. The rest of the world has yet to follow, however. In 1999, Big Tobacco companies received more than $31 billion in revenues, making this industry, which results in the death of one smoker every eight seconds, one of the largest industries in the world.[5]

The antismoking campaign in America demonstrates how shareholder activism can provide cause-oriented activists with a natural ally as new issues emerge.

Activism and the Environment

On March 24, 1989, an American oil tanker, the *Exxon Valdez* hit a reef in Prince William Sound in Alaska. Over the next two days, 260,000 barrels of oil spilled into the pristine waters. It was the worst oil spill in American history. The oil slick eventually covered 1,100 miles of coastline. Tens of thousands of sea mammals and birds died.[6] The Exxon corporation, over the course of the next few years, was found guilty and fined $5 billion in punitive damages. Exxon fought this decision in the courts and ten years later, not one cent of this had been paid. Adding injury to insult, of the 28 affected species, only 2, the sea otter and the bald eagle, have recovered to prespill levels. Some species, including the killer whale, show no sign of recovering.

French Company Feels International Pressure on Labor Rights

In France, shareholder activism is almost unheard of. But a case regarding U.S. workers for a French multinational, **Imerys**, illustrates how continued globalization stands to promote the concerns of shareholder activists in the international arena. At their annual meeting in 2000 in Paris, management heard the concerns of U.S. shareholders regarding a labor dispute in an Alabama plant. The conflict began in June 1999 when the company withdrew recognition of the Paper, Allied-Industrial, Chemical & Energy Workers' Union (PACE) and repudiated its collective agreement with its workers. PACE launched a global campaign to secure the workers' right to be represented. In February 2000, the U.S. National Labor Relations Board threatened to initiate prosecution of the company for allegedly violating the rights of its employees to organize. But shareholder action at the annual meeting drove the message home, and after the meeting PACE organizer Joe Drexler stated, "We are in a much better position then we were six months ago."

Source: *Values 9:3* (July 2000), published by Walden Asset Management, a division of United States Trust Co. of Boston. 40 Court Street, Boston, MA 02108.

An immediate response to the disastrous oil spill came from a group of environmentalists, social investors, churches, and public interest groups, who came together to create an environmental code of conduct now known as the CERES (Coalition for Environmentally Responsible Economies) Principles, originally called the Valdez Principles. Joan Bavaria, founder of Trillium Asset Management, used her extensive network to bring together those who could shape a code of conduct with those who could carry the code into corporate annual meetings. Social investors, such as Trillium, filed resolutions with companies asking them to endorse the principles and pledge to ongoing environmental reporting. By 2000, the CERES Principles had been endorsed by more than 70 publicly traded companies, including giants such as General Motors (GM) that have pledged to adopt ecologically sound operations and standardized, environmental reporting. CERES coalition members currently control $150 billion in assets, so the reach of this nonprofit extends far.[7]

As with tobacco, social investors supported the efforts of grassroots groups. For the first few years, socially responsible mutual funds and religious investors carried on the dialogue. Environmental organizations and foundations did not. It wasn't that environmental groups didn't care but rather that they had no background in shareholder activism. It was churches and socially responsible investors that were experienced enough and willing to carry on the dialogue. Without the environmentalists, the code could not have been crafted, and without socially responsible investors, the CERES Principles would have been relegated to a bookshelf in someone's office. It is a story that exemplifies how the close cooperation between grassroots activists and the SRI field has contributed to real progress.

Steve's Stakeholder Story Stocks: Corporations and Civic Values Customer—Quality and Service

Steven D. Lydenberg, research director at KLD chose these six as examples of how corporations demonstrate commitment to providing high-quality products and giving notably responsive customer service:

- **ArvinMeritor, Inc. (ARM)**, produces high-quality parts and equipment for the automotive industry. In May 2000, the company received three 1999 Supplier of the Year awards from General Motors Corp. In March 1999, ArvinMeritor was awarded the Premier Automotive Suppliers' Contributions to Excellence (PACE) award for its Highway Parallelogram trailer air-suspension system.

- **Commerce Bancorp, Inc. (CBH)**, is a New Jersey bank that competes with its large rivals on customer service. It offers free checking and seven-day-a-week branch banking, and trains its employees to "Wow the Customer" to provide its customers with exceptional and individualized service.
- **Earthlink, Inc. (ELNK)**, is an Internet service provider that seeks information. Its MindSpring division makes customer service one of its core values. It regularly conducts customer satisfaction surveys, offers an array of self-help tools for clients, and provides well-staffed telephone support services.
- **Solectron Corp. (SLR)** is an electronics manufacturing company that adheres strictly to Total Quality Management principles and has been the winner of two Baldrige Quality awards. It has a 99.9 percent on-time delivery record.
- **Southwest Airlines Co. (LUV)** is an airline that is notably successful in stressing customer service. The company's "Heroes of the Heart" award honors employee groups for dedication.
- **Tennant Co. (TANT)** is a commercial cleaning firm that has been a strong proponent of quality and customer service for many years. It carries a line of solvent-free floor recoating systems. The EcoLine division accounts for almost 25 percent of the business.

Source: You can reach Steve at stevel@kld.com, or visit his Web site <www.kld.com>.

At first, only companies that wanted especially to be recognized as socially responsible, such as Ben & Jerry's (now owned by Unilever (UN, UL (ADRs)), The Body Shop (BDSPY), and Seventh Generation (SVNG), signed the pledge to report on environmental impact every year. But in 1993, Sonoco (SON) became the first oil company and the first Fortune 500 company to sign the CERES Principles, and today dozens of large corporations have either signed the principles or have agreed to provide annual environmental audits that provide most of the information asked for in the principles. Each year, conversations with new companies are begun, urging them to sign the principles.[8]

The availability of comprehensive environmental audits was relatively unheard of prior to the CERES Principles and has completely revolutionized the capacity of communities to know what is going on in their backyards.

The Global Reporting Initiative is a more recent outgrowth of the efforts that began with the *Valdez* spill. These guidelines specifically recognize the economic, environmental, and human responsibilities of each corporation. Called together by CERES, a global coalition of corporate social researchers, concerned citizens, and nongovernmental operations put together the initial planning documents.[9]

Through direct dialogue with corporations about the Global Reporting Initiative, it is hoped that issues ranging from sweatshop conditions to environmental sustainability can be framed under a single concept: that of sustainability at an enterprise level, taking the work begun over an environmental disaster to a comprehensive sustainability initiative.

Union Activism: Rio Tinto under Global Attack

Mining giant **Rio Tinto (RTOYL, RTP (ADRs))** came under heavy attack from shareholders at its annual meeting in London on May 10, 2000. At the annual meeting, shareholders put forth a motion stipulating compliance with the United Nation's International Labor Organization conventions standards for workers. In a historic move, an international coalition of unions threatened global workforce problems if Rio Tinto did not adopt these higher standards. Institutional shareholders representing more than 65 billion pounds sterling in assets publicly pledged to back the motion. "We in the trade unions want social dialogue with the multinational companies in general, not least with the big mining companies," said Jack Maitland, president of the International Federation of Chemical, Energy, Mine, and General Workers' Unions.

Source: News from the International Federation of Chemical, Energy, Mine, and General Workers' Unions, e-mail from Kenneth Zinn, kzinn@icemna.org (10 May 2000).

Shareholder Activism Made Easy (or Easier)

What can the individual do? You might feel that activism is too much for you, as an individual investor, to undertake, but there are some pretty simple ways in which you can have a big impact. You can vote the proxies on the shares you own in your own name. You can alert seasoned shareholder activists of issues they might undertake and keep informed about what they are doing so that you can help. You can ask a mutual fund company you bought a fund from to disclose its proxy votes. You can tell a mutual fund you own shares in what issues you want to see it vote in favor of. Social investors active in shareholder advocacy controlled $922 billion in 1999. You can support their efforts.[10]

Shareholder Dialogue Online

Wal-Mart (WMT), the world's largest retailer, is the target of a campaign conducted by socially responsible shareholders to voice concern over the company's shortcomings. In its efforts to be increasingly competitive, some investors feel that Wal-Mart has paid little attention to social issues such as human rights, workforce diversity, and environmental improvement. As You Sow, a nonprofit organization dedicated to promoting corporate accountability, is using the Internet to support its mission. At its Web site <www.asyousow.com>, users can submit electronic petition letters to the heads of major corporations like Wal-Mart to back shareholder resolutions on a range of issues or apply certain standards to their business practices.

Source: <www.asyousow.org/walmart.htm>.

If you have been a shareholder in a company for some time, you probably are used to receiving a large envelope with the legend "Open immediately, important proxy material enclosed" written across the front of it. And if you are like most shareholders, you probably ignored it completely. Now that you know the impact that even a small positive vote can have, you have no reason not to read through the material, make a decision, and cast a vote.

Even proxy materials that do not have a resolution filed by a shareholder can give you an opportunity for action. I, for instance, reject boards of directors unless there is at least some female and/or minority representation. I even go so far as to photocopy my vote and forward it to management with a letter explaining that until they have taken at least a first step toward a board that reflects the demographics of the population at large, I will not support their slate. Responses range from silence or rudeness to solicitousness.

Voting your resolutions will have a welcome, though perhaps unanticipated, benefit. You'll actually look through the materials the company has sent and become a better-informed investor. Every step you take down this path will make you more likely to do a good job in weeding out your underperforming stocks and buying into growing companies.

The Interfaith Center on Corporate Responsibility (ICCR) still serves as the central exchange for shareholder activism. Its members frequently become interested in issues because an activist took the time to alert it to an unfolding situation. Issues such as violence on children's television or an unsafe working environment have worked their way through this network to become a dialogue. ICCR operates as a loose federation so when issues are raised, it is up to individual members to decide which ones to work on. Subscribing to the ICCR newsletter, *The Corporate Examiner* (ICCR, 475 Riverside Drive, Room 550, New York, NY 10115 <info@iccr.org>) is an inexpensive and simple way to stay abreast of the 200 or so actions going on at any given moment.

For instance, if you find that dialogue is occurring on an issue you know something about, you can lend a hand. General Motors' decision in the spring of 2000 to leave the Global Climate Coalition (GCC), an association of energy and automobile companies that questions the existence of global warming, was based in part on the mounting evidence of global climate change. GM's action followed Ford Motor Co. (F), DaimlerChrysler (DCX), Texaco (TX), and the Southern Co. (SO), all of whom withdrew from the GCC. General Motors' decision came at the end of the warmest U.S. winter on record. Information from scientists at the National Oceanic and Atmospheric Administration, knowledgeable about the impact of burning petrochemicals had assisted activists like Sister Patricia Daly, a Dominican Sister , in her dialogue with the company. Sister Daly notes, "As the impact of global warming worsens, corporations and countries must rise to the challenge."[11]

In April 1999, the Domini Social Equity Fund (DSEFX) became the first mutual fund to publish its proxy votes on the Web. As president of the fund, I used the opportunity to challenge the mutual fund to greater transparency by revealing the stands it took on shareholder resolutions. Pax World Fund (PAXWX), the oldest socially responsible mutual fund in the United States, now also publishes its proxy voting policy. TIAA/CREF publishes its policy and Vanguard has announced that it will. But less than a handful of other funds do.

Money you invest in a mutual fund belongs to you. You should have an absolute right to know whether fund management is voting for or against a resolution that would create environmental standards or standards governing sweatshop contracts. The fact that this is conducted behind closed doors is absolutely unacceptable, and financial planners who are concerned about shareholder dialogue have begun an informal campaign of phoning mutual fund managers and asking how they are voting on an issue. By making your opinion known, you can become part of creating accountability over proxy voting by mutual funds, and with mutual funds owning close to half of the financial assets in America today, this is urgently necessary.

While you are urging greater transparency, you could also tell your mutual funds how you feel they should be voting. Lacking input, they probably follow management and ignore their responsibility for the environment or human rights. If they hear that these things matter to their shareholders, they should respond and support greater social responsibility. That would add a lot of weight to the debate. Mutual funds own more than $4.2 trillion worth of stocks of U.S.-based companies.[12] If they begin supporting the whole person, rather than simply the investor's wallet, they can alter the course of human events.

Direct dialogue through social shareholder resolutions is an exciting, dynamic, and successful way to create a real impact. Sometimes I wonder if it might be better to own just any stock and bring about change at the company through dialogue. But I do not believe in entering battle with one hand tied behind my back so I want to use every tool I have, and activism is but one. As a social investor I use three: screened portfolios to create a seismic shift in corporate behavior by placing it under the spotlight, shareholder activism to achieve specific remedies, and community economic development to help bring distressed communities back to life.

The 24 Most Heavily Unionized Companies in the United States

Company	Percent Unionized
Safeway Inc. (SWY)	90%
Burlington Northern Santa Fe Corp. (BNI)	88
Great Atlantic & Pacific Tea Co., Inc. (GAP)	88
Yellow Corp. (YELL)	86
Norfolk Southern Corp. (NSC)	85
US Airways Group, Inc. (U)	84
Southwest Airlines Co. (LUV)	83
Consolidated Freightways Corp. (CFWY)	82
UAL Corp. (UAL)	82
AMR Corp. (AMR)	80
Alaska Air Group, Inc. (ALK)	77
Bethlehem Steel Corp. (BS)	77
Delphi Automotive Systems Corp. (DPH)	77

Company	Percent Unionized
Roadway Express, Inc. (ROAD)	75
Consolidated Papers, Inc. (CDP)	73
Northwest Natural Gas Co. (NWNG)	73
Stillwater Mining Co. (SWC)	73
Union Pacific Corp. (UNP)	73
Kroger Co. (KR)	70
SBC Communications Inc. (SBC)	70
Bell Atlantic Corp. (BEL)	69
Navistar International Corp. (NAV)	69
Niagara Mohawk Holdings Inc. (NMK)	69
Ameren Corp. (AEE)	68

Source: Kinder, Lydenberg, Domini Socrates database <www.kld.com>.

Community Economic Development

Investing to Make a Difference Locally

Philanthropy is commendable but it must not
cause the philanthropist to overlook the circumstances of
economic injustice which make philanthropy necessary.

—MARTIN LUTHER KING, JR.

Caught up in the excitement of shareholder activism and big corporations, it often is easy to forget the individual who, along with five dependents, is living in one of our decaying inner cities under conditions a civilized society should not tolerate for any of its own. For one reason or another, whole populations exist outside of the economic mainstream, and the economic boom of the 1990s only increased their misery. In California, for instance, wage earners in the bottom 20 percent saw their buying power drop by 10.3 percent between 1988 and 1998.[1] But lending a helping hand to those in need can be as simple as being deliberate about where you do your banking. By using a community development bank or credit union, you get the basic banking services you need while also stretching the capacity of that local community-based institution to meet the sometimes overwhelming challenges of its service area. Holding cash in a community development loan fund, bank, or credit union is not charity. Community development financial institutions (CDFIs) empower people to help themselves, one at a time.

CDFIs directly connect you, the investor, with those in need. Every CDFI faces a similar challenge: The needs it seeks to meet take more funds than the institution itself is capable of providing. And that's where you come in. To do their work, CDFIs enter into partnerships with nonprofits, government agencies, enlightened citizens, and any other resources they can find. Furthermore, as we saw in our Chapter Two review of Shorebank Corp., CDFIs must actively solicit deposits into their institutions from sources outside geographic areas.

CDFIs come in three basic types: community development loan funds, community development banks, and community development credit unions. Taking the industry as a whole, they lend to at-risk populations and experience loan-loss ratios that put conventional lenders to shame, proving what many have long suspected: low-income people are actually more likely to repay their loans than are large businesses. Grassroots lending institutions play a crucial role in revitalizing communities globally and conscientious investors play a crucial role in supporting them.

Community Development Loan Funds

Community development loan funds (CDLFs) are nonprofits that borrow from many sources and lend to many borrowers. They offer help with budgeting, building, or whatever technical assistance the borrower may need to ensure success of the project. Generally the borrower is a collection of people who would otherwise never hope to qualify for credit of any kind. CDLFs serve the most at-risk populations and do so in the most innovative fashion. One exciting example is the McAuley Institute, which runs a project in rural northern Mississippi. The area has undergone rapid change, largely the result of an influx of casinos into the region, and land once used for agriculture is becoming more valuable for other purposes. In 1994, a crisis erupted in the rural town of Walls, when 11 families were evicted from their sharecropper shacks. Alerted to the situation by the priests of the Sacred Heart, McAuley moved quickly to coordinate other partners, including Union Planters Bank and the United Way, to develop a 38-unit rental property. Rents are set at 30 percent of household income.[2]

Regional Community Development Loan Funds

Boston Community Capital (Metro Boston, MA)	Housing, Business
Capital District Community Loan Fund (Metro Albany, NY)	Housing, Business
Cascadia Revolving Fund (Washington, OR)	Business, Community Facilities
Chicago Community Loan Fund (Metro Chicago, IL)	Housing, Community Facilities
Common Wealth Revolving Loan Fund (Northeast, OH)	Housing, Business
Community First Fund (Lancaster County, PA)	Housing, Business
Community Loan Fund of SW PA (Metro Pittsburgh, PA)	Housing, Business
Cooperative Fund of NE (New England)	Housing, Business, Community Facilities
Cornerstone-Homesource (Cincinnati, OH, No. KY)	Housing
First State Community Loan Fund (DE)	Business, Community Facilities

Florida Community Loan Fund (FL)	Business, Community Facilities
Genesis Fund (ME)	Housing, Business, Community Facilities
Greater New Haven CLF (New Haven, CT)	Housing, Community Facilities
Hawaii Community Loan Fund (HI)	Business
Illinois Facilities Fund (IL)	Community Facilities
Lakota Fund (Pine Ridge Reservation, SD)	Business
Leviticus 25:23 Alternative Fund (NY, NJ, CT)	Business, Community Facilities
Montana Community Development Corp. (MT)	Business
New Hampshire CLF (NH)	Housing, Business, Community Facilities
New Jersey Community Loan Fund (NJ)	Housing, Business
New Mexico CDLF (NM)	Housing, Business, Community Facilities
Northcountry Cooperative Development Fund (8 Midwest States)	Housing, Business
Rural Community Assistance Corp. (10 Western States)	Housing, Community Facilities
Vermont Community Loan Fund (VT)	Housing, Business
Worcester Community Housing Resource (Worcester, MA)	Housing, Business

Source: National Community Capital Association <www.communitycapital.org>.

Here's how it often works: A nonprofit working in a hard-hit part of the city finds a group of desperate people squatting in a boarded-up building. If the building has been seized by the city for unpaid taxes, it may be available. The nonprofit will negotiate with the city to get the building. But even if it is successful, it won't be given much time to get the building up to a standard that meets the city's building code. Materials will be needed and cost money. While future residents may have enough income between them to cover the interest payments of a loan, they have no track record as a cooperative, and no one of them can individually guarantee the loan. The deal falls outside the rules a conventional bank follows and will not be financed. For the lucky few, there is an answer. Sometimes the nonprofit finds a partner, a CDLF, that makes the loan and offers technical assistance to teach the formerly homeless owners to function as a co-op.

Investing in Affordable Housing: Spotlight on East and Oak Estates Community Lending at Work— Project of the Reinvestment Fund

Eloisa Mayr has undertaken her largest project yet: constructing 52 single-family homes in Vineland, New Jersey. Originally from Costa Rica, Mayr began as a real estate agent whose clients depended on her bilingual ability. To gather support for this project, Mayr approached everyone from the neighbors to City Hall, explaining her goal of providing affordable housing to those in the low- to moderate-income range. The response she received was overwhelming, and plans for the construction of East and Oak Estates were under way.

The Reinvestment Fund of Philadelphia, financed the $6.3 million project in conjunction with the Urban Home Ownership Recovery Program and the New Jersey Housing and Mortgage Finance Agency. East and Oak Estates is strategically located near the Vineland-Millville Urban Enterprise Zone, providing ample employment opportunities. Residents can now look forward to three-bedroom homes and a better life, all made possible by Mayr and investors who chose to put their money to good use.

Source: "Entrepreneur Borrowers Seize the Moment for Success," *Reinvestment News,* a publication of the Delaware Valley Community Reinvestment Fund (Spring 1999). Its Web site is <www.trfund.com>.

The loan fund works in partnership with the nonprofit that brought the situation to its attention so that the project has a maximum likelihood of success. After three or four years of on-time payments, the loan fund helps the occupants find a more conventional financial institution, such as a bank, to take over the loan. Then the CDLF can go out and meet the needs of a new at-risk group.

In rural areas, the almost universal form of low-income housing is trailer parks. But the United States has gone through an economic boom and real estate prices have been rising even in rural communities. Consider the position of an elderly couple that has owned land and rented it, for instance, to 22 families as trailer sites. When they are approached by a developer to sell the acreage for what seems like a figure beyond their wildest dreams, they wish to do so. The kindest will notify residents that an offer has been made and give them a chance to match it.

Remember, trailer housing is delivered as a mobile unit but then plumbed and wired into place. It has a foundation under it and a garden around it; it cannot be moved. These families are facing financial disaster. Not only are they losing a place to live, they are losing the money they put into acquiring it. They will move mountains to match the offer. But like the formerly homeless in an urban squatter's building, they do not have a track record as a co-op and no one of them will be able to sign for the loan. Rural CDLFs are frequently their only hope.

These two illustrations are fairly typical. Most CDLFs based in the United States focus on housing, though a healthy percentage make loans to create businesses. Those that lend overseas frequently focus on business creation first. Either way, they share a vision of creating healthy communities. Roughly 40 vital CDLFs exist, and most serve a clearly stated constituency. For instance, Boston Community Capital is in the business of building healthy communities in the Greater Boston area. Shared Interest makes small business loans in South Africa, and the Lakota Fund makes small business loans to residents of the Pine Ridge Reservation in North Dakota. The Low Income Housing Fund is based in San

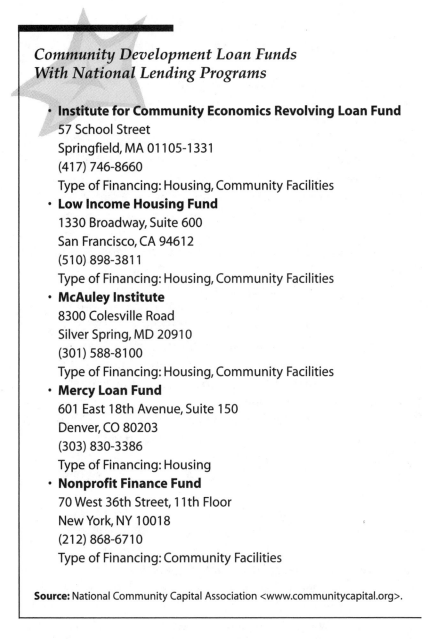

Community Development Loan Funds With National Lending Programs

- **Institute for Community Economics Revolving Loan Fund**
  57 School Street
  Springfield, MA 01105-1331
  (417) 746-8660
  Type of Financing: Housing, Community Facilities
- **Low Income Housing Fund**
  1330 Broadway, Suite 600
  San Francisco, CA 94612
  (510) 898-3811
  Type of Financing: Housing, Community Facilities
- **McAuley Institute**
  8300 Colesville Road
  Silver Spring, MD 20910
  (301) 588-8100
  Type of Financing: Housing, Community Facilities
- **Mercy Loan Fund**
  601 East 18th Avenue, Suite 150
  Denver, CO 80203
  (303) 830-3386
  Type of Financing: Housing
- **Nonprofit Finance Fund**
  70 West 36th Street, 11th Floor
  New York, NY 10018
  (212) 868-6710
  Type of Financing: Community Facilities

Source: National Community Capital Association <www.communitycapital.org>.

Francisco but lends nationally. Loan fund managers recognize that housing alone cannot build a healthy community. When San Francisco–based Rubicon Bakery, owned by Rubicon Partners, a not-for-profit that serves the homeless and very poor, sought capital for expansion, local banks turned it down. The Low Income Housing Fund considered the benefits of hiring and training the homeless at the bakery and felt that the expansion was the right move. They made the loan, thus allowing the bakery to triple its jobs and training slots.[3]

A note of warning! "Loan fund" is not a specific term. Thousands of parishes, community development corporations, and even food cooperatives run a program they call a loan fund. Here I am speaking of a fairly small group of established non-profits that are in the primary business of borrowing from the many to lend to many different groups among the needy. Their national membership organization is the National Community Capital Association (NCCA), based in Philadelphia, Pennsylvania. The NCCA was formed in 1986 to create and support a national network of community lenders that combines principles of social and economic justice with solid business practices. Today, the membership includes credit unions and banks , but it was originally community development loan funds that formed the NCCA, and they still represent an important constituency. NCCA members receive ongoing technical training conferences, access to new capital sources, and peer review of their own practices. They are spread across both the nation and the world, offering investors of goodwill the chance to diversity their portfolios of loans to the poor. The NCCA Web site is at <www.com munitycapital.org>.

CDLFs do work that by its very nature requires heavy subsidies and patient money. As a socially responsible investor, you choose to lend funds for a period of years, two at a bare minimum. Five years are really what it takes to nurture projects through to completion. Remember the story of the trailer park? A CDLF cannot start the process until the money is available; next the fund will review several identified projects to decide which one to assist. It might be six months before the transaction is complete. Then the collection of payments from the co-op begins and needs to be seasoned for a minimum of three years before even the most friendly of community banks is ready to take on the debt. That's three and a half years if the entire project goes without a hitch.

Making an uninsured loan to a nonprofit for five years at 2 percent interest? This is not your typical investor's concept of making money, and it is a wonderful testament to the powerful caring nature of people that CDLFs are so widely used in social investment portfolios. Most social investors make the loan at 2 percent interest or less. They allocate a portion of their portfolios to them, not caring about making money, but wanting to stay even with inflation. Investors in these funds now increasingly even add a line to their will or estate plan, instructing that any loans to nonprofits that are outstanding at the time of death be forgiven.

Why support CDLFs? Here's one way to think about it. You might not hit a home run with every dollar you invest. You are likely to have some money in a bond, certificate of deposit, or even money market account that is just there because, as my father likes to say, "The revolution might come and we want to be ready." You probably give to charity. Whatever amount you loan to a CDLF is money you get to "give" to something you care about, but you still have the money to "give" again next year. If you loan $5,000 at 2 percent when you could get 6 percent elsewhere, you're paying out $200 to get $5,000 worth of impact every year the loan is outstanding.

Community Development Banking

The movie classic *It's a Wonderful Life*, starring Jimmy Stewart, is shown every holiday season. In it we see the world as it exists with and without the caring community banker. Without the lending institution, the future is grim; the town deteriorates into a mean and dangerous place; Main Street is largely boarded up, and lives are shattered. Our hero chooses life and returns home to find that the community is gathered to support him as best it is able so that it can benefit from his kindness and generosity as a lender. Such stories, dusted off at the holiday season, are a lost part of our shared popular culture. Most of us, and most banks, have forgotten what it is that we, and they, were created to be.

Community development banks and bank programs are, in a way, simply a return to the origins of banking. Early bank charters were granted to encourage saving and thrift by the population. Today's community development bank programs are innovative and aggressive in meeting the needs of community organizations. The best-known community development bank is the South Shore Bank of Chicago, which was profiled earlier in this book. A bank is a natural vehicle for community building.

Wainwright Bank & Trust

Mission statement: "With a sense of inclusion and diversity that extends from the boardroom to the mailroom, **Wainwright Bank & Trust Co. (WAIN)** resolves to be a leading socially responsible bank. The bank is equally committed to all its stakeholders—employees, customers, communities, and shareholders." The bank's social justice agenda has become a unifying theme that embraces its mission statement, literature, and products while providing a unique identity to a publicly traded corporation. The bank's commitment to affordable housing, community development, women's rights, and the gay and lesbian community have brought it both recognition in the form of awards and a committed, indeed passionate, customer constituency.

Source: <www.wainwrightbank.com>.

Many community development banks and bank programs are members of the NCCA, which was discussed in the CDLF section of this chapter, but not all are. No more than a dozen have been successful in gaining national recognition so many work relatively anonymously, happy with the simple designation of "community bank."

Community Development Banks and Bank Programs

Albina Community Bancorp	Portland, OR	503-287-7537
Bank of Cherokee County	Park Hill, OK	918-772-2572
Berean Fed. Savings Bank	Philadelphia, PA	215-472-4545
Blackfeet National Bank	Browning, MT	406-338-7000 x200
Boston Bank of Commerce	Boston, MA	617-457-4400
Central Bank of Kansas City	Kansas City, MO	816-483-1210
City National Bank of NJ	Newark, NJ	973-624-0865
CityFirst Bank of DC	Washington, DC	202-332-5002
Community. Bank of the Bay	Oakland, CA	510-271-8400
Comm. Bank of Lawndale	Chicago, IL	773-533-6900
Community Capital Bank	Brooklyn, NY	718-802-1212
Community Comm. Bank	Los Angeles, CA	323-888-0065
Douglass National Bank	Kansas City, KS	913-321-7200
First Bank of the Americas	Chicago, IL	773-523-3145
Int'l. Bank of Chicago	Chicago, IL	773-769-2899
Legacy Bank	Milwaukee, WI	414-342-6900
Louisville Comm. Dev. Bank	Louisville, KY	502-778-7000
Metro Savings Bank F.S.B.	Orlando, FL	407-293-7320
Mutual Fed. Savings Bank	Atlanta, GA	404-659-0701
Neighborhood Nat'l. Bank	San Diego, CA	619-544-1642
Pan American Bank	Chicago, IL	773-254-9700
ShoreBank Cleveland	Cleveland, OH	216-268-6100
South Shore Bank	Chicago, IL	800-669-7725
Southern Bank Corp.	Arkadelphia, AR	870-246-3945
United Bank of Philadelphia	Philadelphia, PA	215-829-BANK
Unity Nat'l. Bank of Houston	Houston, TX	713-620-4350

Source: <www.socialfunds.com>.

Some community development banks were formed expressly for the purpose they now serve. These include Community Bank of the Bay in San Francisco, California; Community Capital Bank, in Yonkers, New York; and Newport Bank, in Oregon. Others, like the Wainwright Bank & Trust (WAIN) in Boston, Massachusetts, have essentially transitioned from more conventional banking to integrating innovative support for communities into all their work. Finally, there are community development banks that are subsidiaries of conventional banks. First Community Bank is a subsidiary of the Bank of Boston (now itself a subsidiary of Fleet Bank (FLEW)) that serves Boston's low-income communities in Mattapan, Dorchester, and Roxbury. It collects its own deposit base but benefits from the resources made available through its parent company.

Many minority-owned banks and savings and loan associations assume the job of revitalizing neighborhoods. Some call themselves community development and others do not. The Blackfeet National Bank is owned and operated by the Blackfeet tribe in Montana and makes loans to businesses on the reservation ranging from pencil manufacturing to a hospital. These businesses, in turn, bring economic opportunity to the reservation's population and to the bank. Mechanics & Farmers Bank, an African-American managed bank in Raleigh-Durham, North Carolina, was for much of its history the primary source of mortgage or small business loans for the African-American population in its region.

Socially responsible investors support community development banks and bank programs by opening an account or by purchasing a certificate of deposit. Because of FDIC insurance, which protects you up to $100,000 on your deposit, you receive greater protection than at a loan fund. The interest rates you earn at these banks are competitive with those paid by conventional counterparts. Best of all, the lending these banks do is specifically tailored to meet the needs of underserved populations, so they give you a chance to extend your personal mission.

Community Development Credit Unions (CDCUs)

Community development credit unions (CDCUs) often trace their roots to either a church or an affinity group (such as the Portuguese American Club) in a low-income area. Many are small and unknown outside their neighborhoods, but these truly grassroots organizations are the first option most poor people have for financial services.

Ten U.S. Community Development Credit Unions

- Alternatives Federal Credit Union, Ithaca, NY
- Appalachian Development Federal Credit Union, The Plains, OH
- Chicanos por la Causa Federal Credit Union, Phoenix, AZ
- First American Credit Union, Window Rock, AZ
- Mission Area Federal Credit Union, San Francisco, CA
- Near Eastside Community FCU, Indianapolis, IN
- Northeast Community Federal Credit Union, San Francisco, CA
- SCICAP Credit Union, Leon, IA
- Self-Help Credit Union, Raleigh-Durham, NC
- Vermont Development Credit Union, Burlington, VT

Source: These were randomly selected from the Web site of the National Federation of Community Development Credit Unions at <www.natfed.org>, which lists approximately 200 credit unions.

CDCUs serve underserved populations in a uniquely empowering way. Most of us are aware of the more conventional, employer-sponsored credit union. The telephone workers of a geographic area will have a credit union that allows employees

to open accounts by becoming a credit union member and paying a $20 or so membership fee. Loans are made only to mem-
bers and are approved by a committee made up of members.
This is the better-known credit union model. But if the credit
union was created to serve a recent immigrant group or urban
parish, members often find that they must be more innovative in
assisting borrowers. Technical assistance to borrowers is the hallmark of community lending. Roughly 200 credit unions have
been federally designated as community development, which
means that they can accept deposits from nonmembers.

Like other credit unions, CDCUs are democratically controlled, nonprofit, insured, government regulated, and overseen
by a voluntary board. But unlike other credit unions, federally
designated CDCUs have the privilege of raising deposits from
nonmembers. To do this, the credit union must demonstrate a
commitment to meeting the needs of low-income people.
CDCUs come in many sizes and shapes. Some are large lending
institutions with hours and facilities that make them look like
banks. Others operate in a church hall for a few hours a week.
All of them make small personal loans, exclusively to their members. Some are capable of making larger loans. Loans are
approved by a committee of volunteer members, making these
credit unions unique in this method of empowering both the
lender and the borrower.[4]

Through CDCUs you can lend support in a geographic area or
to an issue that you select. Alternatives Federal Credit Union
lends to organic farmers (among many loans) in New York State.
First American supports the needs of Navajos living in Arizona.
Self Help loans to day care centers in North Carolina. As with
banks, you simply open an account.

The credit union movement is international in scope.
Innovative models exist in Mexico, the Congo, and England, to
name but a few. VanCity Savings Credit Union, Canada's largest
credit union with more than $6.4 million (Canadian), is an exam-
ple of how much these institutions can accomplish. With more
than 262,000 members, VanCity plays a progressive role in

financing new businesses. The Family of Ethical Funds, an initiative of VanCity, is now Canada's largest family of socially responsible mutual funds. More recently, Citizen's Bank was formed as an Internet banking subsidiary. VanCity stands out as a progressive force among Canadian financial institutions.

In the United States, the National Federation of Community Development Credit Unions (NFCDCU), which offers its roughly 200 members ongoing technical assistance, has been an effective lobbying organization. Recognition for its work came in the form of the largest federal CDFI grant ever awarded. By visiting its Web site at <www.natfed.org>, you can find the community development credit unions that will help you achieve your goals.

Institutional Support for CDFIs

Community development financial institutions count on support from a broad array of sources. Banks, churches, and local government play an important role in capitalizing CDFIs. Most established CDFIs receive strong support from local conventional banks, which make loans and grants to the CDFIs as a means of improving their community reinvestment banking records. National legislation written in 1977—the Community Reinvestment Act (CRA)—encourages this. The CRA declared banks to be created by government to serve public purposes, or, in the words of economist Robert Kuttner, "not just to siphon money out of communities, but to put the money back in."[5] A bank's CRA rating can affect that institution's ability to acquire another bank, and gaining CRA credits is an important-enough goal that many banks view CDFIs as important strategic partners. But CDFIs largely operate outside of the mainstream, buffeted from the decisions made in settings beyond their reach. Increasingly, their members are forced to address matters of public policy and to spend their precious resources trying to influence potentially damaging changes in the CRA or other banking regulations.

Community Reinvestment Act Takes a Hit:
Accountability to Communities Fades

When the Financial Services Modernization Act passed in
November 1999, low- and moderate-income communities were
robbed of protections they had once had. Under the new banking overhaul, banks and financial services conglomerates will
have far less accountability to communities. Effective enforcement of nondiscriminatory lending has been undermined perma-
nently by legislation making most of the nation's banks immune
from Community Reinvestment Act (CRA) examinations for periods of four to five years. What's more, the government will not
impose any sanctions, even if the banks fail to maintain satisfac-
tory ratings under the CRA. What does this mean for low- and
middle-income people? Community development banks will
become even more desperately needed with the coming era of
CRA dismantling.

Source: Stanton McManus, "Sunburn: A New Banking Law is Set to Silence
Consumer Advocates," *In These Times* (17 April 2000): 10–11.

Insurance companies also support CDFIs. The Equitable
(owned by AXA Financial (AXF)), Aetna (AET), and Connecticut
General (now CIGNA (CI)), for instance, have had long-standing
community investment programs. It makes sense. After all,
insurance companies pick up the cost of societal problems. They
cover the building damage or health care costs that result from a
two-class society, so enlightened self-interest leads many to support local and national community development initiatives.

Both the Ford and MacArthur Foundations offer strategic and
ongoing support for CDFIs as an integrated aspect of their work,
but few others do. It is hard to see why so few foundation
endowments offer such support. Foundations can allocate 5 percent of their portfolio values to a diversified portfolio of loan

funds. Specific legislation clarifyies that a "program-related investment" of this size is consistent with fiduciary and charitable obligations. By giving away 5 percent and investing 5 percent, foundations can effectively double their annual budget for good works. To go one step further, the foundation could then put 5 percent into certificates of deposit at a community development bank or credit union. Because these are insured at market rate, this could be viewed as simply a part of the fixed-income (bond) portion of the portfolio, tripling the foundation's impact each and every year.

Stingy Foundations

Did you know that foundations are required by law to spend only 5 percent of their assets per year? But their assets have been increasing at a much higher rate. Over the past 20 years, investments in the Standard & Poor's 500 have returned 17.6 percent a year, all of which is tax-free to foundations. Foundations are beginning to look more like investment banks than groups established to give away money.

Source: *The Washington Monthly*, May 2000, 6.

A few large pension funds like the New York City Employees Retirement System and the California State Public Employees Retirement System allocate hundreds of millions of dollars into community development initiatives. California's Treasurer's Office increased deposits with several community lenders such as Broadway Federal that serves South Los Angeles by $1.3 billion as of April 2000. The office is also purchasing $1 billion in home loans made to low- and moderate-income people from community lenders. "Investment vehicles, targeted to distressed communities and sectors have emerged. The success of these ventures is breaking down old myths about the risk and return of community reinvestment," states Philip Angelides, California's state treasurer.[6]

Investing in CDFIs Made Easy (or Easier)

Compared to buying a stock, investing in a CDFI can be a somewhat cumbersome process. You must first find the organization, phone it, and talk with someone to get literature and fill out a form. In this day and age of e-trade, CDFI investments seem out of sync with the mainstream. Nonetheless, in 1999 $5.4 billion was invested in U.S.-based CDFIs.[7]

One Loan Fund's Investment: SelecTech, Inc.

The business practices of SelecTech, Inc., can be summed up in the words of Chuck Dwyer, chief financial officer: "We keep unwanted plastics out of landfills by making them into products." A producer of injection-molded polymer products made from mixed plastic wastes, SelecTech was established in 1996 and has been growing ever since. SelecTech utilizes a unique manufacturing process that does not require that plastics be excessively cleaned, allowing the company to make products with a high value at a low cost.

The Boston Community Venture Fund, a program of Boston Community Capital (BCC), has invested funds into the Taunton, Massachusetts–based company that will enable a production growth of 25 percent. This growth means the creation of jobs for low- to moderate-income workers in an area that needs these jobs. And while investors in BCC can feel good about creating new jobs, the new employees can feel good about what they are doing.

Source: "Spotlight on SelecTech, Inc.," *Healthy Communities: The Newsletter of Boston Community Capital Association* (Spring 2000).

Mutual funds and financial planners working with the socially responsible investor have had great success in finding ways to make it easier for you to support community development initiatives. Some, like the Pax World Balanced Fund (PAXWX), the MMA/Praxis Growth Fund (MMPAX), Parnassus (PARNX), and the Calvert Social Balanced Fund (CSIFX), dedicate a portion of their portfolios to CDFIs, the investments as either an aspect of their cash management or bond portfolios.

A second model is to offer investors a way to directly invest in CDFIs. Domini Social Investments has partnered with Shorebank to offer the Domini Money Market Account at South Shore Bank. Shorebank gains new depositors at their banks in Chicago, Detroit, and Cleveland. Domini Social Investment clients gain access to and information about the good news of community investing, something many of them might otherwise never have learned of. Investors have the comfort of federal insurance, market rates of interest that float with rates in general, and check-writing capacity.

Innovative ideas for getting the word out about community development opportunities are just beginning to take hold. One of the easiest ways to invest in a portfolio of CDFIs is offered by the Calvert Group. This mutual fund management company created a foundation that gives you an easy way to invest in communities. You can purchase a Calvert Community Investment Note with a one-, three-, or five-year maturity and then you select the rate of interest; depending on how charitable you want to be, you can go up to 4 percent (as of this writing). Your money is pooled with other investors into a portfolio of loans for affordable housing, microcredit loans, and community development.[8]

Partners for the Common Good Fund, managed by Christian Brothers Investment Services, is an investment currently available only to Catholic institutions, such as schools, cemetery associations, hospitals, parishes, and congregations. The fund is a pooled community development investment vehicle that makes investments intended to support women- and minority-owned enterprises, promote worker-owned or democratically controlled enterprises, and support community development through collaboration with other organizations sharing similar values.[9]

My own survey indicates that support for community economic development institutions is one of the strongest motivations people have in becoming socially responsible investors. CDFIs can fit into just about everyone's portfolio. They are money market alternatives with solid track records. Many are equivalent to the bank deposit you may already have in terms of interest earned and safety. They have special appeal to those who believe in a hand up rather than a handout. The support of CDFIs is one of the unique aspects of the social investment industry. As social investors face the increase in challenges to building a more livable world, especially in the global economy, these grassroots community lending institutions will continue to provide us with innovative solutions.

Global Finance and Its Impact on the Global Economy

6

When growth increases poverty, when real production becomes a negative economy, and speculators are defined as "wealth creators," something has gone wrong with the concepts of wealth and wealth creation.

—DR. VANDANA SHIVA

Socially responsible investors share a belief that through our investments we can build a world in which human dignity and environmental sustainability become guiding principles for commerce. While we begin our efforts at home, we know that the world is at stake and we must do what we can to understand and influence global financial forces as well as those within our own borders. We see that the world is rapidly becoming a single global economy. Already simple consumer goods such as Coca-Cola soft drinks and Gillette razor blades are available almost universally, at least in urban settings.

The capitalist or for-profit system has been the largest single force in opening up new countries and cultures to both the exploitation and the rewards of the more economically developed nations. How did this happen? Consumer goods are often the beachhead upon which the spreading of Western culture depends. There is a traditional pattern for the assault of Western ways. First, a curious or missionary-minded person leaves an initial consumer good, such as a frying pan, near an indigenous outpost. It is hoped that this simple gift will encourage the recipient to want to learn more about these generous strangers. As trust and relationships grow, larger, more complex products such as bicycles and farm equipment follow the simple goods.

International Manufacturers of Firearms

Name	Country
Amadeo Rossi SA (ROS14)	Brazil
Companhia Brasileira de Cartuchos (CCTU4)	Brazil
Forjas Taurus (FJTA4)	Brazil
Devtek Corp. (DEK/A)	Canada
SNC-Lavalin Group Inc. (SNC)	Canada
Ceska Zbrojovka AS (CSZB)	Czech Republic
Sellier & Bellot AS (SLBL)	Czech Republic
Metso Oyj (ME01V)	Finland
Thomson-CSF SA (HO)	France
Verney-Carron SA (VRCR)	France
DaimlerChrysler AG (DCX)	Germany
MG Technologies AG (MET)	Germany
Rheinmetall AG (RHM)	Germany
Asahi-Seiki Manufacturing Co. Ltd. (6111)	Japan
Howa Machinery Ltd. (6203)	Japan
Komatsu Ltd. (6301)	Japan
Miroku Firearms Manufacturing Co. (7983)	Japan
Raufoss ASA (RAU)	Norway
Scana Industrier (A/S)	Norway
Reunert Ltd. (RLO)	South Africa
Daewoo Telecom Co. (0506)	South Korea
Saab AB (SAABB)	Sweden

Name	Country
Swiss Industrial Co. Holdings, Ltd. (SIG)	Switzerland
BAE Systems Plc (BA/)	United Kingdom
IMI Plc (IMI)	United Kingdom
Tomkins Plc (TOMK)	United Kingdom
Alliant Techsystems Inc. (ATK)	United States
Ellett Brothers, Inc. (ELET)	United States
Olin Corp. (OLN)	United States
Primex Technologies, Inc. (PRMX)	United States
Sturm Ruger & Co., Inc. (RGR)	United States
Venturian Corp. (VENT)	United States

Source: Kinder, Lydenberg, Domini & Co., Inc. Socrates database <www.kld.com>.

Eventually, the indigenous population becomes integrated into the global economic machinery. The implications of such a tale are simultaneously hopeful and horrifying. On the one hand, at least in theory, whole populations need not starve in a global economy. On the other, whole populations can be easily oppressed. Certainly globalization has led to blandness. The gradual loss of diversity of languages, of alternative ownership systems and marketplaces, and of alternative sciences is more than sad. It is wasteful and wrong.

Most importantly, global commerce has destroyed the ability of governments to either protect their citizens from harmful practices or to benefit from taxing, since a company can move elsewhere. Finance is still more fluid, capable of moving in a manner of minutes from continent to continent. With such freedom, money movers can literally dictate the terms under which they will operate.

Alternatives to modern capitalism do exist. Anyone who has traveled to a third-world nation has seen the vibrancy of the local marketplace. One observes a tremendous variety of choice as well as an overall order with a density of square footage that is well beyond what is imaginable in modern economies. There exists an ability to both sell a product and provide livelihood in a structure that is a complete alternative to the one that the New World has become used to. This is collectivism at work, not capitalism. This marketplace is not owned by a corporation, does not have shareholders demanding profits, and exists only for its obvious purpose: to provide goods and services in exchange for a livelihood.

Three Picks from Axel Wilhelm and imug

Axel Wilhelm, head of research of imug, a social and environmental rating agency in Hanover, Germany, chose these three German companies as innovative ideas for social investors.

- **Henkel KgaA (HENKY (ADR))** is listed in the DAX 30 and is one of the leading manufacturers of "applied chemicals" in Germany, using a high percentage of renewable raw materials for its products. Henkel combines a high environmental profile with a very solid performance of social responsibility toward its employees. The company won several prizes for environmental stewardship and is praised as one of the most ecoefficient companies of the industry worldwide.
- **T-Online** is a provider of Internet services in Germany. T-Online recently introduced a program to deliver free services to all 44,000 public schools in Germany. In addition, the company will give 20,000 PCs to these schools. German Chancellor Gerhard Schroeder regards this initiative as "a very important contribution to acquaint the next generation with the possibilities of the Internet."
- **Wedeco** is a German company designing and manufacturing ultraviolet (UV) disinfection equipment and systems that remove microbial and toxic pollution from water and wastewater. UV disinfection is very low-cost and ecoefficient and has several advantages over traditional disinfection systems such as chlorination. Wedeco is currently

number two on the world market. The company is constantly expanding its business activities and has excellent prospects to profit from the growing demand for clean and healthy water.

Source: imug is in the business of social investment research as well as in sustainability consulting. You can visit its Web site at <www.imug.de> or write Axel at wilhelm@imug.de.

Yet Wal-Mart (WMT) has arrived in Mexico. The frying pan left in the forest has reengineered whole societies. Having trained a population to desire ever more goods, we now easily convert population after population to depending on the global corporation and, with it, the inherent financial structure that so dominates how business is done.

Billionaire hedge fund manager George Soros observes, "We live in a global economy that is characterized by free trade in goods and services and even more by the free movement of capital. As a result, interest rates, exchange rates, and stock prices in various countries are intimately interrelated and global financial markets exert tremendous influence on economic conditions everywhere."[1] Finance will dictate how corporations are managed and how goods and services are distributed. When the economic engines of the world (companies) owe allegiance to only one stakeholder (the shareholder) and that stakeholder has only a three-month view of the world, the only logical result is that companies will cease to provide goods and services at reasonable returns, instead demanding ever higher ones. These higher returns will come at the expense of the other stakeholders, whose needs are no less pressing than those of the shareholder but whose voices are weaker.

The corporate dominance model is being rolled out globally. World debt paved the way. The International Monetary Fund (IMF) and our biggest banks made loans but saw no moral imperative to do basic due diligence on the borrower's willingness or ability to repay. Any ordinary lending organization would take the hit and that would be that. But our global lending institutions are "too important" to be allowed to fail. The result? Governments in Uganda, Argentina, and Thailand, to name a few, must spend 30 percent or more of their receipts not on serving their public, not on building schools or providing health care, but on debt service. And how are these governments paying down debt? Because of pressure from global financial institutions, such public institutions as phone companies and water systems are being privatized, a fancy way of saying being sold.

Privatization: A Case Study in Taking from the Poor and Giving to the Corporations

In 1999, the Bolivian government succumbed to World Bank pressure and sold off Cochabamba's public water system to a privately held American company, **Bechtel**. Within weeks of assuming control, Bechtel more than doubled water rates, forcing families earning less than $100 per month to hand over $20 or have their taps shut off. "This is a struggle for justice, and for the removal of an international business that, even before offering us more water, had begun to charge us prices that are outrageously high," said the mayor. In January and February 2000, residents shut down Cochabamba for four days with strikes and transportation stoppages. President Hugo Banzer's police force moved in to protect American corporate interests with two days of tear gas, injuring more than 175 and leaving 2 youths blinded. More strikes in April resulted in a declaration of martial law, midnight arrests of protest leaders, and interrupted radio stations, until the Bolivian military shot a 17-year-old in the face. Protest leader Oscar Olivera said, "The blood spilled in Cochabamba carries the fingerprints of Bechtel."

Source: Jim Shultz, "Water Fallout: Bolivians Battle Globalization," *In These Times*, 15 May 2000, 11–12.

The result is that anything that might have been profitable for government is being removed. Resources to meet basic human needs are being stripped away and delivered to private corporations who then sell shares to investors around the world. Now the goods and services they deliver must also provide maximum financial results for shareholders. And so the global corporation, and not local sovereign governments, becomes the dominant force in another society.

In Switzerland: Investing for Sustainable Development

As of year-end 1999, the Ethos Foundation administered approximately 460 billion euros in global equities and bonds on behalf of 74 pension funds from all over Switzerland. Director Dr. Dominique Biedermann describes his organization: "The Ethos Foundation was created by pension funds for pension funds. The aim was to forge an instrument of asset management enabling them to analyze companies according to the criteria of sustainable development, in an approach based on classical financial criteria and on a set of environmental and social criteria. A further aim was to exercise shareholders' voting rights in a responsible fashion." The investment strategy includes a mixture of avoidance, positive selection, and engagement.

Source: "What's New in Social Investment," April 2000, Prepared for the members and affiliates of the U.K. Social Investment Forum.6.

Against the argument that globalization leads to a gradual improvement in the standard of living and human rights of populations emerging from subsistence lies the stark reality of evidence. As an example, each year the United States purchases billions of dollars worth of oil from Saudi Arabia, which in turn purchases billions of dollars worth of weapons from U.S. arms dealers. Yet the human rights group Amnesty International

points out the pervasive use of torture and systematic discrimination rampant throughout that country. The public flogging
and imprisonment of Faustino Salazar for entering the nation
with two chocolate bars containing liquor fascinated and horri-
fied the world, but did nothing to affect the oil-for-arms trade.[2]
The global struggle for basic human dignity will depend on the
role of global economics. Global trade and finance structures are
still taking form, and the manner in which they do so will determine the capacity of a people to live in dignity.

The financial services industry has yet to acknowledge its
potential role in creating a just world. In fact, it is still struggling
with the mechanics of globalization. Individual nations still have
vastly different regulations of corporations, financial service
intermediaries, and investment vehicles (such as mutual funds).
Beyond these barriers are the ongoing issues of corruption,
cronyism, and a general breakdown in civic society prevalent in
so much of the world. The evolution toward global standards is
accelerating. It has both positive and negative potential and the
emergence of the mutual fund as a dominant actor on the stage
of international finance—and therefore global corporate governance—is beginning to be understood.

Japanese Green Investment Movement Takes Off

Four green investment funds were launched in Japan in 1999.
Nikko Securities Co., Yasuda Fire & Marine Insurance, Dai-ichi
Mutual Life Insurance, and **Sumitomo Bank (SUBJY (ADR))** offered
the funds, which quickly grew to a combined asset base totaling
over $1 billion. Only firms meeting environmental performance
standards are included in the portfolios. The fast-growing industry
of Japanese green funds seems to appeal primarily to individuals
rather than institutions, with women slightly outnumbering men.

Source: "Japan Green Movement Emerging," *Connections Networking for
Responsible Business and Investing* 30 (Spring 2000).

Because U.S. investors invest globally and exert such a strong voice, they shape global corporate behavior. According to the Investment Company Institute, a trade organization serving mutual funds in the United States, Americans had invested more than $1.12 trillion dollars abroad by year-end 1999 through mutual funds alone. That's out of about $6.8 trillion in mutual funds in America. The U.S. mutual fund industry is by far the largest in the world. The combined assets of all other mutual funds (based in Europe, Asia, etc.) are only $3.5 trillion.[3]

Investment abroad by Americans is not always positive for the nations in which we invest. It is the work of responsible investors to build a strong voice within the financial services industry, a voice that calls for profits within the standards of decency. While this may seem self-evident, consider the events of this past year. PSA Peugeot Citroen (PEUGY (ADR)), France's second largest car manufacturer, was forced to lay off thousands of Belgian workers. The size and abruptness of the layoffs violated the expectation of secure employment that Europeans had held dear for more than 50 years.

Prime Minister Jacques Chirac of France made a nationally televised speech in which he attributed the layoffs to the fact that France was no longer in control of French companies. Rather, American mutual funds were now calling the shots about how business would be conducted in France. While you can argue the facts and state that we were scapegoats, the structure is in place to allow exactly that: money managers, whether U.S.-based or not, running what has been the work of government—making policy guidelines for business practices. This makes the building of an SRI mutual fund presence all the more strategically important.

The Three Aspects of SRI in One World

Some argue that global cultural differences preclude the construction of a uniform global value system and that there can be no global definition of socially responsible investing. But in screening portfolios, shareholder activism, and community economic development, socially responsible investors and their managers learned from global partners and found ways to implement best practices.

SRI in Italy

A survey of depositors in Italy's ethical bank, **Banco Etica**, found the typical Italian ethical investor is a young female with middle to high family income, high levels of education, a midlevel professional position, and active membership in political parties, voluntary associations, and the Catholic Church. Over 28.5 percent of surveyed individuals were positive about entrusting their savings to an ethical bank, meaning that 12.5 million Italians are potential ethical investors. Italy has the fastest rate of SRI growth in the world.

Source: Vatican News Service, "Ethical Investor is Feminine, Young, Committed and Practicing," 3 May 1999.

Screening certainly can transcend national boundaries. While SRI investors in the United States avoid alcohol, tobacco, gambling, nuclear power, and military weapons, a French investor might find this stand completely unbelievable. But the stakeholder model can transcend the cultural specificities of each nation. When I talk with French investors about the fact that for-profit systems are very efficient at delivering a product as cheaply as possible to as many people as possible and that I don't think tobacco, alcohol, gambling, or weapons should be distributed as cheaply as possible to as many people as possible, they frequently agree. Government should distribute these products exclusively, as they always have until quite recently in France.

SRI in Sweden: KPA Takes It to Heart

KPA, a large asset management firm in Sweden, has chosen to invest only in ethical investment funds. In February 1998, KPA's Board of Directors decided that the company should work actively for a better future for people and the environment. The decision is based on Agenda 21—the document from the World Conference in Rio de Janeiro 1992 is an action plan for sustainable development during the 21st century.

CEO Ingemar Alserud writes: "Ethical issues are important to our clients. They are to us too. Furthermore, companies that value ethics will have a future competitive advantage, both domestically and worldwide." KPA imposes environmental standards for its service and product suppliers, thereby inducing a ripple effect much greater than the firm alone might have. To structure the environmental initiative, KPA chose to implement the environmental management system ISO 14001. In 1998, KPA was the first Swedish financial institution to become so certified, signifying its commitment.

Sources: KPA's Environmental Report 1999, pp.1–4. Company brochure "Our Responsibility—For a Better Future for People and the Environment." KPA's Web site is www.kpa.se. To date it is in Swedish only.

The reverse is also true. American social investors have been slow, relative to the Europeans and Japanese, to build models for rating the sustainability impact of a company's action. Models for how to evaluate the long-term environmental impact of manufacturing techniques have largely come from Europe. One primary example is the Dow Jones partnership with Sustainable Asset Management, which developed the Dow Jones Sustainability Group Index. While many companies on this index wouldn't appeal to a U.S.-based social investor, the thinking about sustainability criteria is one which U.S. investors are finding helpful.

This index incorporates five corporate sustainability principles: innovative technology, corporate governance, shareholder relations, industrial leadership, and social well-being. In addition, the management believes that there are two major drivers to the trend to sustainability. The first driver is that corporate sustainability is attractive to investors because it aims to increase long-term shareholder value. The second is that the companies that integrate the five principles will do better because of their enlightened and disciplined management.[4] In the United States, this approach is being studied for possible application to our portfolios.

New organizations—such as Businesses for Social Responsibility in the United States and Canada, European Business Network for Social Cohesion, and EMPRESA in Latin America—offer companies a network for sharing ideas and best practices toward a goal of greater corporate social responsibility. They offer members practical advice and information. Ideally, a drive for greater transparency and disclosure will result from these associations, and successful corporate initiatives over environmental sustainability and human dignity will be shared and replicated. In the meanwhile these organizations, through sharing of what works, have created an environment within which corporations themselves can identify issues and work together toward positive solutions. Consultants have entered the field as well. Arthur D. Little, a worldwide consulting firm offers, through its Cambridge, England, division, services for companies wishing to manage corporate responsibility in actions. States consultant David Brown, "Corporate performance on social and ethical, as well as financial, accounts cannot be hidden, at least for the large corporations. Demands for transparency, accountability, and public reporting are steadily increasing."[5]

Europe Takes the Lead—Holds Companies Accountable for Environmental Impact through Extended Producer Responsibility Laws

Extended producer responsibility (EPR) got its start in Germany in 1991, when the Christian Democratic government, responding to citizen concerns about the scarcity of landfill sites, passed a law requiring manufacturers to take back and recycle all packaging material, boxes, cans, and bottles. Within two years, 12,000 companies were participating in an industry-funded recycling program, which shifted the costs of managing packaging waste from taxpayers, who still foot the bill in the United States, to waste producers. Companies now have economic incentives to act in an environmentally responsible manner. The initiative has been wildly successful, prompting similar programs in Holland, Sweden, France, Austria, Finland, Spain, and Belgium. Now the European Union is finalizing legislation that will standardize EPR for packaging across 15 member states.

Canada, too, has followed suit; seven of the ten provinces have adopted an EPR system that requires producers to take responsibility for beverage container waste. These provinces have achieved a recovery rate for beverage containers that far exceeds that in most American states. In *Beverage Industry* magazine, E. Gifford Stack of the National Soft Drink Association notes, "Producers also have a financial incentive to design their products to make less waste."

Source: Joel Bleifuss, "The Big Stick Approach: The European Union Quietly Holds Corporations Accountable," *In These Times*, 17 April 2000, 2.

As investment markets become increasingly global, security analysts struggle with alternative accounting systems, unexpected consumer preferences, different legal systems, and a host of other complicated new issues that must be evaluated before an investment decision can be made. The same is true for corporate social responsibility analysts. Looking at companies through the eyes of the stakeholder is an especially useful evaluative method now, as investors increasingly ignore national boundaries when making purchase decisions. Although the specific data available vary tremendously from country to country, the underlying themes of stakeholder analysis, with an eye toward human dignity and environmental sustainability, are universal concepts that can be applied in every stock market situation. The approach has the advantage of being adaptable to other legal systems and cultures. For instance, in the United States, the Environmental Protection Agency mandates that corporations report on their emissions of certain toxic chemicals. This law does not exist in other countries, but most nations do have some public access to certain environmental impact information that allows us to view the corporation though the eyes of the natural environment. Consumer watchdog groups evaluate product safety in most countries. Whether through a voluntary recall a company might issue, a write-up in *Consumer Reports* or through an exposé on the front page of *The Paris Match*, it is relatively simple to collect data about a company's product safety record. This provides a way to look at the company through the eyes of the consumer. Once separate stakeholder analysis takes place, it is compiled into the comprehensive social profile.

Nonetheless, good data sources need to be developed. Seb Below, a senior consultant at SustainAbility, a London-based consultancy that advises companies on environmental policy, says European ethical funds are forced to rely almost entirely on information from the companies themselves to judge their environmental and social credentials, "We need more rigorous, audited information," says Mr. Below. The demand from the social investment community for screened portfolios will help make the data available. Portfolio screening creates the corporate accountability infrastructure, which should give consumers, regulators, investors, and corporate management teams worldwide the opportunity to work together to address issues of concern to all persons.

Already, the growing demand from socially responsible investors abroad is creating new demand for corporate social reporting. The screened portfolio industry abroad is growing far more rapidly than most U.S.-based investors recognize. In Spain, there were 7 SRI funds by the end of 1999 and in Sweden there were 20; France has 17. The United Kingdom has more than 40 funds itself and GBP 3 billion under management. Japan has 4 ecofunds and Malaysia has 1 fund screened on issues relating to women and children. The WAFA bank in Morocco has launched two "solidarity" funds to finance social development, the environment, culture, and health.[6]

Mizue's Miracles

Mizue Tsukushi is president and CEO of the Good Bankers Co., Ltd., a corporate social research firm based in Tokyo, Japan. She chose these three Japanese companies for social investors.

- **Kibun Food Chemifa** is a leading manufacturer of soybean milk. Soybeans are now recommended by the World Health Organization for they contain nutrients that have improved Asian women's health for a long time, making their menopause less stressful than that of their Western counterparts. The company has always opposed the development and use of genetically modified soybeans, starting long before genetically modified foods became controversial.
- **Nikko Securities (KIKOY (ADR))** is one of the top securities firms in Japan and has led its sector in promoting a sustainable society by launching Japan's first green fund, the Nikko Eco Fund. The company is also the first in Japan to have signed for the United Nations Environmental Programme (UNEP) Financial Institutions Initiative and is persistently working hard to obtain ISO 14001. In May

2000, the company published the first environmental report
in the industry—*Sustainability Report 2000.*
- **Sumitomo Forestry Co., Ltd. (SUBJY (ADR))** is a promoter
of sustainable forestry and the largest single-house manufacturer in Japan. In 1999, the company was the first in Japan
to obtain the manufacturing excellence designation ISO
14001 for forest management for all its divisions. The company supports the concept of sustainable "Forest
Ecosystems" by working with citizen volunteers to plant
young trees in the badly damaged woodlands. In 1997,
Sumitomo Forestry recycled 80 percent of the wood and 90
percent of concrete and metal scrap by-products from its
construction waste in 1997.

Source: You can reach Mizue at Gbtokyo@aol.com. The Good Bankers; Asako
Kyobashi Building; 10th Floor; 1-6-13 Kobashi, Chou-ku; Tokyo 104-0031 Japan.
<www.members.aol.com/gbtokyo/home.htm>.

Just as unique national aspects to screening are being studied
and a system of sharing is developing, so are unique aspects of
direct dialogue gaining from approaches taken in other parts of
the world. Today, governance standards are still quite different
from one nation to another. Consider this: the Italian Borsa
(stock exchange) recently commissioned a study on how to make
the companies they trade more palatable to global investors. The
study came back with recommendations, including such things
as an independent board and an annual meeting available to all
shareholders at which management is present to answer questions.[7] While these standards seem pretty basic to U.S. investors,
they, in fact, do not exist in much of the world.

Between the lack of governance standards and the possibility of
corruption at many companies, many non-U.S.-based investors are
afraid to invest hard-earned money in even their own stock markets. Furthermore, there is currently no universal standard for
what ownership of a stock means in terms of rights. The appropriate response may be to institute U.S.-type corporate governance

procedures as a "best practice" globally without imposing such standards legally. With the sovereignty of nations at stake and with the natural disinclination of corporate leadership to add burdens to those they already carry, it seems unlikely that nations will impose such standards as law. Indeed, with U.S. institutional investors and mutual funds demanding that their interests come before those of other stakeholders, perhaps it is not a model we should seek to emulate. Most likely, civic society will have to become more creative and assertive in identifying innovative new ways to bring corporate actions under public scrutiny.

SRI in Malaysia: UNIFEM Supports Gender Equity Efforts

United Global Bank Asset Management and the United Nation's Development Fund for Women (UNIFEM) have launched a fund that invests only in companies that have socially responsible policies toward women. This fund was launched in Singapore in 1999 for non-U.S. residents. The fund managers survey companies on their hiring practices, female representation on their board of directors, and child care facilities. The fund contributes one-third of its annual fund management fee to UNIFEM. The bank's Managing Director Daniel Chan said, "Social and ethical investing is being done in the United States and in parts of Europe, and it has worked. We think it's a good concept."

Source: UNIFEM press release, 13 December 1999.

In the meanwhile, the heads of states of the European Union are studying the issue of appropriate corporate governance closely. A few have begun to institute new policies. A particularly creative one has been launched in England. Beginning July 3, 2000, all U.K. pension funds were obliged to state whether or not they have a policy on socially responsible investing. The early indications are that although they are free to say that they do not, and leave it at that, the majority wants to be able to state that they have a policy. This is causing policies to be created and changes to be implemented. Environmental Resources Management surveyed the 25 largest U.K. pension funds and found that 21 of them intend to institute socially responsible investment principles.[8] It now appears that Norway, Sweden, and Denmark are actively exploring copying the model.

Under the best of circumstances, a system of transparency and governance that includes true checks and balances and true cost accounting will be implemented universally. Under the worst of circumstances, corporations will continue to enjoy the tremendous power that their revenues give them and the globe will have only a checkered accountability system, allowing companies to locate in countries with low governance standards.

While cultural relativists led by Edward Said have argued that nations of the "Orient" and other developing regions should maintain their independent standards, a growing number of developing nations have signed such international agreements as the Kyoto Accord. This agreement called for sharp reductions in the usage of heat-trapping greenhouse gases by 38 industrial nations. By signing it, less industrialized nations confirmed their acceptance of a universal standard of environmental justice that may be Western in origin, but is universal in its significance and impact. Such international agreements, generally formulated under the auspices of the United Nations or other voluntary multilateral organizations, put into place the structure to monitor and enforce standards on a global scale.

Global shareholder dialogue is evolving rapidly. Although no nation recognizes the rights of small shareholders to the extent that the United States does, many do have mechanisms for addressing issues at the annual meetings. An exciting example of shareholder activism was the result of an export of dialogue from the United States to Britain.

In 1999, British Petroleum acquired Amoco and became BP Amoco (BP (ADR)). Environmental groups based in the United

States had been in shareholder dialogue with Amoco about drilling in Alaska's pristine wilderness and were urging the company to develop meaningful alternatives to petroleum by developing their solar manufacturing capacity. But in England the filing requirement is that 100 shareholders who together own an average of 10,000 pounds sterling of the company must act jointly. Trillium Asset Management, a U.S.-based firm specializing in SRI, had a client who owned enough stock to get the issue on the ballot. Ninety-nine Greenpeace members each acquired one share to achieve the filing minimum. The vote received 13 percent rather than the typical 1 percent that most shareholder resolutions in England receive. Management had clearly misread investor and public sentiment. It was a wake-up call and though clearly shaken, they have taken steps to rebuild their reputation. They announced plans to accelerate the solar development part of their business.

Through shareholder activism, socially responsible investors owning shares of companies based in the United States offer a helping hand to indigenous people struggling for justice. Occidental Petroleum (OXY) received a resolution filed by Mercy Health Services, the Sinsinawa Dominicans, and Walden Asset Management over the issue of drilling on indigenous land. The U'wa people living in the rain forest of Colombia consider the land in question to be sacred. The U'was have threatened to commit mass suicide if the company carries through with its plans to drill there. The potential damage of this ill-advised drilling initiative is staggering to contemplate.

Burma has become recognized as home to a repressive regime and Unocal has been receiving shareholder questions on doing business in Burma for several years. Yet the company continues to assert that it is a voice for positive change in that country. A report issued in May 2000 by EarthRights International indicates the extent of Unocal's involvement in the use of forced labor. It contained eyewitness reports from dozens of civilian victims of forced labor and torture at the hands of the Burmese military. "This report reveals what Unocal officials knew and when they knew it," said Tyler Giannini, codirector of EarthRights and principal author of the report, *Total Denial Continues*. "They knew forced labor was likely to be used before they went into Burma, and they knew with certainty no later than 1996 that forced labor was, in fact, endemic to their project. Despite this knowledge, they went forward in their business partnership with the Burmese military, and continue the partnership today." Ka Hsaw Wa, codirector of EarthRights International, coordinated the clandestine fieldwork to gather the evidence in the report. "Villager after villager tells the same story. Before the pipeline, there was little army presence in the region. The pipeline brought the soldiers and it brought misery to thousands of innocent people. So in a very direct way, Unocal brought this misery to my people," she said.[9] Socially responsible investors are probably the greatest hope these villagers have for relief from the misery their lives have become. We own the stock, we know how to file resolutions, and now we have a global infrastructure that is growing more connected every day.

Community economic development plays a far more important role in certain emerging nations than it plays in the United States. However, many common threads again emerge. The need for public and private partnership is universal. The debate over models that affect 10 or 12 people and models that affect several thousand continue to rage. The repayment record by poor people, especially poor women, is excellent, and as poverty lessens, the entire community becomes healthier.

Oikocredit is probably the best alternative for social investors who want to pick their corner of the globe to lend funds for community economic development. This loan fund supports more than 350 marginalized groups in 66 nations worldwide. Oikocredit lends to groups rather than to individuals. A cooperative of coffee growers, for example, may wish to purchase its own roasting facility. Coffee beans rot very quickly once picked if not dried, so an easy way to oppress coffee farmers is to stall in purchasing their beans. The desperate farmers will take whatever they can get rather than face a complete loss. By making loans to the cooperative, Oikocredit is doing more that giving people a way to earn a living, it is helping to build a more just society. Lenders come from the United States and Europe and most of the borrowers are in the Southern Hemisphere.[10]

Women's World Banking (WWB) operates primarily from grants rather than investors' loans and was founded on the belief in the central importance of economic access and, in particular, credit for poor women. This translates into supporting local initiatives and trusting that local practitioners and institutions are best able to decide the right mix of credit, savings, training, and commercial links, as well as the most appropriate delivery mechanisms, that will move their clients from survival to growth. From 1979 to 1994, WWB Affiliates have made, brokered, or guaranteed more than 200,000 loans averaging approximately $350 each. The weighted average repayment rate was more than 95 percent, with less than 1 percent of defaults.[11]

Emerging Contractors in South Africa: Supporting a Democracy in the Making—Project of Shared Interest

Greg Nthatisi is one of South Africa's "emerging contractors," skilled builders who were prohibited from forming their own businesses under apartheid and who have since faced difficulty obtaining sufficient credit. With more than two million people currently in poor living conditions, housing is one of South Africa's most pressing needs. Loan guarantees collaboratively issued by a consortium that included Shared Interest made possible the completion of 5,207 low-cost houses; 30 local contractors in 34 communities built these homes. With the help of American investors who lend their money to Shared Interest, contractors like Greg Nthatisi can move from "emerging" to "established" and provide the housing and jobs that South Africa desperately needs to become an economically viable nation.

Source: "Building Houses in the Free State," *Shared Interest: In Focus* VI, no. 1 (Spring 2000).

In a developing economy, $350 is a potential alleviation of poverty for generations to come. Most poor venders or crafts-people in emerging economies must start their day going to a loan shark. They borrow enough to pay for the supplies, perhaps a barrel of dried beans. Next, the beans must be hauled to a market and sold. The loan shark is repaid at a rate that can be as high as twice the amount loaned, even though the loan was for one day. A theft or accident can be calamity. To be able to purchase inventory once, without a loan shark, can break the cycle of poverty forever.

Community Development Loan Funds That Make International Loans

- **Accion International**
  www.accion.org
  617-492-4930
  Provides microeconomic loans and technical assistance throughout Latin America.
- **Nicaraguan Credit Alternatives Fund**
  608-257-7230
  Provides microloans in Nicaragua.
- **Shared Interest**
  212-337-8547
  Provides microloans for small business and housing in South Africa.
- **SEED Haiti Community Development Loan Fund**
  (c/o LWC Office) 617-523-6531
  Business loans to peasant cooperatives in rural Haiti
- **Fonkoze**
  202-667-1277
  Provides business loans in Haiti
- **Nitlapan**
  847-866-4592
  Provides small and medium-sized loans in rural Nicaragua.

> • **Oikocredit**—www.oikocredit.org
> 212-870-2725
> Supplies credit to productive enterprises in disadvantaged
> areas all over the world.
>
> Also Worth Noting:
> • **INAISE**, the International Association of Investors in the
> Social Economy is a network of social finance organizations,
> including banks, loan funds, and credit unions that you can
> find at <www.inaise.org> or phone in Brussels, Belgium, at
> (32-2) 234 57 97.
>
> **Source:** National Community Capital Association <www.communitycapital.org>.

Sometimes U.S.-based CDFIs offer technical assistance to start-up CDFIs abroad. Shorebank Corp. is particularly active in this regard. With teams in Romania, Georgia, and Azerbaijan, this Chicago-based CDFI has helped create microlending pools throughout the former Soviet Union, Eastern Europe, and elsewhere. Recently it, along with Triodos Bank of the Netherlands and others, helped launch KREP Bank in Nairobi, Kenya.[12]

As in the United States, CDFIs abroad come in the form of banks, credit unions, and loan funds. Many do not operate from loans or deposits but rather from grants. Others are self-sufficient, indigenous models. Almost every culture has a history of "lending circles" by which each member of the circle contributes a small amount and then the circle decides which business one of its members wants to start will be financed first. When that business repays its loan, the next entrepreneur is selected. It is likely that these circles will continue to make good partners for CDFIs operating out of the United States. Several community development loan funds that are based in the United States make loans globally and are profiled in boxes throughout this book. But there is so much more that could be done. As socially responsible investors create more innovative and accessible vehicles to hold CDFI investments, more of these assets can flow to the rest of the world. In the meanwhile, we must study indigenous models and support them with grants or by partnering with them on projects.

Getting the Best of Each Culture in One World

Economic or financial systems no longer fit into simple national frameworks. The global village is here on Wall Street, and it offers tremendous opportunities and challenges toward achieving our twin goals of justice and environmental sustainability. One reason for this is the Internet. In moments I can visit <www.1worldcommunication.org> and review a score of articles written by activists reporting on conditions in East Timor from the ground, three dozen written from Columbia, and so forth. I don't need the *New York Times* to tell me how my favorite foreign correspondent feels about the events unfolding in the jungles of Brazil. I read 15 letters from tribal leaders there and form my own opinion. Or I can visit the Irrawaddy Web site at <www.irrawaddy.org> to follow events in Burma. Such sites proliferate daily, and they are all healthy for the future of the world.

Access to alternative news sources better arms SRI to evaluate the impact of globalization and to act with local organizations to address the worst effects of globalization. Armed with knowledge, social investors have demanded companies that source from sweatshops to conduct audits of their suppliers' factories. One of the most highly regarded monitoring organizations is Verité, a nonprofit that publishes reports on the dynamics of the global assembly line. The Verité Index points out that the percentage of sweatshop laborers that are women between the ages of 15 and 22 is 90 percent. The number of hours per month commonly worked in a factory in Bangladesh audited by Verite was 100. The total sewing/assembly cost of $20 Disney 101 Dalmatians pajamas in Haiti is six cents.[13] By adding screens that support corporate social research on sweatshops, by filing shareholder resolutions on sweatshop sourcing, and by supporting community development investment institutions that operate abroad, socially responsible investors use the knowledge base that grassroots groups provide us to come up with constructive solutions.

I have come to feel that the different corners of the world have fairly definite strengths to share in building a strong global social investment community. By working with these strengths, social investors should be able to help craft one world that benefits from all the parts. A good team usually has more than one star. Each star has a special talent, sometimes poorly developed in other team members. Although different from one another, together they have a winning combination.

The emerging economies offer their vibrant alternative models to business as usual. The most innovative and exciting community development work, like MiBanco in Panama and the Grameen Bank in Bangladesh, emerge from these "outside of the box" thinkers. Furthermore, emerging economy citizens have a capacity for personal transformation that first-worlders cannot conceive of. Prida Tiasuwan, founder of the world's largest gold jewelry manufacturing company, lives in Thailand. When he was 12, his father took his family north, away from the troubles of southern Thailand by traveling along the river, a journey that lasted months. Today, his daughter attends a university in England and his gold is sold at Wal-Mart and on the Home Shopping Network. But in spite of his tremendous transformation, he remembers the reality of poverty and fear.

Panama's most popular guide, simply known as Jimmy, left the bush at age 22. Today he runs executive retreats. He flies a seaplane into Panama's jungles with top executives from global corporations and runs survival training courses that are geared toward team building. He is as comfortable spending six days in a jungle barefoot and without supplies of any sort as he is eating at a fine French restaurant with visiting royalty from Europe. His son attended a university in the United States and now works with him. He is both worlds in one man.

With amazing capacity for adaptation and comfort with alternative economic models, the emerging nations contribute not only evidence of the hardships our current global economic vision has created but also the visions and capacity to come up with answers. But social investors must do their part, too, and work to free these nations from the debt loads, corporate-sponsored military oppressors, and criminal destruction of their natural resources.

Thomas's Top Two

Thomas Thijssens does corporate social research for Triodos Bank NV, one of the primary managers of social investment portfolios in the Netherlands. He likes the following two companies' social stories.

- **Van Melle NV** produces confectionery brands including Mentos, Fruit-Tella, and Air Heads. The company has a policy of avoiding genetically modified foods. Van Melle publishes a social report for all Dutch branches, and was one of the first companies in the Netherlands to publish an environmental report. Where possible, sustainable energy from solar systems or wind turbines is used, and the company has set up a green office program to minimize the environmental impact of office activities. This led to use of chlorine-free recycled paper and double-sided copies. Van Melle aims to build production locations in each geographic territory to minimize the environmental impact of transporting its products. The company gives 1 percent of its profits to initiatives of environmental causes, and sets up environmental education programs to plant trees. The Van Melle mission statement says, "We are involved with the environment and are determined to reduce our environmental impact to a sustainable level."
- **Wolters Kluwer NV (WTKWY (ADR))** publishes legal, financial, business, medical, and educational books, journals, and

training manuals. A consistent social policy is firmly embedded in the organization. The company has nonfinancial performances as a part of its management information and salaries system. The company puts great effort in the training and education of its employees, and has a leave program in which employees are able to exchange days for salary and vice-versa. Moreover, 30 percent of its employees work on flextime and others telecommute. The company is known for its good relations with its Works Council and unions and annually publishes a detailed and comprehensive social report.

Source: You can reach Thomas at triodos@knoware.nl or visit his Web site at <www.triodos.nl>.

When I read that the citizens of Japan felt personal humiliation at the banking collapse in their nation, I was startled. We had had a banking collapse in the United States and I had felt no shame. I had felt no connection to the events at all. This sense of personal responsibility for the reputation and reality of the society one belongs to is something that could become a best practice in a global economy. Additionally, the Buddhist and Hindu cultures almost completely reverse all the truths we know in the West. Factories such as Pranda Jewelry in Thailand, whose founder I introduced above, run on Buddhist philosophy, and each room offers a peaceful spot of beauty for the workers to gaze on and center themselves.

Europeans continue to enjoy an enlightened leadership that is still willing to speak out openly on issues of the meaning of civilization and on environmental sustainability. They understand that with position and power comes responsibility and they humbly shoulder it. By and large, society in Europe still equates living well with the quality of an evening stroll and not with the number of television sets you own. The evening stroll brings you in contact with fountains, plazas, structural harmony, flowering plants, and other people. There is a sense that the nation's status is diminished if the status of the least of its citizens is diminished. Finally, there is an intellectual enjoyment of examining the philosophical underpinnings of a decision undertaken.

Pool's Passions: Venture Capital and Socially Responsible Investing

Adam de Sola Pool is the chief investment officer of Environmental Investment Partners. He invests venture capital into environmental companies in central Europe. He chose to share the following story with us.

Organica is a Hungarian wastewater treatment company that converts old barges (coal, sand, etc.) into floating wastewater treatment systems. This solves many of the land permitting issues. A wastewater plant can be towed into place within 48 hours of signing the contract versus months to get land use permits. Moreover, it can be towed away if the client does not pay the usage fee (thus solving the financing issue because leasing companies easily finance mobile assets). Furthermore, the company plants 2,000 species (plants, fish, and snails) in the converted barges to do the wastewater treatment processing, dramatically reducing the chemical and biological additives necessary to do tertiary treatment of the wastewater.

Source: You can reach Adam de Sola Pool at <pool@eip.com.pl>. His VC fund details are at <www.ceeeif.com> and <www.eip.com.pl>.

In the United States, we are great systems people. We know what we want, and it is to get the job done. We have experimented with and found an effective means of distributing financial assets through our mutual funds. We have found a reasonably empowering, if less protected, means of providing for retirement through our various plans. Americans have a profound respect for individual rights and, relative to the rest of the world, a true comfort with a cacophony of voices. Our corporations will hire the best and the brightest no matter what their national origin, gender, sexual orientation, faith, physical disabilities, military service, or geographic location. If the employee has the talents we want, we truly don't see any impediment.

A Global Village of 100

If we could shrink the earth's population to a village of precisely 100 people, with all existing human rations remaining the same, it would look like this:

- The village would have 57 Asians, 21 Europeans, 14 North and South Americans, and 8 Africans
- 51 would be female, 49 male
- 70 would be nonwhite, 30 white
- 70 would be non-Christian, 30 Christian
- 80 would live in substandard housing
- 70 would be unable to read
- 50 would suffer from malnutrition
- 1 would be near death, 1 near birth
- 1 would have a college education
- No one would have a computer
- 6 would control 50 percent of the entire world's wealth
- Those 6 would be U.S. citizens

Source: "Globalization: Why Should We Care?" Presentation at the National Network of Grantmakers Conference, 15–18 March 2000, Boston, Massachusetts.

These attributes, taken together, should add up to a tremendous formula for advancing the causes of peace, justice, and a sustainable environmental policy. The fact that the socially responsible investment community is still small and in close communication with each other globally gives us an opportunity to help shape the way in which global financial services, through the companies they control, affect the lives of people. By addressing the root cause of so much hardship in so much of the world, socially responsible investors will make it possible for all the planet's citizens to enjoy the fruits of global prosperity.

Applying Social Criteria to Your Investment Decisions

7

You Can Make Money This Way

Each time a man stands up for an ideal, or acts
to improve the lot of others, or strikes out against injustice, he sends a tiny ripple of hope, and crossing each
other from a million different centers of energy and dar-
ing, those ripples build a current which can sweep down
the mightiest walls of oppression and resistance.

—ROBERT KENNEDY IN SOUTH AFRICA IN 1966

We've seen how to integrate social and ethical criteria into portfolio management. This chapter and the next address why to do it. Here we look at the investment case in the chapter, next we examine the impact on the planet. Socially responsible investing makes so much sense because it makes you a participant in a more complex analysis of a company, and it has had real success in creating a more livable planet.

Steve's Stakeholder Story Stocks: Corporations and Civic Values Environment—Sustainability and Efficiency

Steven D. Lydenberg, research director, at KLD chose these as examples of companies that promote energy efficiency, recycling, alternative fuels, and pollution prevention.

- **AstroPower, Inc. (APWR)**, is a developer and marketer of solar electric power products. Among its environmentally progressive manufacturing practices is the use of silicon wafers discarded by the computer chip industry, which it recycles for its products.
- **Baldor Electric Co. (BEZ)** is a manufacturer of highly energy-efficient motors through its Super-E and High Efficiency lines. Another line won top prize in the "Electric Motors, Drives, and Controls" category from *Plant Engineering* magazine.
- **Interface, Inc. (IFSIA)**, is a carpet manufacturer notably devoted to recycling and environmentally sustainable manu-facturing practices. The Terratex line is made entirely from 100 percent recycled polyester fibers. The company publishes a sustainability report and is a CERES Principles signatory.
- **Plug Power Inc. (PLUG)** develops power generators that uti-lize fuel cell technology rather than combustion. These fuel cells are designed for use off the grid, at home or at commer-cial sites. Plug's stationary fuel cells generate electricity through chemical reaction rather than through combustion, resulting in zero emissions other than water and, depending on the fuel source, small amounts of carbon dioxide.
- **Real Goods Trading Corp. (RGTC)** products include ener-gy-efficient water heaters, dryers, and heaters; environmen-tal books, videos, and CDs; and products for water, air, and

outdoor gardening and healthy activity. The company promotes living off the grid through using alternative energy
sources.
- **Schnitzer Steel Industries (SCHN)** operates metal-process-
ing and recycling facilities and minimill steel plants. The company's metal recycling contributes to the efficient use of
existing resources and provides its minimill with a steady
supply of raw material. Its operations contribute to reducing
waste and the minimill uses recycled waste material to produce useful metal products.

Source: You can reach Steve at stevel@kld.com or visit his Web site at
<www.kld.com>.

How does the application of social criteria to the investment
decision-making process create value? Part of the answer lies in
the fact that the basic principles of social investing, if allowed to
continue to their logical conclusions, will reduce other costs on
investors, allowing them to invest more. A broader distribution
of wealth should lead to spending less on protecting yourself
and your family; a cleaner environment should reduce your
health care costs; getting business out of weapons production
should mean fewer lethal weapons are in the hands of fanatics.
But perhaps of greatest interest to the investor is the fact that
even over the relatively short run, social investing can actually
enhance the investor's involvement and results.

In this day and age of day trader and dot-com boom times,
you might easily forget that the tortoise won the race. But care-
ful evaluation of a corporation's expectations and business practices has been the hallmark of every great portfolio manager
since the dawn of Wall Street. The corporate social responsibility research process evaluates a corporation's impact on its various stakeholders and allows even the conventional securities
analyst or stock picker to learn whether or not the management
team is effective at handling a broad range of issues, any one of

which might escalate to a crisis if poorly dealt with. Through social impact profiles, an analyst sees aspects of the corporation that are missed in conventional analysis. It reveals whether a top-flight management team is in place and whether a progressive, enthusiastic corporate culture exists. The socially responsible investor is interested in the long term. Only professional, capable managers think and plan that way.

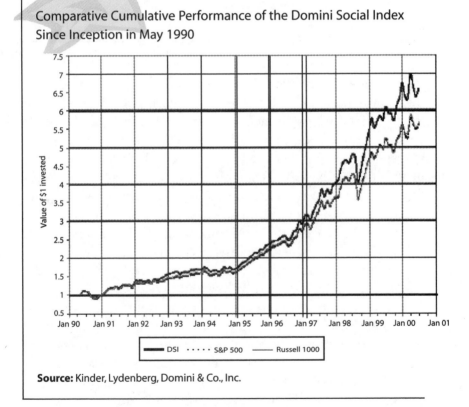

Remember: The Tortoise Won the Race!

Comparative Cumulative Performance of the Domini Social Index Since Inception in May 1990

Source: Kinder, Lydenberg, Domini & Co., Inc.

The Domini 400 Social Index taught us that the application of broad social criteria to the investment decision-making process does not hinder the investor from achieving superior results. In fact, it seems that the application of social criteria may have led to superior investment results for the index's first ten years. From May 1, 1990, through April 30, 2000, the Domini Social Index returned an average annual 20.83 percent versus 18.70 percent for the more conventional Standard & Poor's 500 Index.

There is growing evidence that social screens do not hinder performance. Morningstar, the major mutual fund-rating service, conducted an analysis of the performance of SRI funds in 1999. The results show that 21 percent of the SRI funds that they track earned the coveted five-star or four-star rating. That compares with 12 percent of all mutual funds in the Morningstar universe.[1] That's almost a two-to-one ratio.

Screening Large Funds: Some Are Better Than Others

In 1999, Kinder, Lydenberg, Domini & Co., in collaboration with Morningstar, took the top domestic stock mutual funds and ran them through the screens KLD uses to maintain the Domini 400 Social Index. The funds were separated by style, five growth, five value. The three largest growth funds did fairly well, with only 5 percent to 14 percent of their assets failing the screen. These three, AXP New Dimensions, American Century Ultra, and Janus, invest heavily in service, health, and high-tech industries, which usually have negligible environmental issues and progressive employment practices. In contrast, the study found that the large value funds, such as MSDW Dividend Growth Securities and DIVAX, with their heavy holdings in utilities, energy, and industrial firms, had a harder time passing social screens. Failure rates for the five large value funds examined ranged from 29 percent to 45 percent. Morningstar cautioned that the study does not conclude that growth funds are inherently more socially responsible than others, but merely shows market conditions lending themselves to investments in high-tech, service, and health companies result in a relatively clean portfolio.

Source: "KLD & Morningstar Examine Large Funds," *Connections Networking for Responsible Business and Investing* (Spring 2000).

The belief that SRI makes sound investment sense is shared by portfolio managers around the world. Alfred Kool, a representative of PGGM, a large pension manager in the Netherlands with more than $46 billion in assets, stated, "We believe that it increases returns," as part of an announcement that the company is now beginning to manage funds according to SRI principles.[2] Other European Union portfolio managers concur. "We don't invest in companies that cause some form of damage to the environment," says Derek Bartlett, manager of the City Financial's Acorn Ethical Fund. "We invest in companies that are trying to improve the environment." The fund had a total return of 19.3 percent for the 12 months ended June 12, 2000.[3]

How do each of the three arenas of social investing affect portfolio performance? Screens reveal the quality of management and the corporate culture. Activism helps companies avoid future problems. Community development makes a reasonable alternative to cash reserves.

Social Screens Make Better Decisions Possible

The excellent performance of socially screened portfolios may well be a result of looking at a company through the lens of the stakeholder model. To make this case, I will compare two companies, one in the Domini 400 Social Index, one not. By walking through the process of deciding which of these large companies to add to the index, you can see that corporate social analysis adds a startlingly significant depth of knowledge about a company that even conventional asset managers should value.

I draw from social audits of fairly similar companies, Johnson & Johnson (JNJ) and American Home Products (AHP). Both are large consumer goods and pharmaceutical companies. The sample full audit of JNJ found in Appendix A at the back of this book was written by Kinder, Lydenberg, Domini & Co., Inc., and is drawn from Socrates: The Corporate Social Ratings Monitor. Looking it over will give you a sense of what goes into selecting a company buy for an SRI portfolio. Although I do

More of Carsten and Leslie's Picks

Carsten Henningston and Leslie Christian are the founders of Portfolio 21, a global mutual fund investing in a sustainable future. They think these companies are of special interest to social investors.

- **STMicroelectronics (STM)** is in the semiconductor industry, an industry fraught with high energy and resource consumption, which makes it all the more outstanding to see the company embrace sustainability. ST believes the world is priceless; ecology is free. As a result, ST has committed to working toward achieving environmental neutrality, following CEO Pasquale Pistorio's belief that sustainability can provide a real competitive advantage. ST's goal is to communicate the success of its commitment and to encourage other businesses to also strive for sustainability. Hopefully, ST's influence will contribute to reducing the environmental impact of semiconductor manufacturing throughout the industry.

- **Swiss Re (SWCEY (ADR))**, a Swiss company, is a clear leader in the insurance industry through its early recognition of environmental issues and leadership role in lobbying for strong public policies to combat climate change. The company creates incentives for clients to reduce their impact on the environment. In short, the company's insurance rates are based, in part, on a client's environmental impact and the risks associated with that impact. As a global insurer, Swiss Re provides insurance products and policies that motivate companies throughout the world to follow sustainable business practices, reduce their impact on the environment, and save money.

Source: You can reach Carsten at carsten@portfolio21.com or at the fund's Web site <www.portfolio21.com>.

not append the full audit of AHP, I draw from it as well. By comparing these two companies, the value of reviewing a social profile emerges clearly.

According to the JNJ audit, the company offers 52 weeks of childbirth leave, and family benefits include phaseback for new mothers, adoption aid of $3,000, resource and referral services, and a lactation program. The company contributes more than 50 percent toward the operating costs of six on-site child care centers—the balance comes from fees parents pay. AHP's profile reveals that the company offers 24 weeks of maternity leave, and other family benefits track those at JNJ. AHP has two on-site childcare centers and covers 33 percent of the costs of these. That's 52 weeks versus 24 weeks of maternity leave, similar benefits on adoption, and 50 percent versus 33 percent of child care costs at six versus two on-site centers.

The grants programs at the two companies also reveal disparities. JNJ gives about $1 million a year to the Head Start Program, which targets early education for economically disadvantaged preschoolers. JNJ funds research on how to develop better child care centers and early childhood programs. The company supports INROADS, a national program for placing minority youth in summer internships. JNJ gives about 1.5 percent of earnings before taxes to charity, a significant level, and it provides estimates of its in-kind noncash contributions. The company's giving is strategic and related to its core business; it is innovative and transparent; it specifically supports community-based institutions such as public schools.

In 1999, AHP told KLD that it did not disclose figures for its corporate charitable giving. But in 1996, the company informed KLD that it had donated 114 million pills of its hormone replacement therapies for a ten-year worldwide study of the effectiveness of estrogen in the prevention of osteoporosis, heart disease, and other conditions. It estimated the value of its donations at $50 million. One could argue that this is not charitable giving and would be better allocated to the company's research budget. When you compare the two companies' charitable giving programs, you find JNJ to be transparent and strategic, with a focus on giving support to at-risk populations, while AHP is silent about most giving and considers some noncash gifts for scientific research to be an act of charity.

Corporations' Performance Closely Linked to a Strong Ethical Commitment

Corporations that publicly declare the importance of an ethics code to their management philosophy perform better in both financial and nonfinancial terms than corporations that do not make such declarations, according to a 1999 study of 500 large public U.S. companies performed by DePaul University Professor Curtis C. Verschoor. "The most plausible cause of superior perform- ance relates to the nature of the values that have infused an organ- ization over time. The resulting code of conduct merely reflects these values," comments Verschoor. This premise is consistent with the results of a recent study by Arthur Andersen that found that an ethics program created to guide behavior and reinforce company values is significantly more successful than one that employees believe was established strictly for compliance purposes.

Verchoor concludes, "an emphasis on proper values deals with setting examples, interpreting ethical principles, and structuring appropriate reward systems. Ethical culture spreads from clear and unequivocal goal setting at the top and openness through- out the organization. On the other hand, compliance has to do with rules, hierarchy, and sanctions. Legalistic codes of conduct designed only to protect an organization from conflicts of inter- est or rogue managerial behaviors are unlikely to motivate loyal employee behavior and result in long-term retention of favorable relationships with suppliers, customers, and other stakeholders."

Source: Robin Florzak, "Corporate performance is closely linked to a strong ethi- cal commitment, DePaul professor's study finds," DePaul University press release, 12 February 1999.

Next, let's compare the way the two companies impact the communities they operate in. Since the late 1970s, JNJ has played a substantial role in the revitalization of its headquarters city of New Brunswick, New Jersey. In December 1996, AHP reported it had agreed to pay a civil penalty of $129,000 to settle allegations relating to inadequate provision for emergency planning and

Ethical Investment Web Sites in Europe, the United States, and Australia

Ethical Investment Services maintains an online fund selector for the European ethical investor. The Ethical Fund Selector allows an investor to specify his or her own ethical and financial priorities. The investor can then view and order the funds that most closely meet his or her own preferences. Other features of the site include a polling tool that presents the arguments for and against a topical ethical investment issue and invites visitors to cast their vote. The site is at <www.ethicalservices.co.uk>.

SocialWorld.com and the **Social Investment Forum** offer online fund selection tools for the social investor looking for U.S.-based funds. Both sites offer a large resource base for financial planning, shareholder activism, academic studies, community economic development, and upcoming conferences. Socialfunds.com also offers a news service for those who want to stay abreast of the field. The sites are <www.socialfunds.com> and <www.socialinvest.org>.

Ethical Investor is an online magazine, or "e-zine" for the ethical investor in Australia. It has updates on corporate social research reports, product information, and thought pieces from portfolio managers of ethical investment portfolios. Most Australian mutual funds advertise on the site so they can be reached through links. You can find them at <www.ethicalinvestor.com.au>.

agreed to donate emergency response equipment to the community that brought the suit.

A picture is emerging here: one of a company that is ahead of the curve on issue after issue, despite some areas of real concern, versus a company that isn't. JNJ is in the Domini 400 Social Index and AHP is not. Through social analysis, I believe that a portfolio bias toward companies with forward-looking, multi-tasking, and on-the-ball management teams is introduced. Higher-quality management teams and strong corporate cultures help companies' performances and our investment. During the two years leading up to my writing this book, the companies have differed in returns to investors as well. JNJ has returned 21 percent, while AHP has risen 14 percent.

Even simply avoiding problems should lead to superior performance. Why wouldn't any security analyst struggling to select the finest company within his or her industry seek out a tool to evaluate the quality of the management team? The stakeholder screening process is an almost universally overlooked tool on Wall Street. Outside of those managing social accounts, it is unknown. The feminist in me attributes this to a hangover "macho" attitude on Wall Street by which it is somehow considered soft to use the vocabulary of socially responsible investing. But the results speak for themselves, and the performance of the Domini 400 Social Index cannot be denied.

When the Domini Social Index (DSI) was constructed, I hoped that simply avoiding trouble would add performance value to the index. Although today I believe the index has benefited both from emphasizing the positive and from avoiding the negative, it is true that social screens help identify a company with problems. Appendix D at the back of this book was provided by KLD and briefly lists the indicators of a company's strengths and vulnerabilities. What are some of these? Thirty or more Superfund sites, class-action suits, product safety fines, excessive compensation for the board, complete lack of diversity at the top, excessive emission of toxic chemicals, underfunded pension accounts, and operations in Burma are all considered to indicate problems brewing.

Good Governance Pays

In a landmark finding, according to a survey by McKinsey & Co. conducted in cooperation with the World Bank, domestic and foreign investors say they would pay a giant 24 percent premium for stock in a Latin American corporation equipped with good governance practices. That's twice as large as the 11 percent premium U.S. investors said they would pay for a well-governed U.S. company in 1996, when McKinsey last published such a study. The finding concisely translates the theoretical benefits of good corporate governance into hard cash terms. This is a powerful argument for corporate governance reform in Latin America and elsewhere. In fact, disclosure was the top governance priority for Latin American investors surveyed. The World Bank is likely to sponsor similar tests on investments in eastern Europe next. Authors gathered responses from 90 institutions holding $1.6 trillion in assets.

Source: *Global Proxy Watch* IV, no. 22 (2 June 2000): 1; OECD/World Bank Global Corporate Governance Forum, <www.gcgf.org>.

There's a saying on Wall Street that "the easiest way to make money is to not lose money." Staying out of troubled companies is one way to limit your risk. Nobody wants to make a financial bet on management teams that have a problem staying out of the kind of trouble just listed. They've already displayed a level of incompetence and there are plenty of good management teams out there to bet on. Corporate social research is actually just good solid research. It generates valuable insights into a company and the team at the helm. By screening an investment portfolio in a manner that considers this information, whether positive or negative, the investor is both reducing risk and adding focus on the quality of management and the corporate culture. You can make money while screening an investment portfolio.

Shareholder Dialogue
Keeps Companies out of Trouble

The real financial benefit of shareholder dialogue lies in the fact that it accomplishes several things simultaneously. Companies are made aware of potential liabilities before they grow larger, and investment managers have access to more information about the company they are considering investing in. Most shareholder-sponsored resolutions simply ask for reports about progress in addressing certain problematic issues. Any fiduciary would ask for the same, once made aware of the issue. It is, after all, only prudent to want management to report on progress toward removing risks. It is hard to argue that shareholder responsibility through filing and/or voting costs anything to investors and easy to see that it acts to reduce risks. Finally, it is only prudent for the owners of a company to support requests for greater disclosure. Active shareholder dialogue such as we see in the United States, Canada, and England is an effective means of assisting both the corporation and its various stakeholders to achieve positive results. Reducing risk is one of the primary ways investors enhance return. Shareholder actions do just this for investors. Consider some of the avoided costs in a few recent cases.

Polyvinyl chloride (PVC) is used in the manufacture of containers for intravenous solutions. In early 1999, Greenpeace and several health groups issued a report on findings that the possible carcinogen DEHP (a chemical used in the manufacture of PVC) can leach into fluids in IV bags that hospitals use. Catholic health care systems, which faced the potential liability of lawsuits arising from DEHP exposure, approached Abbott Laboratories (ABT), a manufacturer of IV bags. The company made a rapid decision to find an alternate to PVC. Shareholders now avoid a risk that they once unknowingly faced.

In 1999, after years of fighting with environmentalists and church groups over the issue, General Electric agreed to spend nearly $250 million to help clean up the Housatonic River in Massachusetts. Cancer-causing chemicals allegedly had been dumped into the river for years. Activists may have saved investors hundreds of millions of dollars' worth of liability.

More of Bobby Julian's Best Picks

Bobby Julian is finance director at Preferred Energy, Inc., a Manila-based nongovernmental organization with direct investments in renewable energy enterprises. He also develops projects in other areas of the environmental infrastructure space—e.g., water and waste. His main interest is in technology that provides access to new or improved basic services for the many, which, ironically in this day and age, means his choice investments lean toward the speculative.

- **Essential.Com (ESSE)** is a leading online communications and energy marketplace, offering a broad range of branded "Essential Services" to residential and small business customers. It is not limited to environmentally friendly services but rather covers a much wider array, ranging from energy to telephony and cable television. Its business model explores new distribution channels for delivering basic services.
- **Ocean Power Corp. (PWRE)** is dedicated to becoming the world's leading innovator of mass-produced, modular, water desalination, and renewable-energy power systems. Its success will depend on its ability to make desalinating sea water cost-competitive with pumped ground water. To achieve this, the company mass-produces modular systems powered by renewable energy. A recent Memorandum of Understanding with Wind Harvest Co. to develop an exclusive license agreement to provide Windstar turbines for use with Ocean Power's H2OkW Seawater Desalination Systems seems headed in the right direction. The impending global water problem will provide Ocean Power vibrant markets for its systems.

- **Startech Environmental Corp. (STHK)** manufactures waste treatment systems that break down both hazardous and nonhazardous waste into usable materials. Its most promising technology is the Plasma Waste Converter (PWC) that allows for the development of urban resource recovery centers that can process up to 500 MTs of mixed urban waste a day. Startech has formed a strategic alliance with Skidmore, Owings & Merrill LLP (SOM) to design and construct these centers worldwide. SOM has committed to selling the PWC systems and securing PWC-based contracts. If the centers can be built with a relatively small footprint and if the PWC technology will have little or no impact on its immediate surroundings, then the company would have a lock on waste disposal postlandfill.

Source: You can reach Bobby at Preferred Energy, Inc., 10th Floor, Strata 100 Building Emerald Avenue, Ortigas Center Pasig City, Philippines 1605; telephone 632-631-2826; fax 632-632-7097, or e-mail him at pei@info.com.ph.

When RJR decided to separate its tobacco business from its food business, the company stated that the decision had been a purely economic one and that it had not grown out of the shareholder actions requesting the company to do so. Again, activists were asking for something that the company management found to be in the best interests of the company.

Rapid response to activists may be an indication of a better decision-making process in management. In 1999, Coca-Cola took a $103 million (110 million euros) charge after a contamination scare in Belgium and France forced the company to recall its products. The direct financial cost was compounded by the damage done to the company's reputation in Europe by then Chief Executive Douglas Ivester's sluggish handling of the crisis; it took him ten days to fly to Brussels and apologize.[4] A year later, a young Italian boy staying with me told me he doesn't drink Coke because they don't even tell you when their cans are bad.

Most shareholder filings address an issue that could potentially cost the company a great deal, whether in product liability suits, a bad reputation, or human health issues. In 2000, Placer Dome Inc. (PDG), a Canadian company, made the responsible decision to circulate a shareholder proposal asking for a corporate commitment to provide shareholders with independent information concerning risks and liabilities from environmental accidents. While Canadian law would have allowed the company to exclude the resolution had it been considered simply social, the financial implications convinced Placer Dome to allow the issue to come to a vote.

While these examples show the importance of shareholder activism in reducing risks at the company, there is also the role of the person voting the resolutions to consider. Whether you manage your own money or sit on the board of a library and hear reports from money managers, you have the right and, I believe, the responsibility to hold management accountable. It costs you nothing and it builds the possibility that the company will avoid costs. Furthermore, any prudent fiduciary would ask for reports on issues where the well-being of either the company or the beneficiary is at risk. It is possible and prudent to support shareholder activism while making money with your investments.

European Commission's Statement on the Corporation's Responsibility to Its Employees

Companies have responsibilities not only to their shareholders but also to other stakeholders. The corporate entity has a responsibility to maintain the employability of its workers. The employability of an individual is his or her ability to find a niche in the labor market. Employability encompasses more than just training: It also provides individuals with a better understanding of change, of the need for mobility, and of the means to upgrade skills. In short, it means that individuals have confidence in their own ability to adapt to change.

The responsibility for becoming employable, and for maintaining employability, is shared. All actors have a role. Companies have a duty to maintain the employability of their workers, while workers have a duty to participate fully in training to maintain their own employability. For the unemployed, ensuring employability is a responsibility shared with government and local authorities.

Top-performing companies have a good social dialogue with their employees because motivated people are the vital component for commercial success. Regular, transparent, comprehensive dialogue creates trust.

Source: Excerpts from "Managing Change: Final Report of the High Level Group on Economic and Social Implications of Industrial Change," *EC Commission on Employment & Social Affairs*, 1998, 7–9.

Community Economic Development

Community economic development investments suffer under a cloud of below-market returns because many loan funds can offer only below-market interest rates. Even credit unions and banks are unable to provide investors with the long-term upside that equities or bonds can return. But that is an unfair comparison. CDFIs pay as well as a saving account. Some pay better. Many are insured. In an earlier chapter, we reviewed the argument that using these investments can triple the impact of charitable contributions, which is no mean feat. CDFIs make good investment sense for several reasons. It is the right thing to do; it's safe; you'll be a more involved investor; you might be saved other expenses; and it stretches your giving budget.

Sometimes a person should make an investment because it is the right thing to do. Many are rich enough, or care enough, to lend resources to enable these extraordinary grassroots organizations to do their work. Support systems around the world are being stripped away. In the United States, government, traditionally the largest source of support structures, has been subjected to 20 years of successful "get government off our backs" campaigns. These campaigns haven't stopped an obscene escalation in corporate subsidies via environmental or defense legislation. Rather, they accomplished just what many argue their framers desired: the rich have gotten richer and the unwanted minorities have paid for it. In the United States, as abroad, CDFIs offer a rare and slender lifeline to lives being shattered by these events. If we take individual responsibility for the future, then we recognize that the right thing to do is to support CDFIs with our investment dollars, with our voting policies, with our volunteer hours, and with our charitable contributions.

Ralph's Rage—Nuclear Power's Wastefulness

Ralph DeGennaro is cofounder and president of Taxpayers for Common Sense. What really make Ralph and his colleagues mad is wasteful government spending and subsidies, including corporate welfare. Here's a section from Ralph's testimony before the U.S. House Committee on Science, Subcommittee on Energy Hearing on Fiscal Year 1998 Research Budget:

"Anyone who doubts that the agencies like the Department of Energy have become the Department of Corporate Welfare needs to know the story of the Advanced Light Water Reactor (ALWR) program. The ALWR subsidizes a consortium of corporations like **General Electric (GE), Westinghouse (now a wholly owned subsidiary of British Nuclear Fuels BNFL), and Asea Brown Boveri/Combustion Engineering (ABB Group Zurich Exchange ABBZn.S)** to develop new nuclear reactor designs and to obtain regulatory approvals from the Nuclear Regulatory Commission. But nuclear fission is a mature technology that has received more than 50 percent ($47.2 billion in 1995 dollars) of all federal energy R&D support between 1948 and 1995. Despite these subsidies, no

American utility has successfully ordered a nuclear power plant since 1973 and a poll found that 89 percent of utility CEOs said that their company would never even consider ordering a nuclear power plant.

"ALWR was to be a five-year program that would be completed in fiscal 1996. Amid promises that fiscal 1997 would be the last year, Congress appropriated $38 million for a sixth year of funding. But now the Department of Energy has requested another $5.5 million for fiscal 1998 for termination costs, including a study, for a program that was long scheduled for termination and should not require any extra spending to end.

"General Electric had revenues of $70 billion in 1995. Westinghouse had revenues of $6.3 billion in 1995. Asea Brown Boveri/Combustion Engineering had revenues of $33.7 billion in 1995. Taxpayers have already provided more than $310 million for these corporations' consortium between FY92 and FY97. It is outrageous to ask hardworking Americans to keep paying money to these corporations."

Source: You can reach Ralph at ralph@taxpayer.net or visit his Web site <www.taxpayer.net>.

The second reason to invest in CDFIs is the investment case. A depositor at a community development credit union or bank enjoys all the protections and gets as good a rate of interest as could be received banking elsewhere. When you buy a certificate of deposit at Self Help Credit Union, your interest rate is equivalent to the rate a certificate of deposit at a conventional credit union would give you. Your services are equivalent as is your insurance protection. CDFIs make a good asset allocation with the portion of your funds you might be holding for cash reserves or a rainy day. They offer equivalent returns to other money management vehicles and do much more then the conventional choices can.

The third reason to invest in CDFIs is that you are a more interested investor. You will read the newsletter that is sent; you will notice the financials; you will be a more involved investor. A more knowledgeable and involved investor is a better investor. The very act of involvement will lead you to make more deliberate decisions. You will think more carefully about whether to purchase a two-year certificate or one that comes due in six months. You will notice when negative news comes out on credit unions. You will treat your cash management portion of your investments more seriously and will therefore make more money.

There is yet another reason investing in CDFIs makes good financial sense. Because you are going to bank somewhere, why not also see some benefit to your community? If you are fortunate enough to live near a community development financial institution, then the choice should be clear. By lending funds or by placing a deposit with the CDFI, you are going to see the value of your community enhanced. A strong community lender will create a healthier community. Your pocketbook will benefit in a dozen ways. You'll experience lower crime rates, better social safety nets, affordable housing, an increase in entry-level jobs, and an infrastructure for community growth. Without the community lender, you might have to pay for these things in higher taxes, a less pleasant lifestyle, a longer and more dangerous commute, subpar schooling for your children, and a less vibrant community. Even the most conventional investor can quickly tally up the costs in not supporting CDFIs.

The final reason a prudent investor uses CDFIs is that your money does two jobs for you at once. While it is earning interest it is also acting in much the same way that your charitable contributions act. You might give money to a soup kitchen sponsored by your place of worship or perhaps you contribute to the local community foundation. Maybe you lend volunteer hours as a soccer coach or school tutor. These are all things that cost you money yet are also supported by community development financial institutions. When you place funds with a CDFI, your money does more than earn interest for you, it also stretches your charitable impact.

CDFIs make a good asset allocation with the portion of your funds you might be holding for cash reserves or a rainy day. They are no worse for your returns than other money management vehicles and do much more than conventional choices can. They are safe, often even insured; they are saving you money; and they fit well into any portfolio.

Screening a portfolio, active engagement of corporate management teams in dialogue on stakeholder issues, and investments in at-risk communities—all work well in a soundly managed investment portfolio. They make money and they make good sense. They build what futurist Hazel Henderson calls a win-win world.[5] Social investing allows us to build an environment within which commerce and people can both survive and thrive while not harming investment results.

The Power of SRI   8

Better Investing Will Result in a Better Tomorrow

Never doubt that a small group of thoughtful, committed citizens can change the world. Indeed, it's the only thing that ever has.

—MARGARET MEAD

Investors stand at the fulcrum of two worlds, the world of finance and the world of commerce. By building a caring presence at this essential juncture, socially responsible investors make possible the use of the financial engine of the planet, surely the strongest human-made force at work today, as a tool for building a future that encompasses human values along with monetary ones.

Cowboy shows were still popular when I was growing up. One scene was replayed in almost every episode. It had variations, but always the essential elements remained. Generally, a vulnerable person or family, often a grandmother, mother, and three young children, in a wagon or stagecoach were being drawn by two or four strong horses. Something would cause the horses to stampede without purpose, which spelled disaster for the helpless family hugging each other in terror. Cowboy Bob would gallop up alongside the lead horse and, in a magnificent display of heroic athletic ability, manage to either pull the beast to a more moderate pace or actually mount it and steer the wagon to safety.

Today, the financial engine of the world is engaged in a purposeless stampede, carrying the world's population as we helplessly cling to the slim security of the buckboard. We do not know where this ride will end, but we know that the lack of purpose spells disaster for our helpless "family of man." And

---

The 14 Companies Most Dependent on Tobacco Product Sales from around the World

Company	Country	Percent of Revenues from Sales of Tobacco
Papastratos Cigarette SA (PAPAK)	Greece	100.0
Massalin Particulares SA (PART)	Argentina	99.9
Nobleza-Piccardo SA (PICA)	Argentina	99.9
Austria Tabakwerke (ATBK)	Austria	99.9
Tabak AS (TABAK)	Czech Republic	99.9
VST Industries Ltd. (VST)	India	99.9
JT International Bhd (RJR2)	Malaysia	99.9
West Indian Tobacco Co. Ltd. (WIT)	Trinidad and Tobago	99.9
British American Tobacco, Plc (BATS)	United Kingdom	99.9
Gallaher Group Plc (GLH)	United Kingdom	99.9
Imperial Tobacco Group Plc (IMT)	United Kingdom	99.9
Holts Cigar Holdings, Inc (HOLT)	United States	99.9
R.J. Reynolds Tobacco Holdings (RJR)	United States	99.9
Pakistan Tobacco Co. Ltd. (PTBC)	Pakistan	99.0

Source: Kinder, Lydenberg, Domini & Co., Inc. Socrates database <www.kld.com>.

where is Cowboy Bob? Is he in government? No, finance has brought governments to their knees, forcing them to sell their water systems, roads, and basic infrastructures to private owners. Is he in consumer power? No, consumers are still bamboozled into using tobacco, petroleum, meat, and a dozen other more tangibly dangerous products than finance. Is he in benign management at multinational corporations? No, corporate management has come under the relentless pressure of finance to enhance shareholder returns. There is only one possible Cowboy Bob in this picture, an investor class that introduces purpose and direction to this powerful set of beasts. Without an investor class that is able to mount, or at least steer, the thundering forces of finance, and thereby commerce, disaster is certain.

Social investors' primary impact results from their unique capacity to reintroduce purpose into finance. By operating from within the financial services world, social investors alter the course it takes. Furthermore, social investing reintroduces and empowers personal responsibility for doing what can be done. It is an action step that a person can take to build a livable world. And as individuals take responsibility for the world, their weight will tip the scales toward a new civic ethic.

The word "investing" makes socially responsible investing uniquely capable of having the impact we desire. Investors are the strongest voice at the table. Money movers have replaced God, government, and commerce; theirs are the tallest buildings in our cities. Their demands are the first voice management at companies responds to. They are too strong a force to operate safely without purpose. Adding "socially responsible" to investing has impact because investors operate at the essential point, the juncture of finance and commerce.

Building a Voice for Decency within the Financial Services Industry

Mutual funds are far and away the fastest-growing force in the financial services industry today. With assets of roughly

$7 trillion, mutual funds own almost half of the market capitalization of the United States. The implication of the shift to their dominance in the financial services industry is profound, for it means that essentially no one owns the economic engine of the planet. The average holding period of a company's stock in a fund is under 12 months (index funds have a longer holding period). Clearly, the portfolio manager's sights are set on the very near term. This inclination will be reinforced by the structure of mutual fund management companies, which have a financial incentive to deliver excellent results, for that is how to get more money under management. This is all good news for the small investor's wallet.

But the small investor is more than a wallet; the investor is also a living being. Unlike an "excellent investment result," you and I need air to breathe, and, furthermore, we hope to live in pleasant surroundings. Because responsible environmental practices are not counted in corporate profit calculations, they are not important to fund managers. The steady demand for immediate improvement in profit margins forces management teams at companies to make decisions, which, while good for our wallets, adversely affect our health, our safety, or freedoms. This is not a matter of bad people but of bad structure.

Steve's Stakeholder Story Stocks Corporations and Civic Values Employee Relations—Diversity and Pluralism

Steven D. Lydenberg, research director at KLD, chose these as examples of companies that provide tangible benefits to their employees by promoting equal opportunity in their workplaces and communities.

- **Avon Products, Inc. (AVP)**, is a cosmetics company with numerous women in top management. An Asian-American woman, Andrea Jung, is CEO. Women account for 85 percent of the company's U.S. managers and officials.

- **Complete Business Solutions (CBSI)** is an information service company. Raj Vattikuti, an Asian-American, is CEO and Karen Fast is an executive vice president. The company hires graduates from Focus HOPE, an innovative job training initiative for inner-city high school students in Detroit.
- **First Tennessee National Corp. (FTN)** is a regional bank that has taken remarkably thorough steps to address work and family issues for its employees. The company supports near-site day care centers and offers alternative work schedules and a phaseback program after maternity leave.
- **Imation Corp. (IMN)** is an image and information storage company that provides notably strong work and family benefits. Barbara Cederberg serves among the company's senior executives. She is a vice president of the company and one of its five most highly compensated officers.
- **McDonald's Corp. (MCD)** is a fast-food restaurant that has done much to support African-American entrepreneurs in economically disadvantaged neighborhoods. The company purchases about $600 million a year in goods and services from minority-owned and women-owned businesses.
- **Siebert Financial Corp. (SIEB)** is a woman-owned investment banking and brokerage firm headed by Muriel Siebert, who, for many years, has been a staunch advocate for women within the financial services industry. Ms. Siebert was the first woman to own a seat on the New York Stock Exchange. Three of the five members of the board are women.

Source: You can reach Steve at stevel@kld.com or visit his Web site at <www.kld.com>.

Mutual funds give small investors access to the benefit of professional asset management, but the benefit received is too narrowly defined: financial benefit. That would be fine if there were checks and balances in the world, counterweights to the power of money, but there are none. Nothing that protects the living, or organic, nature of humankind is as strong as the power wielded by money movers. To define the goals of an industry that controls half the financial assets of the United States as narrowly as "make me money next year" is a mistake of formidable proportions. I focus on mutual funds because they are so uniform in the message management gets, but pension funds, endowments, and the managers of the other half of the financial assets of the United States are also just visitors, along for a nine-month "make me money" ride. Who then will stand up for corporate practices that create the world we want to live in? Where is Cowboy Bob?

Only socially responsible investors, operating from within, are a voice for tomorrow in the current structure. Our message— "Make money for me, yes, but stealing money is different from making money; stealing from the poor, from the natural environment, from civic society is not making money"—is urgent. By operating from within, you and I harness the tremendous power of the world's economic engine for the creation of a more livable tomorrow.

Screening an investment portfolio is the keystone upon which a whole new structure for oversight and dialogue is being built. Simply the demand for corporate social research, in and of itself, created the framework within which so much positive social change has already been accomplished. This was the lesson we learned from the Sullivan Principles: systematic data collection leads to knowledge, which leads to civic action. And it is screening that sets into place a structure to capture data, such as information on toxic releases or contributions to local communities, or board compensation.

There are other ways screening leads to positive results. It impacts corporate behavior by providing a profiled company with a copy of its audit, allowing that company to take steps. Sharing a social profile with activist groups or the public can give them the knowledge they need to take action. It's all about constructing the framework that allows evaluation, dialogue, and ideas for a new way of doing business.

Paolo's Picks for Social Accountability

Paolo Ivo is an auditor with Bureau Veritas Quality International (BVQI), a firm that provides independent verification of working conditions, corporate codes of conduct, and international standards. The company's mission is "to deliver economic value to clients through [Quality, Health, Safety, and Environmental Management] of their assets, projects, products, and systems." The firm has a presence in more than 120 countries. Paolo chose the following two social responsibility stories.

- **Celtipharm** is a private, leading French company producing galenic, or plant-based, pharmaceuticals. The company operates as an "e-hub" for pharmacists and veterinarians. It manufactures most of its products but sometimes has to buy some of its products from abroad. It wishes to contribute to the evolution of the labor laws in developing countries and to ensure that these laws are abided by. Celtipharm is the first French company to be awarded SA8000 certification (a social accountability in sourcing audit) systemwide. The company conducts internal audits to be certain it is not engaging in the use of child or forced labor and has a written policy against discrimination on the basis of sex, race, religion, or opinions. Celtipharm carries out regular audits on suppliers and subcontractors to be certain that they abide by the same rules.
- **Kesko Oy (KKOYX)** is Finland's largest retail company and the biggest company in the country. The company is seeking certification that its suppliers are socially responsible. Its stated mission is to be the best and most respected trading company. Kesko has been among eight Finnish companies to be included in the new Dow Jones Sustainability Group Index. With more than 5,000 existing suppliers producing out of Finland, the company decided to focus on 700 suppliers in 30 countries that seemed to

need assistance most in meeting the supplier standards Kesko seeks.

Source: You can reach Paolo at grantpsi@dglnet.com.br or check out the Web site <www.bvqi.com>.

How else does the need for data create positive social change? To collect data, the information must first be made available. Therefore, corporate social profilers must be active supporters of initiatives to create new and credible data sources. Here's how it works. Today, socially responsible investors need information about how companies source their products. Are they made in sweatshop conditions or with child or prison labor? This is a newly identified need so the data have never been collected in any systematic way. The best a researcher can do is assume that a company purchasing T-shirts in Vietnam is not very interested in the conditions under which those T-shirts are manufactured. This assumption is both unfair and lacking in credibility.

So the researcher searches for data sources. Human rights groups can be good sources of information about conditions in factories that manufacture consumer goods, and even about specific company practices, but their information is just too idiosyncratic to be useful in the social evaluation process. Furthermore, the complexity of sourcing itself poses a barrier. With Disney (DIS) sourcing from thousands of vendors in nations all over the globe, it is simply not reasonable to expect a good assessment of the overall impact from a struggling group whose primary purpose is to alleviate suffering.

Shareholder activists worked with human rights groups to help frame the sweatshop issue and give screeners something to go on. For instance, the concept of paying a living wage is one that is quantifiable and should be relatively ascertainable. By asking companies to agree to conduct surveys that discover what a living wage is and then pay it, activist organizations such as Coalition for Justice in the Maquiladoras create data points. Shareholder dialogue also called attention to the need to have third-party inspection of factories. The existence of a third-party inspection then becomes another ascertainable data point. Third-party evaluators have been on the job long enough now that they themselves have become an important resource in the process of learning what can and cannot be readily changed in a manufacturing plant. Already it is clear that because of marketplace demand for sweatshop data, the process of quantifying what heretofore was not quantifiable—steps to alleviate human suffering—has begun.

An International Coalition of Corporate Social Research Firms

Sustainable Investment Research International (SIRI) Group is a coalition of nine research organizations devoted to the global advancement of social investing. Address is P.O. Box 55, NL–3700 AB Zeist, the Netherlands, telephone +31-30-693.65.79, fax +31-30-693.65.55, e-mail info@sirigroup.org. Web site <www.sirigroup.org>.

Member Contact Information:

- **AReSE SA** covers France and Portugal. Created in July 1997, AReSE is the first French environmental and social rating agency. Telephone 33-1-60 39 50 10, e-mail arese@sirigroup.org, Web site <www.AReSE-sa.com>.
- **Avanzi, s.r.l** covers Italy and was created in 1997 to provide independent research to organizations engaged in designing and implementing sustainable development strategies. Telephone 39-02-480 270 24, e-mail avanzi@sirigroup.org, Web site: <www.avanzi.org>.
- **CaringCompany AB** covers Sweden, Denmark, Finland, Norway, Poland, and the Baltic states and has been active in the field of social investing since 1992. Telephone 46-8-660

2630, e-mail caringcompany@sirigroup.org, Web site <www.caringcompany.se>.

- **Centre Info SA** covers Switzerland. Founded in 1990, it provides corporate research, country sustainability research, and consulting services to clients interested in corporate social responsibility. Telephone 41-26-322 06 14, e-mail centreinfo@sirigroup.org.
- **Fundación Ecología y Desarrollo** covers Spain and is a nonprofit organization established to promote business sustainability that provides social and environmental research on Spanish companies. It also publishes the first e-newsletter dealing with corporate social responsibility issues in Spain. Telephone 34-976-29 82 82, e-mail ecodes@sirigroup.org, Web site <www.ecodes.org>.
- **Kinder, Lydenberg & Domini & Co., Inc. (KLD)**, covers the United States. Founded in 1990, it is dedicated to researching the social records of publicly traded companies. Telephone 1-617-426-5270, e-mail kld@sirigroup.org, Web site <www.kld.com>.
- **Michael Jantzi Research Associates (MJRA)** covers Canada and provides a full range of social investment research and support services to institutional clients and financial professionals. Telephone 1-416-861-0403, e-mail mjra@sirigroup.org, Web site <www.mjra-jsi.com>.
- **Pensions & Investment Research Consultants Ltd. (PIRC)** covers the United Kingdom and Ireland and has been providing socially responsible investment research to institutional investors since 1986. Telephone 44-20-7247-2323, e-mail pirc@sirigroup.org, Web site <www.pirc.co.uk>.
- **Triodos Research BV** covers the Netherlands, Belgium, and Luxembourg and is a division of Triodos Bank. In 1996 it began screening companies and providing social investment consulting to institutions. Telephone 31-30-693-6500, e-mail triodos@sirigroup.org.

Source: Kinder, Lydenberg, Domini & Co., Inc.

The core long-term strategic impact of SRI lies in screening. Screening is the driver. It changes the rules. Remember, it was social investment portfolio managers who, seeking a way to screen for environmental criteria, convinced environmentalists of the need to construct the code of conduct regarding the environment, now known as the CERES Principles. By seeing the need and addressing it, convener Joan Bavaria, founder of Trillium Asset Management, completely altered the landscape of environmental reporting, so that today it is far more in-depth and routine than could have been imagined 20 years ago. Only because of social screens on investments are data systematically collected on corporations and their stakeholder impacts. This plants the seeds of change. As we saw in the South African debate, the very existence of data encourages ongoing evaluation and reporting and this, in turn, allows civic society to take action.

Another important result of screening comes from sharing a corporate social profile with that company's management team. By sharing this information on an annual basis, corporate social research firms, such as KLD in the United States, Triodos Research in the Netherlands, and the Good Bankers in Japan, receive a deeper understanding of the company's culture, and the company also has a chance to point out any progress it may have made. Corporate responses to a profile range from extremely helpful to hostile. Some companies immediately send back cartons full of pamphlets and information bulletins that might improve the report. Others indignantly demand to know who we are and what we intend to do with this information. But all learn something about the way they affect their various stakeholders.

When a corporate social research firm receives an inquiry from a company about how to improve its profile with regard, for instance, to diversity, we have a chance to go further in the education process. A fairly typical corporate response is to point out that several top managers are female. Research companies then have the chance to point to the fact that in our universe the company is only in the better half with regard to women in management, not in the best 10 percent—a level we consider significant.

Innovation at Whirlpool: Meeting the Challenge of Diversity

In the past five years, the Muslim population of Nashville, Tennessee, has jumped from practically zero to 20,000 as the area has become the home of immigrants from Somalia and Kurdistan. Muslims now make up 10 percent of the peak-time workforce of a Whirlpool plant in the vicinity, and the company has altered some production schedules to allow time for daily prayer. (Muslims pray five times a day, first washing their hands and feet.)

Accommodating Muslim workers' religious needs has caused some friction with non-Muslim workers, according to a spokesman for the Benton Harbor, Michigan–based **Whirlpool Corp. (WHR)**, but management has persisted in trying to adapt to their religious needs with a minimum of disruption to established practices.

Source: "Changing Times: Diverse Workforce Emerges as Result of Multicultural Population," *Chicago Tribune,* 1 January 2000, Chicagoland Final, sec. C, 12.

It isn't just funky little companies that take an interest. In 1990 when the Domini 400 Social Index was being launched, International Business Machines (IBM) inquired what it would take for it to qualify for inclusion in the index. At the time, IBM was in South Africa and was also a military contractor, so the profile allowed us to enter into a discussion with the company about the role it had in each of these areas. When the call to reinvest in South Africa came and after IBM sold off most of its military units, the company was added to the index, only to be removed again as its military involvement grew.

The Domini Social Equity Fund (DSEFX) has spent several years in shareholder dialogue with Home Depot (HD). Our concern grew out of several class-action suits the company has faced, information we gathered through our social profiling. These indicated a structural failure with regard to hiring and promoting women and minorities. But the company has taken a number of innovative steps in other issue areas and meets our basic criteria, so we own them. Being a member of the Domini 400 Social Index is by no means a validation of a company's social citizenship. It does mean that the company is better than others we profile and is typical of the type of company a socially responsible investor might buy. Nonetheless, several companies, including Home Depot, have announced in their annual report to shareholders that they are members of the Domini 400 Social Index.

Corporate social screening also creates a structure for comparing one company to another in a way that is useful to activists. For instance, when Domini Social Equity Fund joined activists and entered into dialogue with Disney (DIS) on the issue of sourcing in Haiti, we were able to come prepared with innovative solutions that The Gap stores (GPS) had in place. The Gap had developed guidelines after being faced with evidence of harassment of workers that were organizing at a plant it sourced from in El Salvador. The social-screening process, coupled with activism results, had given us a tool to assist another company to look at the issue creatively and thereby leverage our impact.

Activists sometimes use research originally generated to help screen portfolios as a way to evaluate which company to enter into discussion with on a certain topic. Several years ago, concern that women were slotted into traditionally female jobs and that these jobs paid less than men's jobs led us to examine the database for the Episcopal Church. From the data we were able to establish that the financial services industry was particularly prone to this way of thinking and the church entered into a successful dialogue with Aetna (AET) on the issue. Today the company has a solid record on comparable-worth analysis and diversity in general.

Aetna: Using Technology to Retain Diverse Employees

Technology tools are helping employers create custom programs that both improve the bottom line and help companies hold on to valuable employees. At **Aetna Inc. (AET)**, the Hartford, Connecticut–based insurance and financial services company, women make up three-quarters of the workforce; and the company recognizes flexibility as a competitive advantage. Aetna offers flexible hours, part-time work, job sharing, compressed workweeks, variable schedules, and telecommuting options. Special software tools designed for customer care centers have helped Aetna accurately predict the number of customer service representative needed at a given time. Schedules for the department are based on predicted levels of coverage needed both for peak and non-peak times. Since implementing the program in its call centers, Aetna says retention has increased. The company has been named one of *Working Mother's* 100 Best Companies for ten years running. "When it comes to achieving work/life balance, we get it. And that's a huge competitive advantage," Christine Curtin, a human resources consultant, says.

Source: Carol Stavraka, "Aetna: Using Technology to Retain Diverse Employees," *<www.diversityinc.com>*, 6 June 2000. © 2000 www.diversity.com.

Imagine a world where corporate social responsibility information didn't exist, and remember that only with the advent of socially responsible investing did it come about. Ongoing universal corporate accountability research was simply not available 20 years ago. Only socially screened portfolios have created the structure within which the research takes place. Government doesn't do it, foundations don't do it, academia doesn't do it, and corporate trade organizations don't do it. A quiet revolution occurred when socially responsible investors began to request that their investments be made only in more responsible companies.

The revolution is being carried forward in academic literature. Social research databases are generally made available to academics wishing to research a broad range of issues. Studies attempting to find a relationship between greener companies and profits or diversity and strong corporate cultures, as well as brand management studies and evaluations of corporate identity, are but a few of the ways academics have used the research. The interrelationship between academics and business management is deep. Business ethics, corporate culture building, and brand management as well as the assessment of the quality of management, the importance of integrity in product excellence, and the implications of diversity all go directly to issues of better business management practices. The provision of data to the academic community is quietly building a body of knowledge that reinforces the argument that better managers can be spotted by their concern for stakeholders.[1]

Although most of us understand that the role of shareholder activists in the South African debate was pivotal, few realize what a tremendous influence it has had in shaping the flow of information on and improvement to the environment, working conditions in the Maquiladoras of Mexico, alleviation of world debt, and a host of other issues. More than 300 shareholder conversations that address human dignity take place each year, changing for the better the lives of largely desperate and helpless people around the world.

Shareholder activists also teach management at companies something that they carry with them throughout their long careers, and activists might even turn managers into advocates themselves. For example, several years ago General Motors (GM) signed the environmental code of conduct, the CERES

Principles, discussed in earlier chapters. This agreement means that the company conducts ongoing assessments of the impact on the biosphere at each of GM's facilities across the globe. The process itself brings managers into an educational circle that

Making a Difference at MiBanco

"Around the end of June 1996, community leaders in Panama met with Michael Chu, president of ACCION International, to talk about microfinance. It had a great impact on me and made me feel impatient because so many people here in Panama are poor and need credit. I began by working with 110 banks in Panama to put **MiBanco** together.

"After considering several models, we Panamanians decided to create our own. We felt that if you want to help the poor in a country, you need to find a form of business that permits rapid lending. Lending circles, known here as little banks, make this possible. We wanted the spirit of a cooperative organization to be combined with the lending power of a bank.

"The poor that are looking for work are much more numerous than those that are employed and generating income for our country. To alter this requires access to credit. Poor people may be selling wares in the markets or baby-sitting others' children—in other words, they have jobs. Nonetheless, traditional financial institutions ignore honest and hardworking poor people and will not lend them money. Our bank has found that the poor are good credit risks—the repayment rate is 98 percent at MiBanco."

Source: This piece was contributed by Roberto Eisenmann, founder, president, and CEO of MiBanco. Eisenmann is a national hero in Panama for having stood up to the dictator Noriega. Only his personal commitment to creating a community development financial institution for the poor in his country made it possible.

involves legal, health and safety, shipping, sourcing, human resources, and other departments. General Motors' own pension fund now votes in favor of resolutions that support the CERES Principles when the question is raised at other companies. In such an environment it is not surprising that when Ford (F) announced an initiative to greatly improve fuel consumption by its vans, GM immediately announced that it would do the same and attempt to do better.

Community economic development creates almost immediate betterment in people's lives. Tens of thousands of women have a greater degree of political and economic freedom in Bangladesh today because of loans and technical assistance they received from the Grameen Bank, a microlender operating there. And beyond the actual loans, the bank has served as a model for other community development initiatives so that programs such as MiBanco in Panama or Shared Interest in South Africa had something on which to shape their own programs.

Consider the groundbreaking work of MiBanco. This is a conventional bank in structure, and banks need equity, or ownership capital. To meet the capital requirements set by Panama, the founders appealed not only to friends and family but also to the entire population of that nation. Today, MiBanco stock trades on the Panamanian exchange and is its most widely held company. Furthermore, each time a borrower pays interest, a portion of that payment goes to buying stock for the borrower. This means that in addition to the benefits of lending at the grassroots level, the poorest of the poor in Panama are learning about stocks and are building wealth. It also means that the nonborrower shareholders have learned, through their socially responsible investment in the bank stock, about microlending and the role it can play in building healthy communities.

In the United States, as in much of the world, it is community development banks and credit unions, along with loan funds and nonprofit agencies, that are building one neighborhood at a time, one development at a time, and one business at a time. The two Americas, rich and poor, have become more separate, and the wealthy need not see life as the poor endure it. But poverty remains. There are hundreds of small cities like Camden, New Jersey. As of midyear 2000, 12 percent of Camden's buildings were abandoned, 40 percent of its adults had not completed high school, and 35 percent of its households lived below the poverty level.[2] How can a civilized people allow such disparities to continue? Yet on Native American reservations and in urban centers, in the Mississippi Delta region and in the nation's capital, it is community development financial institutions that offer the best and often the only hope to people that seek to empower themselves to enter the economic mainstream.

Felicia Diaz: An ACCION New York Success Story

After nine years of separation, Felicia Diaz was finally reunited with her family. Felicia came to New York to try to earn a living for the children she had left behind with her husband in the Dominican Republic. Taking what she could get but unable to get ahead, Felicia worked in factories until she met a coworker who was making more money selling jewelry.

Felicia went into the jewelry business full-time and built up a clientele, but was unable to get a loan without a credit history. Then she heard of ACCION New York, a microfinance organization, where she received a $1,500 loan that enabled her to increase her stock, and eventually bring her family to the States. Felicia also began a street stand with the help of a second loan, and a third loan of $20,000 allowed her to open her own restaurant. Thanks to ACCION New York, Felicia is now able to enjoy the reason for her hard work—her family.

Source: "Credit Goes to Felicia Diaz," *Ventures: A Publication of ACCION International* (Winter 1999).

SRI created the first step taken at GM toward instituting a culture that took the environment seriously. The corporate culture may have led to a transformational experience as managers became more aware of their environmental impact and responsibilities. In Panama, the access to credit, pride of repayment, and pride of ownership in something as important as a bank is transforming hundreds of the formerly poor into people with a stake in their nation. Around the globe people are starting to "get it," and as they do, they will tip the scales of justice, bringing balance back into the way finance and commerce relate to the world's populations.

Socially Responsible Investing as a Transformational Experience That Underlies a Tipping Point

One theory on consumption holds some relevance for those who seek ways to institutionalize social change. It is sometimes referred to as the "departure purchase."[3] Certain purchases mark a moment of redefinition or transformation for the purchaser. A woman's new haircut, for instance, might be the first step toward a new suit, a subscription to *Business Week*, and a general redefinition of herself as a serious young professional rather than the graduate student she had been. Sometimes the purchase itself is considered the cause of the transformation. A tree planted in Brooklyn can be the very thing that triggers a chain reaction leading those in the neighborhood to see themselves differently, behave differently, and even create transformation around themselves.

People who decide to become socially responsible investors are often at a transitional or transformational point in their own lives. Perhaps a parent has died or a stock option has been cashed for tremendous value; whatever the reason, the person feels that a change in his or her identity has occurred, that he or she is in some ways not the person he or she was a year ago. To the extent that becoming a socially responsible investor allows one to become educated and deliberate about making investments, it marks a transformation point. And what is it that the investor is transforming into? An advocate for more responsible corporate practices, a watchdog, a more involved citizen? Yes, probably all three.

Deciding how to invest wisely is difficult enough, but there are the additional burdens of emotional baggage money carries with it. Smart, well-educated professionals with exceptionally large vocabularies fumble if asked to define the words *stock*, *bond*, or *portfolio*. Surely some avoidance has to have been at work. These are words we hear every day on the evening news. Why do so many people not know what they mean? Is part of what most people are avoiding a sense that these are the words that have made the two worlds—the one of desperate poverty and the other of spoiled ease?

When people decide to place funds with a professional specializing in SRI or with a mutual fund serving the socially responsible investor, they push through the avoidance and gain a sense of control of their assets and of extending their reach beyond their portfolios. They embark on a journey of redefining themselves. They are finally doing something about it. While they may have admired activists who bravely tie themselves to trees or travel to a distant village in Central America in hopes that the presence of a foreigner will slow the "disappearances," they never could have summoned the courage themselves. But through social investing, anyone with any savings can stand up and be counted; it registers you as a person who will support an infrastructure of ongoing positive social change.

Even when the person taking a first step into social investing has no thought of these implications, they learn them from the investments, just as GM learned from a first step of signing an environmental code of conduct. An SRI mutual fund clearly has tremendous potential as an instrument of positive social change. Through direct dialogue as a shareholder, the fund has access to the decision makers of the world. Through its shareholder base, its management can learn from thousands of individuals in all walks of life. But it can also help give its investors a sense of their own power. It can educate so that even if investors do not know what a corporate dialogue is when they buy shares of an SRI fund, they will learn about their role in it through fund reports. They will begin to define themselves as people who take the extra step.

Institutions also transform when they realize that the act of managing funds in a socially responsible way stretches their mission work. Perhaps the best-known example of this is the work carried on by the Jesse Smith Noyes Foundation, a family foundation based in New York City. A core program area for the foundation is protection of the environment. So it stretches its impact by applying social screens to its investments, by seeking to make venture capital investments in companies that develop solutions to environmental problems, and by not only actively voting its proxies but also actually filing shareholder resolutions that support the work of grantees. Its dialogue with Intel (INTC) led that company to cooperate more closely with concerned environmental activists the foundation had been making grants to in Albuquerque, New Mexico.

The world's population is ready to save itself. Baby boomers have come of age, the Internet and wireless communications have reenfranchised whole populations, and the first world has been rich enough for long enough to begin to look beyond itself. When we do, we see that the emerging and preemerging worlds have been battered to the point of revolution by decisions made on Wall Street or behind closed doors.

The bill has come due. The environmental degradation is no longer in someone else's backyard. The world is too small for that now. Asthma, allergies, childhood leukemia, an epidemic of breast cancer, reports of huge increases in neurological damage, and a host of other health-related concerns are now seen to be the result of ecological damage. Although we continue to clear-cut and burn the rain forests, the equivalent of ripping out the kidneys of a person and expecting the person to survive, blindly relying on a hope that science will save us, we sense that science will not solve all of our problems. We know these things and we are afraid. We see the truth: It is a small planet and time is short.

In this context, perhaps it isn't surprising that a new sort of corporate leadership is emerging. In November 1996, a report was published of tape recordings taken by an employee of

Texaco (TX). The tapes recorded members of management using racial slurs in company meetings about hiring. By coincidence, the reports were published just days before the 25th anniversary dinner for the U.S. network of shareholder activists, the Interfaith Center on Corporate Responsibility. Peter I. Bijur, the chairman of the board and CEO of Texaco, contacted ICCR and asked if he might attend and be available to its membership. For me, it marked a transition moment. The bunker mentality of the past was on its way out. CEOs could admit that they had a problem and that it was being dealt with.

Since then, there have been many indications of a sea change. The war in Bosnia was covered not by the State Department but by refugees themselves, telling their own stories. The World Trade Organization tried to meet in Seattle and was completely unsuccessful in implementing most of the initiatives meant to ease global trading (initiatives many emerging nations saw as a way for the developed world to accelerate its economic imperialism). My 16-year-old son reports to me what the kids online are telling him two days before I read the story in the *New York Times*. There is truly momentum building for something more than grassroots participation: grassroots leadership.

We have the context for seismic shift. We have the understanding: This is not about bad people; it is about bad systems. We have an answer: use the strength of the investment industry to build a better world. We can reach out and touch the dangers. Each of us has traveled back to a place we'd been to 20 years before and been shaken by the explosion in people, tawdriness, and disrespect for pristine spaces. We have only to take individual action.[4]

Like man in Michelangelo's magnificent fresco on the Sistine Chapel's ceiling, humankind reclines in lazy comfort as God (or universal wellness) stretches yearningly toward us, willing us to but raise our dropped finger only an inch or less to touch His own. It would take so little effort to touch that holy place, a world of peace and justice. We have only to integrate these goals into the institutions we most venerate: the financial services industry. Investing in a socially responsible way allows us to do just that.

My parents, like so many of their generation, wrap sandwiches in waxed paper before setting off for the day. They save the paper and use it several days in a row if it is clean enough to do so. If they are heading out early, they'll first make coffee and pour it into a thermos. They clean the plastic bags their fruit comes in; they carefully unwrap gifts, smoothing out the wrapping paper and neatly looping the ribbons for future use. They save candle stubs to use the wax on sticky drawers or windows. They compost food waste for use in the garden, even though they live in a town house with very little green space. They could certainly afford a sandwich in town, and they are sociable people who would enjoy the excuse to sit at a counter with others, but they are not wasteful and to buy a sandwich or coffee is.

What shaped them and the others of their generation to be so completely thoughtful of every small action? For some it was deprivation during the Depression. For my parents it was the war years. My mother came from a well-enough-to-do family to have ignored rationing, but she was caught up in being a part of something bigger than herself. She learned that what she did really mattered. My father came of age in Italy during the war, having been brought up in a socialist labor (and therefore underground) family. He cannot see waste without thinking of what that crumb of food would have meant to him at age 14.

If we are to achieve a world in which there is room for both human dignity and environmental sustainability, then two major initiatives need to be undertaken. At the macro level, financial systems, governments, and corporations must integrate these as primary lodestars to navigate by. At the individual level, each person must see that his or her investment decisions can make a difference, thereby tipping the scales of society to incorporate justice and environmental sustainability into our most powerful civic structures, whether public or private. Socially responsible investing is the catalyst and the vehicle. As a social investor, you release the forces of accountability research; you transform civic society, one life at a time. It matters. The planet is shrinking, and there isn't much time left. Socially responsible investors make every dollar count.

Johnson & Johnson Social Ratings

Strengths	Issue	Concern
◆	Community	
◆◆	Diversity	
◆	Employees	◆
◆	Environment	
	Non-U.S. Ops.	
◆	Product	◆◆
	Other	◆
Alcohol	Gambling	Tobacco
Military Contracting		Nuclear Power

◆ = Strength / Concern

Community		Diversity				Employees	
Cash giving	$57.2 m		Women	Minorities	Total	Employees:	93,100
% NEBT	1.4%	Line:	0	0	0/6	Union:	8%
		Board:	3	1	3/13		
Environment		**Military**				**Non-U.S. Operations**	
Superfund (EPA)	25	Weapons				% International	
		Contracts		$0		Sales	47.0%
Hazwaste		% Revenues		0.0%			
Sites (Co.)	N/A						
Accrued Liabilities	N/A						

All figures are the latest available to KLD.
N/A = Not Available

Business

Johnson & Johnson manufactures and markets consumer products (28 percent of FY 1998 revenues), including Act fluoride rinse, Band-Aid bandages, o.b. tampons, infant formula bottles, Mylanta antacids, and Tylenol pain relievers; pharmaceuticals (36 percent), including contraceptive devices and drugs through its Ortho, McNeil, and Janssen divisions; professional products (36 percent), including sutures, surgical dressings, diagnostic products, surgical caps, gowns, and gloves; and disposable contact lenses through its Ethicon and Vistakon subsidiaries.

In July 1999, the company agreed to acquire Centocor, Inc. In October 1998, the company acquired DePuy, Inc., a manufacturer of orthopedic devices. In 1997, the company acquired Innotech, Inc., Biopsys Medical, Inc., Biosense, Inc., and Gynecare, Inc.

Community
Innovative Giving

Many of the company's grants are targeted at minority neighborhoods. In 1997, with a grant of $610,000, Johnson & Johnson continued its financial support for a program that provides management training to the directors of Head Start programs for economically disadvantaged children. The company's giving to this program has traditionally averaged approximately $1 million per year.

As part of its participation in the American Business Collaborative for Quality Dependent Care, Johnson & Johnson is among the 22 major businesses supporting an $11.8 million project initiated in 1997 to research and develop better child care centers and early childhood programs.

The company's Bridge to Employment program in eight states and Puerto Rico supports the integration of school-based and work-based learning for careers in health. The company also sponsors INROADS, a national program for placing minority youth in summer internships.

. . .

In FY 1998, Johnson & Johnson donated 1.4 percent ($57.2 million) of trailing three-year net earnings before taxes (NEBT) to charity. The company estimated its in-kind giving at approximately $125.4 million.

. . .

Since the late 1970s, Johnson & Johnson has played a substantial role in the revitalization of its headquarters city of New Brunswick, New Jersey, and continues to support community development organizations there.

. . .

As part of the Johnson & Johnson Community Health Care Program, in 1999, the company pledged donations of $100,000 each over two years to the Food for Life Network in Miami, Florida; the Marion County Minority Health Coalition in

Indianapolis, Indiana; the St. Joseph's Mercy Care Services in Atlanta, Georgia; and the Women's Cancer Screening Project in Camden, New Jersey.

Diversity
Promotion

Although there are no women among the company's six senior line executives, Colleen A. Goggins is president of the company's consumer products company, and Carol Webb is president of the company's Ortho Biotech company.

Women in senior staff positions include JoAnn Heisen, who is chief information officer of the corporation and serves on the company's executive committee; Annie Lo, who is vice president for group finance for the Dx group; Helen Short, who is vice president for investor relations; and Brenda Davis, who is vice president for technical resources.

Minorities in nonexecutive senior line positions include Alfred T. Mays, an African-American, who is president of the company's Specialty Products company.

In 1999, Johnson & Johnson told KLD that of its officials and managers, 35 percent were women and 16 percent were minorities.

In August 1998, *Fortune* magazine included Johnson & Johnson on its listing of the 50 best companies for Asians, blacks, and Hispanics. At that time, the magazine reported that none of the company's 25 highest-paid officers were minorities but that 15.5 percent of its managers were minorities. The company was not included on *Fortune* magazine's 1999 list.

Family Benefits

In 1999, *Working Mother* magazine included Johnson & Johnson on its list of the 100 best workplaces for working mothers. The company has been on the list in the past.

Johnson & Johnson offers 52 weeks of childbirth leave, some with full pay, which is 36 weeks longer than the federally required 12 weeks of childbirth leave. Family benefits include phaseback for new mothers, adoption aid of $3,000, resource and referral services, and, since 1998, a lactation program.

In 1998, Johnson & Johnson added two more child care facilities, and the company now contributes more than 50 percent toward operating costs of six on-site child care centers. In addition, the company offers discounts at three child care chains in 45 states to accommodate its widespread sales force. It employs a full-time work-and-family manager and staff, and provides pretax set-asides, discounts at community child care enters, and direct child care subsidies according to family income. Johnson & Johnson is a champion of the American Business Collaboration for Quality Dependent Care, a national organization dedicated to raising funds for the improvement of child and elder care in communities across the country.

Alternative work schedules offered to employees include telecommuting, job sharing, flextime, and compressed workweeks. The company's work and family consultation and referral service has been expanded to include advice on children's education, college planning, adoption, and general work and life issues.

Women and Minority Contracting

In FY 1998, Johnson & Johnson placed approximately 5.9 percent of its total subcontracting for goods and services with women- and minority-owned companies. Of its total subcontracting, approximately $122 million went to women-owned firms and $201 million went to minority-owned firms.

The company has a Minority and Women Business Enterprise Supplier Outreach Program that actively works to diversify its supplier base.

Employment of the Disabled

A 1998 survey by *Careers & the disABLED* magazine ranked Johnson & Johnson sixth among 50 companies with the best reputation for employing and accommodating the disabled. The survey of the magazine's readership (primarily disabled college students and professionals) asked which places of employment they believed would provide the most positive work environment for persons with disabilities. In 1996, the company was ranked 14th.

Three women (Joan Ganz Cooney, Ann Dibble Jordan, and Maxine F. Singer) and one minority (Jordan) serve on the company's 13-member board of directors. Cooney is chair of the executive committee of the Children's Television Workshop. Jordan, who is African-American, is former director of the Social Services Department of Chicago Lying-in Hospital at the University of Chicago Medical Center. Dr. Singer is president of the Carnegie Institution of Washington.

. . .

In 1996, Johnson & Johnson agreed to incorporate in its written policies a statement prohibiting discrimination against employees on the basis of sexual orientation.

. . .

Johnson & Johnson participates in a program at Smith College designed to help prepare female executives for senior management.

. . .

In 1998, Johnson & Johnson was one of a number of American companies found to engage in blatant gender discrimination when advertising for jobs in Asia. Roughly 25 percent of ads placed by these companies specified that positions were for men only or for women only. Typically, the ads directed at men were for senior positions, while the ads directed at women were for lower-level administration positions. Such discrimination is typically not illegal in these countries, where U.S. laws on the subject only apply to American citizens.

Employee Relations
Other Strengths

In January 2000, Johnson & Johnson was included on *Fortune* magazine's "The 100 Best Companies to Work for in America" list. The company has appeared on the list previously. The list was compiled by Robert Levering and Milton Moskowitz, authors of the 1984 and 1993 books of the same title.

Exceptional employee benefits offered by the company include an average of 60 hours of training per employee per year and 100 percent tuition reimbursement with no cap.

Other Concerns

In August 1997, a judge awarded $3.89 million to an employee who filed a lawsuit against Johnson & Johnson alleging that her supervisors and male coworkers had retaliated against her for complaining to the human resources department about gender discrimination. A jury found no discrimination in the company's failure to promote her but did find retaliation following her complaint and awarded her $11.7 million, which the judge reduced to $3.89 million. The company has appealed the decision.

. . .

As of December 1998, the company had approximately 93,100 employees worldwide (up from 90,500 the previous year), 37,968 of whom were located in the United States. In 1999, the company told KLD that labor unions represented approximately 8 percent of its U.S. employees.

In December 1998, Johnson & Johnson announced plans to reduce its workforce by 4.4 percent (4,100 employees) and close 36 factories.

. . .

The January 1996 issue of *Money* magazine ranked Johnson & Johnson ninth among its list of ten U.S. companies with the best benefit packages. The magazine reported that the firm's 401(k) savings plan matches 75 percent of employee contributions up to 6 percent of base compensation. One-third of the match is in company stock. In FY 1998, the company contributed approximately $63 million to this plan. Through the company's defined benefit retirement plan, at age 65, a typical 30-year company veteran will receive an $18,800 annual benefit. Participants may not receive a lump-sum payout.

Money magazine also reported that the company has "superb" health benefits. Employees may choose from a range of HMO, PPO, POS, and indemnity plans. The maximum individual monthly cost (including dental coverage) is $13.75. Johnson & Johnson's wellness programs are particularly thorough. They range from on-site exercise facilities to health food in cafeterias to depression screening. The company markets this program to other corporations and in 1994 granted a five-year marketing license to Nutri/System for the program.

. . .

According to a June 1996 *Industry Week* article, the quality manager at the company's Johnson & Johnson Medical, Inc., plant in Sherman, Texas, credited strong union and management cooperation with making a difficult 1993 downsizing of 23 percent result in a better-functioning, more streamlined plant. The plant shifted responsibility to work groups for handling customer complaints, scheduling, and new process implementation. Employees received an average of 59 hours of training in 1995, compared with 36 hours in 1991. The plant was recognized by *Industry Week* magazine to be among the best plants in the United States.

. . .

The firm has been widely praised for its philosophy of giving business unit managers as much independence as possible. A July 1997 *Investor's Business Daily* article reported that CEO Ralph Larsen has developed a culture in which it is safe to make smart mistakes. A December 1994 *Fortune* magazine article described the company's numerous subsidiaries as operating with "deliberately redundant operations and amazingly independent management." At the center of the culture that unites these disparate operations is the company's credo, one of the first and best-known codes of ethics at U.S. corporations.

. . .

In 1997, Johnson & Johnson joined with several major corporations to pool resources for career management, job training, and recruitment of their workforces. The companies have created a Web site accessible to all employees that includes tests that can be taken to assess career potential and interests. It also helps match employees' needs for training to resources available through the various companies. Information about which jobs are in increasing demand and which are dwindling allows employees to anticipate downsizing and choose to focus on jobs more in demand. Jobs available in all the companies are also posted on the Web site.

. . .

In July 1996, the company was ordered by an arbitrator to turn over control of its AIDS test kit business to a fired executive who had developed the kits and then later sold his company to Johnson & Johnson. The arbitrator ruled that the company had broken its employment agreement with the executive and had to return the assets to him in the event he was terminated "without cause." In October 1996, a judge rejected the company's appeal of the decision.

Environment
Pollution Prevention

Johnson & Johnson was a participant in the EPA's voluntary 33/50 pollution-prevention program in which participants agreed to reduce emissions of 17 high-priority chemicals by 50 percent by 1995, using 1988 as a base year. As of 1995, the company had reduced by 84 percent emissions of the 17 toxic chemicals targeted by the EPA in this program. This was well ahead of the company's stated goal of a 50 percent reduction by 1995.

In late 1992, as part of a special EPA program, Johnson & Johnson's medical division in Sherman, Texas, committed to reducing hazardous emissions by 90 percent by January 1, 1994. In exchange for this voluntary initiative, the EPA agreed to exempt the company from certain regulatory requirements for six years. As of 1998, Johnson & Johnson had achieved a 93 percent reduction worldwide in releases of toxic chemicals from 1991 levels.

The company has an announced goal of reducing hazardous waste generation by 10 percent and solid waste disposal by 50 percent by 2000 from 1991 levels. As of year-end 1998, it had achieved an 11 percent reduction in hazardous waste generation and a 68 percent reduction in solid waste disposal. In 1998, Johnson & Johnson recycled 44 percent of the solid waste it generated. The company is also a member of Waste Wise, the EPA's voluntary solid waste reduction program.

. . .

According to the EPA's 1997 Site Enforcement Tracking System, the company is a potentially responsible party for 25 Superfund sites.

In September 1999, the company told KLD that its environmental remediation accruals were not material.

In November 1996, 54 parties, including Johnson & Johnson, agreed to pay a total of $32.1 million for the cleanup of the Davis landfill Superfund site in Smithfield, Rhode Island. During the 1970s and 1980s, liquid and solid hazardous wastes were dumped in unlined lagoons and seepage pits, contaminating soil, groundwater, and surface water.

. . .

Johnson & Johnson gives to other firms the software it uses to reduce product packaging. The company has a goal of reducing its packaging by 25 percent by 2000 from 1992 levels. As of year-end 1998, it had achieved a 22.3 percent reduction.

In December 1995, the company announced with four other companies that it would be participating in a partnership with the Environmental Defense Fund (EDF) by using its buying power to influence paper companies to improve environmental performance. In August 1993, Johnson & Johnson and four other companies joined with the EDF in a program aimed at increasing the demand for recycled paper. The company's goal was to use 50 percent less paper and to increase its use of recycled paper by 50 percent by the year 1996. It participated in the Buy Recycled Business Alliance. Some environmentalists have criticized the final recommendations of the partnership with EDF, claiming that it identifies many of the (paper) industry's ecologically damaging practices as sustainable.

. . .

In March 2000, the company announced plans to participate in the Climate Saver program, a voluntary program sponsored by the World Wildlife Fund, to reduce its worldwide greenhouse gas emissions. The program calls on companies to cut emissions that equal or exceed reductions listed in the Kyoto treaty. Johnson & Johnson proposed to cut emissions of carbon dioxide, methane, and other gases by 7 percent by 2010. The company proposed to achieve the reduction using energy-efficient equipment, cogeneration, and renewable energy sources. Part of the program requires third-party verification audits.

In 1998, Johnson & Johnson won a Climate Wise Partner Achievement Award. Climate Wise is an EPA program that promotes the voluntary reduction of greenhouse gas emissions by manufacturing companies. It was created to help the United States meet its commitment to reduce greenhouse gas emissions to 1990 levels by the year 2000. Johnson & Johnson pledged to reduce its energy use by 25 percent from 1991 to 2000. As of year-end 1998, it had achieved a reduction of 19.9 percent.

The company was one of 23 charter members in the EPA's Green Lights energy efficiency program. In 1994, the EPA named the firm a "Green Lights Partner of the Year." Johnson & Johnson is also a member of the EPA's voluntary Energy Star Buildings energy efficiency program. In 1998, the EPA awarded the company its Energy Star Buildings Outstanding Upgrade Award for upgrades at facilities in New Mexico and Puerto Rico.

. . .

As of 1999, four of Johnson & Johnson's European sites, two of its Asia-Pacific sites, and two of its U.S. sites were ISO 14000 certified and several more were in the review process. The company has a stated goal of having all of its facilities achieve certification. The ISO is an international standards organization. The 14000 certification series addresses environmental quality management issues.

Non-U.S. Operations

Sales outside the United States represented 47 percent of the company's FY 1998 sales. Johnson & Johnson has operations in 55 countries around the world, including China, Egypt, Hong Kong, India, Indonesia, Kenya, Malaysia, Morocco, Pakistan, the Philippines, Singapore, South Africa, South Korea, Taiwan, Thailand, the United Arab Emirates, Zambia, and Zimbabwe.

. . .

In 1993, the company's Surgikos Maquiladora plant won the Mexican equivalent of the Malcolm Baldrige quality award.

. . .

The company has operations in South Africa, where it manufactures personal care and health care products. (See "Product: Marketing/Contracting Controversy.")

. . .

In 1998, the company donated approximately 10 percent ($6 million) of its total cash charitable giving to overseas programs. The company told KLD in 1997 that the subsidiaries in each country also make their own contributions, which are not tracked by the central giving program. The company's charitable giving overseas includes projects identified by UNICEF and Project Hope as well as projects identified by the corporation. Major programs include continued support in 1998 for UNICEF for a three-year project to eliminate neonatal tetanus in China. In 1996, Johnson & Johnson donated an executive's time to solicit contributions from Philippine corporations for a UNICEF Advocacy Program to promote children's causes. Other contributions have included money to upgrade hospitals in Zimbabwe, South Africa, and Colombia. The firm also makes substantial product donations to international relief agencies.

. . .

In July 1998, Russian tax authorities alleged that Johnson & Johnson Ltd., a unit of the company, had failed to pay back taxes and fines totaling approximately $19 million. In addition, criminal charges were filed against a former director and the chief accountant. The charges were subsequently dropped.

. . .

Johnson & Johnson produces infant formula products for sale internationally. The company is involved in a controversy regarding the international marketing of these products, particularly in developing countries. (See "Product: Marketing/Contracting Controversy" for elaboration.)

Product
R&D/Innovation

In 1998, Johnson & Johnson reported that 33 percent of sales came from products introduced within the past five years. The company's business strategy is based in part on introducing innovative products. In 1998, the company invested approximately 9.6 percent ($2.3 billion) of revenues in research and development.

Product Safety

According to a January 1998 *Forbes* magazine article, in the previous three years as many as 50 lawsuits had been filed against Johnson & Johnson alleging harm from Tylenol. The total number of lawsuits was reportedly more than 100. The company had reportedly settled at least four of these cases. In 1993, Johnson & Johnson agreed to pay $8 million to settle a lawsuit by a person who required a liver transplant after taking Tylenol for a few days following an evening in which he consumed wine. The article asserts that Johnson & Johnson had been remiss in not producing clear labeling with strong warnings about the dangers, including death, of taking too much acetaminophen under certain circumstances. The article also faulted the FDA for not having required clear labeling on all products containing acetaminophen when these problems first appeared. The agency recommended changes in the labeling in October 1997. In October 1998, the FDA mandated that acetaminophen products carry labels that warn against combining them with three or more alcoholic drinks in one day and describe the possible effects of doing so.

The people most at risk of taking too much acetaminophen are children, those who consume alcohol, and the malnourished. Because acetaminophen is considered safer than aspirin for children with flu or colds, for it avoids a potential complication known as Reye's syndrome, parents often administer it to their children. According to the *Forbes* article, the confusing labeling on Johnson & Johnson's infant formulation and the formulation for children has resulted in liver damage for at least one child. *Forbes* reported that the company has changed its labeling one step at a time. After the 1989 death of a five-year-old who received five Extra-Strength Tylenol in one day, a warning against giving that drug to children was added. After the $8 million settlement in 1993, the company added a warning about the consumption of alcohol. As of the writing of the article, the labeling on the children's packaging was under review. As of July 1998, the company was planning to add label warnings regarding the dangers of taking Tylenol or Motrin for people who consume moderate to large amounts of alcohol on a regular basis.

In June 1998, Johnson & Johnson announced it would replace any consumer's SureStep blood-glucose meter manufactured prior to August 1997. Approximately 290,000 home-use meters were manufactured before 1997. A defect in the product could result in an error message instead of a warning that a person's blood-sugar level is very high.

In March 1998, the FDA and the Justice Department in California began a criminal investigation of Johnson & Johnson's LifeScan subsidiary's monitors for diabetics. The company is cooperating with the investigation. Following the publication of news of the investigation, two families notified the company of the deaths of two persons who had faulty meters. A direct link between the cause of death and the meters had not been established as of June 1998. After the company learned of the defect in 1997, it fixed the software problems and developed a test strip to be inserted in packages for customers to use to test for possible defects. After Johnson & Johnson learned of the two deaths, it offered to replace the monitors. Private class-action lawsuits alleging that the product is defective have been filed against the company in state and federal courts in California.

In 1999, a class-action lawsuit was filed against the company's Ethicon subsidiary for allegedly selling contaminated sutures that caused serious infections in a number of plaintiffs and resulted in the death of one person. The company recalled the batch of sutures at issue in 1994, but because hospitals use up sutures quickly, only 25 percent were returned and destroyed.

In March 2000, the company stopped marketing Propulsid, its heartburn drug, after receiving reports of heartbeat irregularities and deaths among patients who used the drug. The company is developing a limited access program in collaboration with the FDA. In April 2000, Public Citizen, a consumer group, asked the FDA to withdraw Propulsid from the market immediately. The group asked for the withdrawal after finding reports of cardiac arrhythmia, including 80 deaths, linked to the heartburn drug between 1993 and 1999. The FDA earlier ruled that Propulsid would be available until July 2000, after which it would be offered through the limited access program.

Marketing/Contracting Controversy

In 1998, Johnson & Johnson was fined $100,000 by the EPA for misleading claims regarding its antibacterial toothbrush. The antibacterial agents in the plastic help keep germs off the handle but do not necessarily have any capacity to kill germs anywhere else, as the company's advertising might lead one to believe.

In October 1996, the company agreed to pay 19 states $2 million to settle allegations that it and the Arthritis Foundation had misled consumers in their marketing of over-the-counter pain relievers bearing the foundation's name. The company's McNeil Consumer Products division marketed four Arthritis Foundation brand pain relievers. The states alleged that the advertising falsely implied that the Arthritis Foundation had been involved in the development of the drugs and that the drugs had been specially formulated.

In 1991, the FDA alleged that Johnson & Johnson had promoted its acne medicine, Retin-A, for a purpose for which it had not been approved, wrinkle prevention, and referred the matter to the Justice Department. An investigation was concluded without charges of unlawful promotion. In January 1995, however, the company pleaded guilty to destroying documents relevant to this investigation, and paid a $5 million fine and $2.5 million to cover the cost of the federal investigation. In January 1996, the FDA approved use of Retin-A for the prevention or reduction of wrinkles. The company now markets the product as Renova.

Johnson & Johnson is involved in a controversy concerning the marketing of infant formula.

Doctors, scientists, public health advocates, and nonprofit groups such as the International Baby Food Action Network (IBFAN) argue that, in general, for the health of the infant, breast milk is superior to breast milk substitutes.

In the 1970s and 1980s, government health agencies and non-government health organizations heavily criticized infant formula manufacturers for marketing their product irresponsibly in poor areas of the world. In particular, women and infants were put at risk by using unsterilized water to make the infant formula.

In response to the controversy, UNICEF, the World Health Organization (WHO), and member countries of the WHO (including the United States) endorsed the International Code of Marketing of Breastmilk Substitutes (the ICMBS). The ICMBS prohibits marketing practices that discourage mothers from breastfeeding. Such practices include offering free and low-cost samples of infant formula, bottles, and nipples to mothers, health centers, and hospitals.

Since 1994, various studies by UNICEF, other UN agencies, and the IBFAN have found that most infant formula manufacturers, including Johnson & Johnson, had consistently violated the ICMBS.

Bristol-Myers is a member of an industry trade association, the International Infant Formula Manufacturers (IFM). The IFM and UNICEF have agreed upon guidelines for eliminating the use of free and low-cost samples in most developing countries. As of 1999, however, members of the IFM, including Johnson & Johnson, had not implemented the guidelines. The companies argue that the regulatory practices and enforcement capabilities are inadequate in the affected countries.

Antitrust

Johnson & Johnson is among several large pharmaceutical companies sued by independent pharmacists, who allege price discrimination. In February 1996, the company chose not to participate in a $408.9 million proposed settlement between 15 of the drug companies and the pharmacies. In April 1996, a federal judge denied approval of the February proposal because it did not alter the two-tier system of pricing by which independent pharmacists had to pay much higher prices for drugs than HMOs and mail-order companies. In June 1996, 11 companies, not including Johnson & Johnson, agreed to a $351 million settlement approved by a federal judge in the lawsuit. In the June 1996 settlement, the companies agreed to stop this practice. Johnson & Johnson is contesting the allegations of the independent pharmacists. In February 1999, several more companies agreed to another settlement of $176 million. The class-action suit continues against seven remaining companies, including Johnson & Johnson.

In a separate case, the company faces allegations of price-fixing from the large drugstore chains, such as Kroger and Rite-Aid.

In December 1996, the attorneys general (AGs) from 22 states sued Johnson & Johnson and two other major manufacturers of soft contact lenses. The AGs alleged that these companies conspired to increase consumer prices by limiting product supplies and access to prescriptions. Several optometrists and optometrist trade associations were also named in the suit. The suit alleged that 25 million consumers might have been overcharged $600 million between 1989 and 1994. In 1998, the company reported that it continued to contest the charges.

In June 1994, Florida regulators sued Johnson & Johnson, Bausch & Lomb, and Ciba, alleging the companies conspired to allow only optometrists to sell replacement contact lenses, driving up the cost of such lenses. The companies asserted their policy was strictly for the protection of customers. The companies later settled.

· · ·

In 1994, *Industry Week* magazine included the company's personal products facility in North Little Rock, Arkansas, on its list of "best plants" for manufacturing excellence in the United States. Previous winners also include Johnson & Johnson Medical's El Paso, Texas, plant and its Sherman, Texas, plant. (See "Employee Relations/Commentary".)

· · ·

Johnson & Johnson, along with other companies including Becton Dickinson and Baxter International, is a manufacturer of latex gloves. Since 1992, federal regulators have required that health care providers wear gloves or similar protective gear to protect against blood-borne viruses. Most medical workers now wear latex gloves. Some of these workers, who are allergic to the proteins in the latex, have sued the manufacturers, alleging that they have failed to reduce protein levels in the product and to warn users about possible allergic reactions. The companies have asserted that adequate alternatives exist for those who are allergic to latex. In February 1996, the California Court of Appeal refused to certify one of these lawsuits as a class action.

· · ·

In February 1998, the FDA required the company's Janssen Pharmaceutica subsidiary to change the labeling on its antihistamine drug Hismanal to warn against potentially dangerous reactions (including fatalities) if the drug is taken with certain antibiotics, widely prescribed antidepressants, and some other drugs. The FDA had not proposed withdrawing the drug from the market. In July 1999, Janssen voluntarily withdrew the drug from the market.

· · ·

A 1995 study by the World Health Organization reported that women using AHP's birth control pills, which contained two progestens, had twice the risk of blood clots as compared with users of an earlier version. The finding led safety regulators in England, Germany, Norway, and New Zealand to issue warnings to doctors that recommend limiting the prescription of the pills. In 1998, the company told KLD that the results of studies funded by AHP indicated that the risk of clotting was very small. In 1998, German regulators reversed their restrictions on prescriptions. Johnson & Johnson's Ortho-Cept product, which is approved by the FDA, contains two progestens.

Other
High Compensation

In FY 1998, nonemployee members of the company's board of directors received a total compensation package that KLD valued at approximately $105,000. This included average fees of approximately $76,000 and a noncash component consisting of stock grants and options that KLD valued at approximately $29,000.

. . .

In 1998, the company told KLD that it used animal testing during the development of nonmedical products. As of April 1999, animal rights groups were targeting the company for testing personal care and household products on animals. The company argues that such tests are necessary for human safety and to continue innovative product development.

As of 1998, it was using 120 alternative tests during the evaluation of new compounds and in new product formulations. The company also said that it relies heavily on human volunteers and on nontraditional tests that require fewer animals.

From 1984 to 1996 it reduced the number of animals used in the testing of nonmedical products by 99 percent. The company is a sponsor of the Johns Hopkins Center for Alternatives to Animal Testing. It has provided financial assistance to the Fund for the Replacement of Animals in Medical Experiments and has funded a five-year study at the University of Texas meant to develop alternatives for tests used to measure skin and eye irritation.

Contraceptive Products
Involvement

Johnson & Johnson manufactures and markets diaphragms, intrauterine devices, spermicides, and oral contraceptives worldwide through its Ortho-McNeil, Janssen-Cilag, Janssen-Ortho (Canada), and Personal Products subsidiaries. Brand names include Cilest, Delfen, Gynol, K-Y Plus, Micronovum, Ortho-Cept, Ortho-Cyclen, Ortho-Novum, Ovysmen, and Trinovum. As of July 1999, the company was developing a contraceptive patch under the brand name Evra, due to be evaluated by the FDA in the first quarter of 2000. Johnson & Johnson manufactures and markets health care products.

In December 1999, the company acquired all of Cygnus Therapeutic Systems's rights to a transdermal contraceptive patch that Johnson & Johnson's Ortho-McNeil pharmaceutical division had licensed to Cygnus to develop. As of September 1999, the product was in Phase III clinical trials.

In the SEC's Own Words

Official SEC Rules on Shareholder Resolutions (Rule 14a-8)

This section is taken from the SEC's Web site.

How to Draft and Defend Shareholder Resolutions
Question 1: What is a proposal?

A shareholder proposal is your recommendation or requirement that the company and/or its board of directors take action, which you intend to present at a meeting of the company's shareholders. Your proposal should state as clearly as possible the course of action that you believe the company should follow. If your proposal is placed on the company's proxy card, the company must also provide in the form of proxy means for shareholders to specify by boxes a choice between approval or disapproval, or abstention. Unless otherwise indicated, the word "proposal" as used in this section refers both to your proposal and to your corresponding statement in support of your proposal (if any).

Question 2: Who is eligible to submit a proposal, and how do I demonstrate to the company that I am eligible?

1. In order to be eligible to submit a proposal, you must have continuously held at least $2,000 in market value, or 1 percent, of the company's securities entitled to be voted on the proposal at the meeting for at least one year by the date you submit the proposal. You must continue to hold those securities through the date of the meeting.

2. If you are the registered holder of your securities, which means that your name appears in the company's records as a shareholder, the company can verify your eligibility on its own, although you will still have to provide the company with a written statement that you intend to continue to hold the securities through the date of the meeting of shareholders. However, if like many shareholders you are not a registered holder, the company likely does not know that you are a shareholder, or how many shares you own. In this case, at the time you submit your proposal, you must prove your eligibility to the company in one of two ways:

   (i) The first way is to submit to the company a written statement from the "record" holder of your securities (usually a broker or bank) verifying that, at the time you submitted your proposal, you continuously held the securities for at least one year. You must also include your own written statement that you intend to continue to hold the securities through the date of the meeting of shareholders; or

   (ii) The second way to prove ownership applies only if you have filed a Schedule 13D (§ 240.13d-101), Schedule 13G (§ 240.13d-102), Form 3 (§ 249.103 of this chapter), Form 4 (§ 249.104 of this chapter), and/or Form 5 (§ 249.105 of this chapter), or amendments to those documents or updated forms, reflecting your ownership of the shares as of or before the date on which the one-year eligibility period begins. If you have filed one of these documents with the SEC, you may demonstrate your eligibility by submitting to the company:

(A) A copy of the schedule and/or form, and any subsequent amendments reporting a change in your ownership level;

(B) Your written statement that you continuously held the required number of shares for the one-year period as of the date of the statement; and

(C) Copyright your written statement that you intend to continue ownership of the shares through the date of the company's annual or special meeting.

Question 3: How many proposals may I submit?

Each shareholder may submit no more than one proposal to a company for a particular shareholders' meeting.

Question 4: How long can my proposal be?

The proposal, including any accompanying supporting statement, may not exceed 500 words.

Question 5: What is the deadline for submitting a proposal?

1. If you are submitting your proposal for the company's annual meeting, you can in most cases find the deadline in last year's proxy statement. However, if the company did not hold an annual meeting last year, or has changed the date of its meeting for this year more than 30 days from last year's meeting, you can usually find the deadline in one of the company's quarterly reports on Form 10-Q (§ 249.308a of this chapter) or 10-QSB (§ 249.308b of this chapter), or in shareholder reports of investment companies under § 270.30d-1 of this chapter of the Investment Company Act of 1940. In order to avoid controversy, shareholders should submit

their proposals by means, including electronic means, that permit them to prove the date of delivery.

2. The deadline is calculated in the following manner if the proposal is submitted for a regularly scheduled annual meeting: The proposal must be received at the company's principal executive offices not less than 120 calendar days before the date of the company's proxy statement which was released to shareholders in connection with the previous year's annual meeting. However, if the company did not hold an annual meeting the previous year, or if the date of this year's annual meeting has been changed by more than 30 days from the date of the previous year's meeting, then the deadline is a reasonable time before the company begins to print and mail its proxy materials.

3. If you are submitting your proposal for a meeting of shareholders other than a regularly scheduled annual meeting, the deadline is a reasonable time before the company begins to print and mail its proxy materials.

Question 6: What if I fail to follow one of the eligibility or procedural requirements explained in answers to Questions 1 through 4 of this section?

1. The company may exclude your proposal, but only after it has notified you of the problem, and you have failed adequately to correct it. Within 14 calendar days of receiving your proposal, the company must notify you in writing of any procedural or eligibility deficiencies, as well as of the time frame for your response. Your response must be postmarked, or transmitted electronically, no later than 14 days from the date you received the company's notification. A company need not provide you such notice of a deficiency if the deficiency cannot be remedied, such as if you fail to submit a proposal by the company's properly determined deadline. If the company intends to exclude the proposal, it will later have to make a submission under § 240.14a-8

and provide you with a copy under Question 10 below, §
240.14a-8(j).

2. If you fail in your promise to hold the required number of
securities through the date of the meeting of shareholders,
then the company will be permitted to exclude all of your
proposals from its proxy materials for any meeting held in
the following two calendar years.

Question 7: Who has the burden of persuading the Commission or its staff that my proposal can be excluded?

Except as otherwise noted, the burden is on the company to
demonstrate that it is entitled to exclude a proposal.

Question 8: Must I appear personally at the shareholders' meeting to present the proposal?

1. Either you, or your representative who is qualified under
state law to present the proposal on your behalf, must
attend the meeting to present the proposal. Whether you
attend the meeting yourself or send a qualified representative to the meeting in your place, you should make sure
that you, or your representative, follow the proper state
law procedures for attending the meeting and/or present-
ing your proposal.
2. If the company holds its shareholder meeting in whole or
in part via electronic media, and the company permits you
or your representative to present your proposal via such
media, then you may appear through electronic media
rather than traveling to the meeting to appear in person.
3. If you or your qualified representative fail to appear and
present the proposal, without good cause, the company
will be permitted to exclude all of your proposals from its
proxy materials for any meetings held in the following two
calendar years.

Question 9: If I have complied with the procedural requirements, on what other bases may a company rely to exclude my proposal?

1. Improper under state law: If the proposal is not a proper subject for action by shareholders under the laws of the jurisdiction of the company's organization;
   Note to paragraph (i)(1): Depending on the subject matter, some proposals are not considered proper under state law if they would be binding on the company if approved by shareholders. In our experience, most proposals that are cast as recommendations or requests that the board of directors take specified action are proper under state law. Accordingly, we will assume that a proposal drafted as a recommendation or suggestion is proper unless the company demonstrates otherwise.

2. Violation of law: If the proposal would, if implemented, cause the company to violate any state, federal, or foreign law to which it is subject;
   Note to paragraph (i)(2): We will not apply this basis for exclusion to permit exclusion of a proposal on grounds that it would violate foreign law if compliance with the foreign law would result in a violation of any state or federal law.

3. Violation of proxy rules: If the proposal or supporting statement is contrary to any of the Commission's proxy rules, including § 240.14a-9, which prohibits materially false or misleading statements in proxy soliciting materials;

4. Personal grievance; special interest: If the proposal relates to the redress of a personal claim or grievance against the company or any other person, or if it is designed to result in a benefit to you, or to further a personal interest, which is not shared by the other shareholders at large;

5. Relevance: If the proposal relates to operations that account for less than 5 percent of the company's total assets at the end of its most recent fiscal year, and for less than 5 percent of its net earnings and gross sales for its

most recent fiscal year, and is not otherwise significantly related to the company's business;

6. Absence of power/authority: If the company would lack the power or authority to implement the proposal;

7. Management functions: If the proposal deals with a matter relating to the company's ordinary business operations;

8. Relates to election: If the proposal relates to an election for membership on the company's board of directors or analogous governing body;

9. Conflicts with company's proposal: If the proposal directly conflicts with one of the company's own proposals to be submitted to shareholders at the same meeting;

   Note to paragraph (i)(9): A company's submission to the Commission under this section should specify the points of conflict with the company's proposal.

10. Substantially implemented: If the company has already substantially implemented the proposal;

11. Duplication: If the proposal substantially duplicates another proposal previously submitted to the company by another proponent that will be included in the company's proxy materials for the same meeting;

12. Resubmissions: If the proposal deals with substantially the same subject matter as another proposal or proposals that has or have been previously included in the company's proxy materials within the preceding five calendar years, a company may exclude it from its proxy materials for any meeting held within three calendar years of the last time it was included if the proposal received:

    (i) Less than 3 percent of the vote if proposed once within the preceding five calendar years;

    (ii) Less than 6 percent of the vote on its last submission to shareholders if proposed twice previously within the preceding five calendar years; or

    (iii) Less than 10 percent of the vote on its last submission to shareholders if proposed three times or more previously within the preceding five calendar years; and

13. Specific amount of dividends: If the proposal relates to specific amounts of cash or stock dividends.

Question 10: What procedures must the company follow if it intends to exclude my proposal?

1. If the company intends to exclude a proposal from its proxy materials, it must file its reasons with the Commission no later than 80 calendar days before it files its definitive proxy statement and form of proxy with the Commission. The company must simultaneously provide you with a copy of its submission. The Commission staff may permit the company to make its submission later than 80 days before the company files its definitive proxy statement and form of proxy, if the company demonstrates good cause for missing the deadline.
2. The company must file six paper copies of the following:
   (i) The proposal;
   (ii) An explanation of why the company believes that it may exclude the proposal, which should, if possible, refer to the most recent applicable authority, such as prior Division letters issued under the rule; and
   (iii) A supporting opinion of counsel when such reasons are based on matters of state or foreign law.

Question 11: May I submit my own statement to the Commission responding to the company's arguments?

Yes, you may submit a response, but it is not required. You should try to submit any response to us, with a copy to the company, as soon as possible after the company makes its submission. This way, the Commission staff will have time to consider fully your submission before it issues its response. You should submit six paper copies of your response.

Question 12: If the company includes my shareholder proposal in its proxy materials, what information about me must it include along with the proposal itself?

1. The company's proxy statement must include your name and address, as well as the number of the company's voting securities that you hold. However, instead of providing that information, the company may instead include a statement that it will provide the information to shareholders promptly upon receiving an oral or written request.
2. The company is not responsible for the contents of your proposal or supporting statement.

Question 13: What can I do if the company includes in its proxy statement reasons why it believes shareholders should not vote in favor of my proposal, and I disagree with some of its statements?

1. The company may elect to include in its proxy statement reasons why it believes shareholders should vote against your proposal. The company is allowed to make arguments reflecting its own point of view, just as you may express your own point of view in your proposal's supporting statement.
2. However, if you believe that the company's opposition to your proposal contains materially false or misleading statements that may violate our antifraud rule, § 240.14a-9, you should promptly send to the Commission staff and the company a letter explaining the reasons for your view, along with a copy of the company's statements opposing your proposal. To the extent possible, your letter should include specific factual information demonstrating the inaccuracy of the company's claims. Time permitting, you may wish to try to work out your differences with the company by yourself before contacting the Commission staff.

3. We require the company to send you a copy of its statements opposing your proposal before it mails its proxy materials, so that you may bring to our attention any materially false or misleading statements, under the following time frames:

    (i) If our no-action response requires that you make revisions to your proposal or supporting statement as a condition to requiring the company to include it in its proxy materials, then the company must provide you with a copy of its opposition statements no later than five calendar days after the company receives a copy of your revised proposal; or

    (ii) In all other cases, the company must provide you with a copy of its opposition statements no later than 30 calendar days before it files definitive copies of its proxy statement and form of proxy under Rule 14a-6.

Raytheon

A Shareholder Resolution on Executive Pay

WHEREAS, despite record profitability in the 1990s, U.S. corporations have laid off record numbers of workers, arguing that cost-cutting is one key to long-term competitiveness and increased profitability;

WHEREAS, only 44 percent of firms that downsized employees saw a rise in operating profits, according to a 1992 study by the American Management Association. The same study found that only 31 percent of corporate downsizers experienced productivity gains following the layoffs, while 77 percent experienced deterioration in employee morale. A second study of 1,000 large companies conducted by the Wyatt Co. found that less than one-third of the companies surveyed hit profit targets projected at the time of the restructuring;

WHEREAS, in 1998, Raytheon announced that it would lay off 14,000 employees by the end of 1999. In April 1999, the company increased this estimate to 15,400 job cuts. In October 1999, Raytheon management announced an additional 2,400 employees would lose their jobs. Raytheon management argued these layoffs would reduce costs and boost profits;

WHEREAS, large layoffs in the recent past have not resulted in the improved financial health promised by Raytheon's top managers;

WHEREAS, since the layoffs were announced, Raytheon's profits have continued to decline and its stock price has dramatically underperformed its competitors. Between January 1, 1998 and November 23, 1999, Raytheon's Class A stock lost 35.8 percent of its value (including dividends). During the same period the S&P Aerospace/Defense Index declined 12.8 percent and the S&P 500 rose 48.6 percent.

WHEREAS, despite having publicly announced the need to cut costs, Raytheon's executives were granted and accepted generous increases in their compensation in 1998. Excluding Mr. Burnham, who did not serve the company during 1997, the company's top four officers collectively enjoyed increases in salary and bonus of more than 30 percent in 1998 (representing $1.79 million, or an average raise of $449,000 per officer). Each of these men also received at least 33 percent more stock options in 1998 than they did the previous year;

WHEREAS, we believe that asking employees to sacrifice, while at the same time enriching executives, sends a poor message to employees, suppliers, and shareholders. We believe that business success over the long term is enhanced when business is viewed as a shared enterprise in which both the rewards and sacrifices are equitably shared among all employees;

RESOLVED, shareholders request that the Board adopt an executive compensation policy that freezes the pay of corporate officers during periods of downsizing in which the lesser of 2 percent of the company's workforce or 1,000 workers lose their jobs. This pay freeze shall continue for a one-year period following the completion of the layoffs.

Supporting Statement

Corporate leaders should have a long-term view when making management decisions. If decisions to cut costs are in the long-term best interest of the company, executives should be willing to defer their rewards until positive results are demonstrated. Rewarding cost-cutting executives for potentially good future performance is in conflict with standards of good corporate governance.

PLEASE VOTE YES.

Source: *The Proxy Resolutions Book,* January 2000. For further information on United for a Fair Economy, please contact:

Interfaith Center on Corporate Responsibility,
475 Riverside Drive, Room 550,
New York, NY 10115,
212-870-2293
or e-mail info@iccr.org

Kinder, Lydenberg, Domini & Co.

Social Rating Criteria 2000

Kinder, Lydenberg, Domini & Co., Inc.
Russia Wharf
530 Atlantic Avenue, 7th Floor
Boston, Massachusetts 02210
Phone: (617) 426-5270
Fax: (617) 426-5299
e-mail sri@kld.com
Web site <www.kld.com>

Introduction

Kinder, Lydenberg, Domini & Co., Inc. (KLD), is using the following social screens during the 2000 research cycle, which runs from November 1, 1999, to October 31, 2000.

Each screen focuses on a particular social indicator and is part of an overall evaluation of corporate social performance. KLD publishes its ratings and analyses as company Profiles. Strength and concern ratings are signified by diamonds in the rating chart on the cover of each Profile. The absence of ratings indicates that there is no significant strength or concern, but Profiles often contain relevant commentary even if no rating is assigned.

KLD's social research is distributed in Socrates—The Corporate Social Ratings Monitor^{SM}. Socrates is a proprietary database program that provides access to KLD's ratings and other data pertaining to the social records of more than 650 publicly traded U.S. companies.

Community
Strengths

Generous Giving. The company has consistently given more than 1.5 percent of trailing three-year net earnings before taxes (NEBT) to charity or has otherwise been notably generous in its giving.

Innovative Giving. The company has a notably innovative giving program that supports nonprofit organizations, particularly those promoting self-sufficiency among the economically disadvantaged. Companies that permit nontraditional federated charitable giving drives in the workplace are often noted in this section as well.

Support for Housing. The company is a prominent participant in public/private partnerships that support housing initiatives for the economically disadvantaged, the National Equity Fund, or the Enterprise Foundation.

Support for Education. The company has either been notably innovative in its support for primary or secondary school education, particularly for those programs that benefit the economically disadvantaged, or the company has prominently supported job training programs for youth.

Other Strength.

Concerns

Investment Controversies. The company is a financial institution whose lending or investment practices have led to controversies, particularly ones related to the Community Reinvestment Act.

Negative Economic Impact. The company's actions have resulted in major controversies concerning its economic impact on the community. These controversies can include issues related to environmental contamination, water rights disputes, plant closings, put-or-pay contracts with trash incinerators, or other company actions that adversely affect the quality of life, tax base, or property values in the community.

Other Concern.

Diversity
Strengths

CEO. The company's chief executive officer is a woman or a member of a minority group.

Promotion. The company has made notable progress in the promotion of women and minorities, particularly to line positions with profit-and-loss responsibilities in the corporation.

Board of Directors. Women, minorities, and/or the disabled hold 4 seats or more (with no double counting) on the board of directors or one-third or more of the board seats if the board numbers fewer than 12.

Family Benefits. The company has outstanding employee benefits or other programs addressing work and family concerns (e.g., child care, elder care, or flextime).

Women/Minority Contracting. The company does at least 5 percent of its subcontracting or otherwise has a demonstrably strong record on purchasing or contracting with women-owned and/or minority-owned businesses.

Employment of the Disabled. The company has implemented innovative hiring programs, other innovative human resource programs for the disabled, or otherwise has a superior reputation as an employer of the disabled.

Progressive Gay/Lesbian Policies. The company has implemented notably progressive policies toward its gay and lesbian employees. In particular, it provides benefits to the domestic partners of its employees.

Other Strength.

Concerns

Controversies. The company has either paid substantial fines or civil penalties as a result of affirmative action controversies or has otherwise been involved in major controversies related to affirmative action issues.

Nonrepresentation. The company has no women on its board of directors or among its senior line managers.

Other Concern.

Employee Relations
Strengths

Strong Union Relations. The company has a history of notably strong union relations.

Cash Profit Sharing. The company has a cash profit-sharing program through which it has recently made distributions to a majority of its workforce.

Employee Involvement. The company strongly encourages worker involvement and/or ownership through stock options available to a majority of its employees, gain sharing, stock ownership, sharing of financial information, or participation in management decision making.

Strong Retirement Benefits. The company has a notably strong retirement benefits program.

Other Strength.

Concerns

Poor Union Relations. The company has a history of notably poor union relations.

Safety Controversies. The company recently has either paid substantial fines or civil penalties for willful violations of employee health and safety standards or has been otherwise involved in major health and safety controversies.

Workforce Reductions. The company has reduced its workforce by 15 percent in the most recent year or by 25 percent during the past two years, or it has announced plans for such reductions.

Pension/Benefits Concern. The company has either a substantially underfunded defined benefit pension plan or an inadequate retirement benefits program.

Other Concern.

Environment
Strengths

Beneficial Products and Services. The company derives substantial revenues from innovative remediation products, environmental services, or products that promote the efficient use of energy, or it has developed innovative products with environmental benefits. (The term *environmental service* does not include services with questionable environmental effects, such as landfills, incinerators, waste-to-energy plants, and deep injection wells.)

Pollution Prevention. The company has notably strong pollution prevention programs, including both emissions reductions and toxic-use reduction programs.

Recycling. The company either is a substantial user of recycled materials as raw materials in its manufacturing processes or a major factor in the recycling industry.

Alternative Fuels. The company derives substantial revenues from alternative fuels. The term *alternative fuels* includes natural gas, wind power, and solar energy. The company has demonstrated an exceptional commitment to energy efficiency programs or the promotion of energy efficiency.

Communications. The company is a signatory to the CERES Principles, publishes a notably substantive environmental report, or has notably effective internal communications systems in place for environmental best practices.

Other Strength.

Concerns

Hazardous Waste. The company's liabilities for hazardous waste sites exceed $50 million, or the company has recently paid substantial fines or civil penalties for waste management violations.

Regulatory Problems. The company has recently paid substantial fines or civil penalties for violations of air, water, or other environmental regulations, or it has a pattern of regulatory controversies under the Clean Air Act, Clean Water Act, or other major environmental regulations.

Ozone-Depleting Chemicals. The company is among the top manufacturers of ozone-depleting chemicals such as HCFCs, methyl chloroform, methylene chloride, or bromines.

Substantial Emissions. The company's legal emissions of toxic chemicals (as defined by and reported to the EPA) from individual plants into the air and water are among the highest of the companies followed by KLD.

Agricultural Chemicals. The company is a substantial producer of agricultural chemicals (i.e., pesticides or chemical fertilizers).

Climate Change. The company derives substantial revenues from the sale of coal or oil and its derivative fuel products, or the company derives substantial revenues indirectly from the combustion of coal or oil and its derivative fuel products. Such companies include electric utilities, transportation companies with fleets of vehicles, auto and truck manufacturers, and other transportation equipment companies.

Other Concern.

Non-U.S. Operations

N.B.: Data for these issues are less complete, less reliable, and more difficult to interpret than the data underlying ratings for U.S. operations.

Strengths

Community. The company has established substantial, innovative charitable giving programs outside the United States.

Other Strength. The company's non-U.S. operations have been praised for their community relations, employee relations, environmental impact, or product innovation.

Concerns

Burma. The company has operations in Burma.

Mexico. The company's operations in Mexico have had major recent controversies, especially those related to the treatment of employees or degradation of the environment.

International Labor. The company's non-U.S. operations have been the subject of major recent controversies related to employee relations and labor standards.

Other Concern. The company's non-U.S. operations are subject to controversies related to the community, diversity issues, the environment, product safety, or product quality.

Product
Strengths

Quality. The company has a long-term, well-developed, companywide quality program, or it has a quality program recognized as exceptional in U.S. industry.

R&D/Innovation. The company is a leader in its industry for research and development (R&D), particularly by bringing notably innovative products to market.

Benefits to Economically Disadvantaged. The company has as part of its basic mission the provision of products or services for the economically disadvantaged.

Other Strength.

Concerns

Product Safety. The company has recently paid substantial fines or civil penalties, or is involved in major recent controversies or regulatory actions relating to the safety of its products and services.

Marketing/Contracting Controversy. The company has recently been involved in major marketing or contracting controversies, or has paid substantial fines or civil penalties relating to advertising practices, consumer fraud, or government contracting.

Antitrust. The company has recently paid substantial fines or civil penalties for antitrust violations such as price fixing, collusion, or predatory pricing, or is involved in recent major controversies or regulatory actions relating to antitrust allegations.

Other Concern.

Other
Strengths

Limited Compensation. The company has recently awarded notably low levels of compensation to its top management or its board members. The limit for a rating is total compensation of less than $500,000 per year for a CEO or $30,000 per year for outside directors.

Ownership Strength. The company owns between 20 percent and 50 percent of another company KLD has cited as having an area of social strength or is more than 20 percent owned by a firm that KLD has rated as having social strengths. When a company owns more than 50 percent of another firm, it has a controlling interest, and KLD treats the second firm as if it is a division of the first.

Other Strength.

Concerns

High Compensation. The company has recently awarded notably high levels of compensation to its top management or its board members. The limit for a rating is total compensation of more than $10 million per year for a CEO or $100,000 per year for outside directors.

Tax Disputes. The company has recently been involved in major tax disputes involving more than $100 million with federal, state, or local authorities.

Ownership Concern. The company owns between 20 percent and 50 percent of a company KLD has cited as having an area of social concern or is more than 20 percent owned by a firm KLD has rated as having areas of concern. When a company owns more than 50 percent of another firm, it has a controlling interest, and KLD treats the second firm as if it is a division of the first.

Other Concern.

Exclusionary Screens

KLD's exclusionary screens differ from the qualitative screens applied to the previous issues in that only concern ratings, but no strength ratings, are assigned for the exclusionary issues.

Alcohol
Concerns

Substantial Involvement. The company derives substantial revenues from the production of alcoholic beverages.

Other Concern. The company derives substantial revenues from the activities closely associated with the production of alcoholic beverages.

Gambling
Concerns

Substantial Involvement. The company derives revenues from the production of goods and services related to gaming or lottery industries.

Other Concern. The company derives substantial revenues from the activities closely associated with the production of goods and services closely related to the gaming or lottery industries.

Tobacco
Concerns

Substantial Involvement. The company derives substantial revenues from the production of tobacco products.

Other Concern. The company derives substantial revenues from the activities closely associated with the production of tobacco products.

Military
Concerns

Substantial Weapons Contracting Involvement. The company has substantial involvement in weapons-related contracting. In the most recent fiscal year for which information is available, it derived more than 2 percent of sales or $50 million from weapons-related contracting, or it received more than $10 million in nuclear weapons–related prime contracts.

Minor Weapons Contracting Involvement. The company has minor involvement in weapons-related contracting. In the most recent fiscal year for which information is available, it derived $10 million to $50 million in conventional weapons-related prime contracts (when that figure is less than 2 percent of revenue) or $1 million to $10 million from nuclear weapons–related prime contracts.

Major Weapons-Related Supplier. During the past fiscal year, the company received from the Department of Defense more than $50 million for fuel or other supplies related to weapons.

Other Concern.

Nuclear Power
Concerns

Derives Electricity. The company is an electric utility that either generates electricity from nuclear fuels or owns an interest in a nuclear power plant.

Design. The company derives identifiable revenues from the design of nuclear power plants. This category does not include companies providing construction or maintenance services for nuclear power plants.

Fuel Cycle/Key Parts. The company mines, processes, or enriches uranium, or is otherwise involved in the nuclear fuel cycle. Or the company derives substantial revenues from the sale of key parts or equipment for generating power through using nuclear fuels.

Other Concern.

American Friends Service Committee

Social Investment Policy and Guidelines

Social Responsibility Considerations

A. Investments should be in companies providing goods and services which people and peacetime industry need by way of food, medicine, clothing, housing, heat and light transportation, communication, recreation, etc.—all the needs of everyday life.

B. Investments *should not* be made in any company which is a developer or a manufacturer of products in the general category of weaponry, including chemical and biological warfare, nuclear weapons systems, antipersonnel weapons, small arms and goods for the automated battlefield.

C. Investments in *other companies deriving revenue from military contacts should be considered individually* to determine the attitude of management to military contracts, their total amount and the percentage of sales they represent, the type of materials and services contracted for, and the direction of the company toward increasing or decreasing military involvement. Major defense contractors or suppliers, major research and development contractors or companies with total military contracts over 3 percent of sales are especially to be avoided. Investments in companies among the top 100 defense contractors should be scrutinized with particular care.

D. Investments *should be avoided* in companies primarily involved in products or services of limited or questionable social value, such as intoxicants, tobacco, some luxury items, or land speculation.

E. In judging investments, consideration should be given as to whether companies have a superior rather than an inferior record within their industry in areas such as the following.

1. Environmental, conservation, and pollution problems.
2. Hiring and personnel practices as reflected in our Affirmative Action Plan.
3. Health and safety of workers.
4. General business practices, including advertising and financial practices.
5. Disclosure to their stockholders of information on business and social responsibility practices.
6. Natural resource companies' recognition of the rights and cultures of native peoples.
7. Relations with unions and with worker-organizing committees.

F. Because of differences in culture and values, it is exceedingly difficult to make judgments about companies with international operations. Further study will be required to determine ways of measuring whether the foreign operation of a corporation: (1) benefits the host country, (2) is consistent with the local culture and fosters human dignity, (3) avoids unnecessary depletion of resources of the host country, and (4) is sensitive to the aspirations of that country. Absolute size of the operation relative to the host country will be a factor. Investment policy should be sensitive to and informed by the experience gained through our program activities outside the United States.

Consistency with Major Program Directions

Investment policies have been influenced by positions of the American Friends Service Committee Board on major program issues. The South Africa program, the nuclear disarmament work, and U.S. Treasury obligations have all generated specific policies on investment.

A. Until January 1994, it had been the policy of the American Friends Service Committee to not hold investments in any company which does business in South Africa. The current policy is to consider firms that do business in South Africa will be guided by the same social guidelines as other firms. A position on nuclear power was developed in 1978 for internal use to guide peace education staff. The corresponding investment guidelines are:

1. Investments in any public utility company which is in the process of constructing nuclear power facilities should be avoided.
2. Over a period of time, holdings in any public utility with significant involvement in nuclear power production should be reduced and eventually eliminated. (The bonds of some public utility companies now using nuclear power should be held until market conditions permit prudent disposal in order to avoid significant losses.)

C. The American Friends Service Committee Board in 1967 decided not to hold any U.S. Treasury bonds for the duration of U.S. military activities in Vietnam. The Investment Committee has continued this practice and held instead bonds of U.S. government agencies. When the investment guidelines were applied to the corporate bond portion of the portfolio in 1983, one result was a large drop in the number of other possible investment choices. In times of rapidly changing investment opportunities, it becomes fiscally prudent to invest temporarily in Treasury bonds which have the advantages of liquidity (can be bought and sold easily at a lower cost), variety, low risk, and noncallability. Appropriate guidelines are:

1. *Investments in U.S. Treasury bonds will be made only in situations where appropriate federal agency or acceptable corporate bond issues are not available or are available at an inordinate investment risk. Treasury investments will be an option of last resort.*
2. During periods of rapidly changing market conditions, temporary investment in U.S. Treasury bonds is appropriate with the understanding that these purchases can be replaced as soon as practical with other acceptable bond investments.
3. The amount of U.S. Treasury bonds which are held should not exceed 15 percent of the total American Friends Service committee portfolio when averaged over any 12-month period.
4. In order to limit to the greatest extent possible the amount of American Friends Service Committee funds invested in Treasury bonds, it is the responsibility of the Investment Committee and the investment advisor to review annually the list of any U.S. Treasury bonds and make every possible effort to find substitute investments.

Endnotes

Chapter 1

1. I am indebted to Ben Cohen, founder of Ben & Jerry's Homemade, for pointing out architecture's implications to me.

2. David W. Moore, "One Out of Nine Households Have 'Socially Responsible' Investments," *Gallup Organization News Service*, 16 May 2000. Online: <www.gallup.com/poll/releases/pr000516.asp> (29 September 2000).

3. Social Investment Forum, *1999 Report on Socially Responsible Investing Trends in the United States*, 4 November 1999. Online: <www.socialinvest.org/areas/research/trends/1999-Trends.htm> (29 September 2000).

4. For a fuller discussion, see Grant D. McCracken, *Culture and Consumption: New Approaches to the Symbolic Character of Consumer Goods and Activities* (Bloomington: University of Indiana Press, 1991).

5. D.B. Horn and Mary Ransome, eds., *English Historical Documents, 1714–1783* (London: Eyre and Spottiswoode, 1957), 821–22.

6. *The Corporate Examiner*, 10 May 2000, 4–5. *The Corporate Examiner* is published by the Interfaith Center on Corporate

Responsibility, 475 Riverside Drive, Room 550, New York, NY 10115. Its Web site is located at <www.iccr.org>.

7. *Ibid.*

8. "Savings Plan Helps Bring Dream Home," *Chicago Sun Times,* 5 June 2000, 54.

Chapter 2

1. Nelson Mandela, *Long Walk to Freedom* (Boston: Little, Brown & Co., 1994), 97.

2. "The Political Impact of Sanctions on South Africa," in *South Africa: The Sanctions Report,* ed. John Hanlon (London: The Commonwealth Secretariat, 1990), 144.

3. Aurent Van Heerdan, "Business Fights Sanctions," in *South Africa: The Sanctions Report,* ed. Joseph Hanlon (London: The Commonwealth Secretariat, 1990), 199.

4. Ann Seidmann, *The Roots of Crisis in Southern Africa* (Trenton, N.J.: Africa World Press, 1990), 96–101.

5. Information is from the Shorebank Web site, located at <www.sbk.com>.

6. Information is from the INAISE Web site, located at <www.inaise.org>.

7. Susana Hayward, "Economic Survival Takes Priority Over Slowly Developing Political Activism," *Los Angeles Times,* 3 June 1990, bulldog edition, A32.

8. Information is from the Vietnam Labor Watch Web site, located at <www.saigon.com/~nike/report.html>.

9. "Top U.S. Clothing Retailers Agree to Settle Saipan Garment Worker Lawsuits," *Sweatshop Watch.*

Chapter 3

1. Kinder, Lydenburg, Domini & Co., Inc., *Working Guidelines for the Domini Social Index* (corporate guidelines, 20 January 2000), 7.

2. Calvert Group, Ltd., *Social and Environmental Criteria For Calvert Group Funds*. Online: <www.calvert.com/investor/ind-sri-about-socialcriteria.html#Product Safety and Impact> (29 September 2000).

3. KLD, 51.

4. Kathy Moore, "Breeding Animals for Food Called Threat to Planet," *Daily University Science News*, 13 September 1999. Online: <unisci.com/stories/19993/0913995.htm> (29 September 2000).

5. *The Corporate Examiner*, 10 May 2000, 3. *The Corporate Examiner* is published by the Interfaith Center on Corporate Responsibility, 475 Riverside Drive, Room 550, New York, NY 10115. Their Web site is located at <www.iccr.org>.

6. Information is from the Kinder, Lydenburg, Domini & Co., Inc., Socrates database.

7. Social Investment Forum, *1999 Report on Socially Responsible Investing Trends in the United States*, 4 November 1999. Online: <www.socialinvest.org/areas/research/trends/1999-Trends.htm> (29 September 2000).

Chapter 4

1. John Glass, "James Gamble: Shareholder on a Soapbox," *Boston Business Journal*, 22 July 1991, 15.

2. Christopher Knowlton, "Ready for Your Annual Meeting?" *Fortune*, 24 April 1989, 137.

3. Paul M. Fischer, et al., "Brand Logo Recognition by Children Aged Three to Six Years," *JAMA* (11 December 1991).

4. Joseph R. DiFranza, et. al. "RJR Nabisco's Cartoon Camel Promotes Camel Cigarettes to Children," *JAMA* (December 11, 1991).

5. Information is from the Web site *The Truth*, located at <www.thetruth.com/tvspot/flash/dailydose.html>.

6. "Exxon Valdez," *Microsoft Encarta Online Encyclopedia 2000*. Online: <encarta.msn.com>.

7. Information is from the CERES Web site, located at <www.ceres.org>.

8. *Ibid.*

9. Information is from the Global Reporting Initiative Web site, located at <www.globalreporting.org>.

10. Social Investment Forum, *1999 Report on Socially Responsible Investing Trends in the United States*, 4 November 1999. Online: <www.socialinvest.org/areas/research/trends/1999-Trends.htm> (29 September 2000).

11. *The Corporate Examiner*, 10 May 2000, 5. *The Corporate Examiner* is published by the Interfaith Center on Corporate Responsibility, 475 Riverside Drive, Room 550, New York, NY 10115. Their Web site is located at <www.iccr.org>.

12. Information is from *Mutual Fund Connection*, the Investment Company Institute Web site, located at <http://www.ici.org/facts_figures/trends>.

Chapter 5

1. Treasurer's Office, State of California, *The Double Bottom Line: Investing in California's Emerging Markets* (2000).

2. McAuley Institute, *Housing Gazette* (Summer 2000), 10.

3. MacArthur Foundation, *MacArthur Foundation Report on Activities 1999*, 23.

4. *Ibid.*

5. Robert Kuttner, "Lessons of the Community Reinvestment Act," *The American Prospect*, 11 November 1997. Online: <www.prospect.org/columns/kuttner/bk971111.html> (29 September 2000).

6. *The Double Bottom Line*, 11.

7. Social Investment Forum, *1999 Report on Socially Responsible Investing Trends in the United States*, 4 November 1999. Online:<www.socialinvest.org/areas/research/trends/1999-Trends.htm> (29 September 2000).

8. Information is from the Calvert Group Web site, located at <www.calvertgroup.com>.

9. Information is from the Christian Brothers Investment Services Web site, located at <www.cbis-fsc.com>.

Chapter 6

1. George Soros, "Open Society—Reforming Global Capitalism," *BBS Public Affairs* (2000), vii.

2. Amnesty International, *Memorandum to Friends of Amnesty International re: End Secrecy, End Suffering—Amnesty International's Campaign in Saudi Arabia* (26 July 2000), 2.

3. Information is from *Mutual Fund Connection*, the Investment Company Institute's Web site, located at <www.ici.org>.

4. Information is from the Dow Jones Sustainability Group Index Web site, located at <www.sustainability-index.com>.

5. David Brown, *The Accountability Business* (n.p.: Arthur D. Little, 1999), 1.

6. Terra Nova Conseil, *SRI in Progress–The French Quarterly Newsletter Dedicated to Promoting Socially Responsible Investing* 7 (July, August, September 2000). Terra Nova Conseil's Web site is located at <www.terra-nova.fr>.

7. Investment Company Institute, "Institute Recommends Mandatory Adoption of Italian Corporate Code of Conduct," *Mutual Fund Connection*, 11 January 2000. Online: <www.ici.org/economy/italian_code.html>.

8. *SRI in Progress*.

9. Information is from the EarthRights Web site, located at <www.earthrights.org>.

10. Information is from the Oikocredit Web site, located at: <www.edcs.org>.

11. Nicola Cunningham Armacost, "Banking on Women," *Business Mexico*, November 1994.

12. *SAS Newsbriefs* 1, no. 5 (June 2000).

13. Verité Inc., *Monitor*, the Verité Web site is located at <www.verite.org>.

Chapter 7

1. Information is from the Social Investment Forum Web site, located at <www.socialinvest.org>.

2. Tamzin Booth, "Ethics Lesson: Principles Pay," *Wall Street Journal Europe,* 2 June 2000, weekend edition.

3. Sara Calian and Tamzin Booth, "Schroders Will Introduce Ethical Investing Practices," *Wall Street Journal,* 15 June 2000, Mutual Funds section.

4. *Ibid.*

5. For a fuller discussion, see Hazel Henderson, *Building a Win-Win World: Life Beyond Global Economic Warfare* (San Francisco: Berrett-Koehler Publishers, 1996).

Chapter 8

1. I am indebted to Lloyd Kurtz for his maintenance of a Web site containing a comprehensive listing of academic work on the field. His literature can be accessed through <www.socialfunds.com>.

2. Edward W. Hill and Jeremy Nowak, "Nothing Left to Lose," *Brookings Review* 18, no. 3 (Summer 2000): 25–26.

3. Grant D. McCracken, *Culture and Consumption: New Approaches to the Symbolic Character of Consumer Goods and Activities* (Bloomington: University of Indiana Press, 1991). Further elaboration of the concepts presented in McCracken's *Big Hair: A Journey into the Transformation of Self* (New York: Overlook Press, 1996) are integrated through this discussion.

4. For a full discussion on the theory of tipping points in history, see Malcolm Gladwell, *The Tipping Point,* (Boston: Little Brown & Co., 1999).

Index